KILLING

Misadventures in Violence

JEFF SPARROW

MELBOURNE
UNIVERSITY
PRESS

MELBOURNE UNIVERSITY PRESS
An imprint of Melbourne University Publishing Limited
187 Grattan Street, Carlton, Victoria 3053, Australia
mup-info@unimelb.edu.au
www.mup.com.au

First published 2009
Text © Jeff Sparrow, 2009
Design and typography © Melbourne University Publishing Limited, 2009

Text design by Phil Campbell
Typeset by TypeSkill
Printed by Griffin Press, South Australia

National Library of Australia Cataloguing-in-Publication entry:

Sparrow, Jeff, 1969–
Killing / Jeff Sparrow.

9780522856347 (pbk.)
    Bibliography.
    Homicide—Psychological aspects.
    Homicide—Social aspects.
    Violent deaths—Psychological aspects.
    Violent deaths—Social aspects.

364.152

Mixed Sources
Product group from well-managed
forests and other controlled sources
www.fsc.org Cert no. SGS-COC-005088
© 1996 Forest Stewardship Council

This project has been assisted by the Australian Government through the Australia Council, its principal arts funding and advisory body.

[T]he drift of modern history domesticates the fantastic and normalises the unspeakable. And the catastrophe that begins it is the Great War.
Paul Fussell

Life is beautiful
Leon Trotsky

CONTENTS

ACKNOWLEDGEMENTS

Some material in *Killing* has appeared, in different forms, in the *Age*, the *Sydney Morning Herald* and *Overland*.

Of the many people who assisted with this book, I thank in particular Kalinda Ashton, David Brophy, Cinzia Cavallaro, Sophie Cunningham, Rjurik Davidson, Lucy Davison, Gill Davy, David Hudson, Foong Ling Kong, Andrew Macrae, Gerard Morel, Sean Scalmer, Alex Skutenko, Jill Sparrow, Rebecca Suter and Katherine Wilson.

The names and locations of some interviewees have been altered. I would like to thank everyone who agreed to talk about a difficult and often personal subject. The conclusions drawn in the book are, of course, mine and not theirs.

NO MERCY HERE

The head lay in a red velvet display case. The eyes had rotted away, as had the lips, but the ears remained and tufts of moustache clung to the black, leathery skin. A 3-centimetre impact hole gaped in the crown, with a matching perforation punched roughly through the bone on the other side.

The head was in the possession of the police in Echuca, a country town in Victoria. Not surprisingly, they wanted rid of it. They telephoned the Turkish sub-branch of the Returned and Services League.

'We've got one Turkish head', a policeman told Ramazan Altintas, the sub-branch president. 'What do we do?' He explained how a local resident, tidying up after a death in the family, came across the grisly artefact, a souvenir, supposedly, from his grandfather's service at Gallipoli. The man brought it to the station. Would Altintas collect it?

The police probably hoped Altintas would make the problem disappear. Severed heads in display cases were not a normal responsibility of country policing, and Altintas seemed an appropriate solution. He was a Turkish community leader in an organisation that commemorated the war. He would know what to do. With luck, he'd take the horrible thing far, far away.

Altintas, however, had other plans. He brought the case back to his office in South Melbourne and he issued a press release. The headline read, 'SCANDAL!' The next day, pictures of the head from Gallipoli featured on the front pages of newspapers across the country. I read the articles over breakfast, without, initially, any interest beyond a certain grisly curiosity. It was May 2002. The invasion of Afghanistan was underway, and speculation was already mounting about an attack on Iraq. The twenty-first century promised so many wars of its own that worrying about the human debris of a battle waged nearly a century ago seemed almost indulgent.

Three years passed. In late 2005, a minor controversy erupted about nowthatsfuckedup.com, a porn website specialising in user-generated content. Specifically, it relied on images provided by readers, allegedly of their girlfriends or wives. Many of nowthatsfuckedup.com's patrons served in the US military, and some complained about difficulties using credit cards from the countries in which they were posted. To encourage their custom, the site owner, one Chris Wilson, offered a special deal: soldiers in Iraq and Afghanistan could access porn freely on the condition they contributed photos from their tours of duty.

Wilson didn't specify any particular kind of photos, and plenty of soldiers simply emailed innocuous snaps of burly young men clowning for the camera or in mock-heroic poses with rifles and helmets. Others sent something quite different. Pictures of corpses arrived by email: horrific photographs of eviscerated torsos, cadavers charred beyond recognition. Sometimes, the dead seemed to be Iraqi soldiers or insurgents. Sometimes, they were civilians. Sometimes, they were just pieces of raw, red meat, sitting wetly in ruined cars or amid the bricks of toppled buildings. Indeed, nowthatsfuckedup.com accumulated so many grisly images that Wilson developed a specific section for his horror show, pages at which digital rubberneckers could scroll past example after example of the dreadful fragility of the human form: a severed head floating in a bowl of blood; an arm; a child with its face torn off.

Some soldiers captioned their work. The labels were often pragmatic, offering 'some pictures in exchange for access' or, more bluntly, 'dead men for entry'. Others made jokes. 'Name the body part', invited one soldier, underneath an image of a glistening lump. Another listed his photo as showing 'an Iraqi driver and passenger that tried to run a checkpoint' and complained 'the bad thing about shooting them is that we have to clean it up'. The viewers, by and large, responded with enthusiasm. 'Awesome', said one. 'Hey, soldier buds', wrote another, 'post some fresh kills for us!'

Eventually, the media learnt of the site and, with the corpses-for-porn deal in the news, the site's URL flashed around the net. Yes, I logged on, too. With the mangled corpses scrolling across my screen, I found myself, quite unexpectedly, remembering the head from Gallipoli.

The scarifying experience of the trenches introduced a new vocabulary for remembrance into English. Prior to the Great War, one spoke of 'keepsakes'. Soldiers posted in France came back with the word 'souvenir' to describe the talismans they collected. In Iraq in 2005, US troops felt less obliged to hoard physical objects. They enjoyed state-of-the-art Internet access, even at the front line. Digital cameras and video recorders were everywhere in Iraq, far smaller and more portable than in previous wars. These soldiers could capture a scene (a desert landscape, the aftermath of a car bombing, a lacerated corpse) on a tiny electronic device and instantly transmit the digital souvenir anywhere around the world. Back in 1915, soldiers at Gallipoli lacked broadband and digicams. But the impulse was the same. Unable to take a photo, someone kept a head: a permanent representation of experienced violence.

At the time of the nowthatsfuckedup.com controversy, I was working on a PhD. Whatever the story of the Echuca head, it definitely constituted a distraction of the kind you were supposed to avoid, and I successfully kept it at bay for several months. But that didn't mean I'd forgotten. In early 2006, with the thesis temporarily stalled, I phoned the Returned and Services League Turkish sub-branch and asked to see Ramazan Altintas.

It was still curiosity as much as anything else. The War on Terror, Dick Cheney had said, would run for a generation—fifty years, Peter Costello suggested. Battles would rage all over the world, not just in Iraq and Afghanistan, but on fronts yet to be determined. There was, it seemed, plenty of violence still to come. In 2006 we were already at war. Yet Iraq and Afghanistan were thousands of kilometres away and directly involved only a handful of Australians, most of whom were soldiers in elite units. The wars played like scratchy old horror movies projected onto a screen: disturbing, yes, but ultimately just shadows flickering on the surface of reality. Each fresh atrocity came and each fresh atrocity went, and there was no trace of its passage. That Friday, the day I phoned Altintas's office, six off-duty Iraqi soldiers had been massacred outside a restaurant in northern Iraq. A few days earlier, unidentified fighters had slit the throats of two teachers in front of their Shiite students, and a car bomb killed seven bystanders in Suleikh in eastern Baghdad. And so on and so on and so on. We became acclimatised so easily.

I'd first been a university student in the late eighties, a time in which you could imagine the planet growing steadily more civilised. Violence, like sexism or racial prejudice, persisted, but in a cosy environment like Melbourne, Australia, it seemed increasingly anomalous, a legacy from an era of darkness, to be slowly but definitively banished by enlightenment's inevitable spread.

The outbreak of a real war in 1990 was akin to finding, somewhere in the outer suburbs, a diplodocus—or, better, a tyrannosaurus. The first Gulf War was a huge, impossible creature rearing up from nowhere, challenging, by its mere existence, the assumptions upon which your life had been based. If something as prehistorically cruel as war could stalk through daylight without the modern world batting an eyelid, then reality was fundamentally other than it had seemed.

Wyndham Lewis's reaction to the Great War described the sentiment exactly: 'Life was good and easy, and I called Life "friend". I'd never hidden anything from him, and he'd never hidden anything from me. Or so I thought. I knew everything. He was an awfully intelligent companion; we had the same tastes (apparently) and he was awfully fond of me. And all the time he was plotting up a mass murder.' In some respects, it wasn't surprising. His war—the Great War—seemed a kind of yardstick, the war against which all others were measured. As the poet Vernon Scannell explained:

> Whenever war is spoken of
> I find
> The war that was called Great invades the mind.

It was particularly so for Australians. The lanky ghosts of the Anzacs had haunted our collective imagination for so long that, in some respects, their battles seemed more real than the sputtering hostilities of our time. The head from Gallipoli might, I thought, make war palpable in a way that the hundreds of thousands dead in Iraq hadn't. Retelling its story might re-create some of the shock Lewis had felt in 1914 and that had gripped me in 1990; it could perhaps puncture through the canopy of indifference spread over the conflicts around us now. A human head collected on a legendary battlefield transformed empty abstraction into the reality of sudden, fatal violence: a bullet thumping into a young man's brain, in a vignette repeated over and over and over again until millions of soldiers lay dead.

But the head was more than simply a reminder of war's toll. The case and its cushion belonged, by definition, to a survivor, so the display was an emblem not just of the dead but of the living, not merely of those killed but of the men who took their lives: perpetrators as well as victims. Because of that, it promised, I thought, insight into the heart of war, into what happened when the fundamental commandment 'Thou shalt not kill' transformed into its opposite. In normal society, only sociopaths hoarded body parts, and if police found a severed head in a display case, it was because they'd raided the apartment of some mumbling serial killer to uncover his makeshift shrine. Yet whoever had carefully detached a head from a neck and then placed it upon red velvet for later contemplation was not a murderer on a secret spree but a man in a time and a place in which killing was not just permissible but obligatory, the highest duty one could perform for one's country.

In that way, the head seemed a cipher: an authentic text waiting for decoding, a message written by bullets on flesh. It pointed to the meaning of war—or more specifically, the meaning of killing, the reason why someone who, as far as anyone knew, lived and died a respected member of the community had felt, some time in 1915, that appropriating a piece of someone else's body was allowed, even appropriate. I wanted to know what had happened—and what, if anything, the story explained about killing and its consequences, of which nowthatsfuckedup.com seemed a particularly ugly contemporary manifestation. That was why I went to see Altintas.

He was a solid, slow-speaking man, middle-aged, with thick eyebrows and salt-and-pepper hair. He clasped my hand and he thanked me for coming. Then he pushed a press release across the table, something about the Anzac Day ceremony and the ceremonial role the Returned and Services League Turkish sub-branch would play in it. I looked at it stupidly, not sure what to do.

'The *Herald Sun*? You're the reporter?'

I wasn't.

'One minute, one minute.' He ushered me back into the featureless waiting room while the real journalist arrived and did a real interview.

With exquisitely bad timing, I'd come only two days before the 2006 Anzac Day celebrations. That year, Turks had been, for the first time, invited to join the march. The Victorian Returned and

Services League president, Major General David McLachlan, explained that the invitation didn't extend to Germans, Italians, North Vietnamese—and especially not to the Japanese. But descendants of Turkish soldiers were welcome because, according to the major general, they were 'a very honourable' enemy. Altintas's grandfather, Veli Cevirgen, had fought at Gallipoli, and Altintas planned to march in his memory. Hence the *Herald Sun* journalist; hence the confusion.

I sat there, with the sharp anxiety of a patient waiting for surgery. This was hardly the time to be confronting him about severed heads and display boxes. But it was too late: I was here now and he'd agreed to see me, so I'd have to tough it out.

Half an hour later, after the journalist had gone, I was called back in. Altintas apologised for the mix-up and asked how he could help. Reminded of the appointment, he nodded. The timing didn't seem to bother him in the slightest. He remembered the head well; he'd always hoped, he said, that someone would investigate it further. Was that what I was going to do? The memory of the thesis, abandoned at home, twinged uncomfortably, but I nodded anyway.

What had it been like to be presented with the box? I'd seen the photo, of course, but what was his reaction to the head? Was it a shocking thing to open the lid and find something like that?

'Shocking, yes. But not frightening. My children saw it and they were not frightened at all. No, it was more ...' He groped for a word. 'It was sad. Not horrible, just very sad.' He'd recognised at once that it wasn't simply a footnote to the Anzac narrative but a story in its own right. Here was a part of a young man: a person who had possessed his own hopes and fears and loved ones; an ancestor, quite possibly, of people living today. That was why Altintas had issued the press release. 'He was only very young. You could see from here.' He moved his finger along under his nose, indicating the first growth of an imaginary moustache. 'Very young. A boy, really, maybe sixteen or seventeen.'

I asked him what he thought had happened.

'Prisoner', he answered softly. He gestured to his forehead. 'Not shot here. But kneel down, like that.' He made a gun shape with his fingers. 'Executed! Yes, I think so. I think that was what happened.'

The bullet hole was, after all, located right in the top of the skull. A trench soldier might take fire in the face or in the neck, but how would he receive a bullet in the crown of his head? At Gallipoli, the Turks occupied the higher positions, with the Australians below them. That was why, at the end of hostilities, the War Graves Commission had identified the bodies of Anzacs by the bullet holes in their skulls. Yet this man was a Turk, not an Australian. How had he been shot from above? The suggestion of a kneeling prisoner, killed by his captor, was ballistically plausible, so when the head became news in 2002, the location of the wound—and the questions Altintas had raised then about a battlefield execution—caused a ripple of shock.

It shouldn't have. Despite Major General McLachlan's rhetoric about the 'honourable enemies' of 1915, the Great War unleashed just as much brutality as in Baghdad today. All the belligerents executed prisoners, not as a systematic policy but with a certain regularity nonetheless. Reading the letters and the diaries of soldiers, the casual references to the disposal of unwanted captives jumped out at me again and again. For instance, after the Gallipoli landing, Private Keith Wadsworth wrote a long letter home narrating his exploits. He talks of wounding a man himself and then explains that, as he ran on, he expected his comrades to bayonet the fellow to death. The Turkish snipers who tried to surrender, he says, 'didn't last as long as a snowflake in hell'. Similarly, from the trenches of France, Captain Lewis Nott sent a letter to his wife describing how the Germans cried out for mercy when cornered. 'My sweet', Nott says, 'there is no mercy here'.

Even Charles Bean, the official historian and a relentless booster of the Anzac legend, explained how he'd come to accept that such executions took place simply because he'd heard officers and men boast so often about them. In his own description of Pozières and its aftermath, Bean describes how the men lit cigarettes while waiting for terrified Germans to emerge from the rubble to be shot or bayoneted. One of the Australians, about to stab a prisoner, discovered that his bayonet wasn't fixed. According to Bean, the soldier calmly secured it and then killed the German, who had been begging for his life the whole time.

Vile deeds were performed on the other side of No Man's Land, too. The behaviour of the German militarists in Belgium prefigured the strategies perfected by the fascists in the next war; the Turks were committing genocide against the Armenians even while the Gallipoli invasion was underway. But the crimes of one army didn't negate the cruelties of the other. Australians had, on occasion, murdered their captives—in *Goodbye to All That*, Robert Graves suggests that 'the troops [with] the worst reputation for acts of violence against prisoners were the Canadians (and later the Australians)'— so Altintas's scenario certainly was not impossible.

The best way to find out would be to track the head's history. Who had kept it all that time? What did they say about its origins?

Altintas laughed. 'We don't know that. No one will say. Even up to now, no one will say. The next day, after all the newspapers came, they changed the story. Suddenly they said there was no young man.' That was one of the more bizarre aspects of the whole episode. The initial news reports were explicit: the head came from a local man who had known about his grandfather's secret but was so shocked when he actually opened the box that he contacted the police. But later the narrative changed entirely. According to subsequent accounts, the head had not been uncovered by a relative at all. Instead, a local painter had taken the box to the police station. He'd borrowed it, many years earlier, from a fellow artist, hoping the grisly item might inspire some grotesque themes in the artwork he was working on. The original painter was now dead; no one in Echuca (or anywhere else) could recall how or where he'd originally come by the head.

It all seemed very strange. How had this tale of the frightened family, so clear and so definite, dissolved into an entirely different story of artists and their work? Altintas offered one explanation. 'They are ashamed.' He shrugged. 'They don't want to talk about what happened. They think we will blame them.'

Would he?

'No. We don't want to blame them. That young man, he did the right thing. When he found it, he could have just thrown it in the rubbish. Instead, he gives it back. I would like to shake his hand, to thank him. He did the right thing. But we would still like to know what happened.' He told me to wait and he went into his files and then came back with a manila folder. It was all the clippings he'd kept about the severed head story. 'Take these. Maybe you will find else something out. If so, please let me know.'

I stood up to leave. But there was one more thing. OK, I understood that he didn't blame the family. But what about the man who took the head in the first place, the soldier responsible for desecrating a corpse? What did he think of him?

'The grandfather?' Altintas paused at the doorway and then shook his head slowly. 'War makes people crazy. I don't blame him. It was not his fault. It's the fault of the people who send young men to invade other people's countries.' He lowered his voice to a confidential whisper. 'Like now, with Iraq. You see, it's just like with Iraq.'

Outside in the sunshine, I still didn't know what to do, but Altintas's comparison, entirely unprompted, reinforced my instinct that there was something in the story that was worth pursuing. There was a contemporary resonance, even if I didn't quite understand how it worked. I might as well keep looking. I was in the library most days anyway. All it would require was fossicking in some different archives.

And there did seem something fascinating about the reaction the head had sparked. The day after the press conference, Detective Sergeant Adrian Kennedy, the police officer who'd handed over the head, told a newspaper that the family involved had been shocked by the media attention: 'They did not want this made public. They thought they were doing the right thing in handing the head over for it to be passed back to the Turkish government. All this publicity means they will probably stay anonymous and we will never know about its origins.' The *Riverine Herald*, the local Echuca paper, headlined its coverage 'A Sad Turn', referring not to the decapitation but to the interest that had been shown in the discovery. 'Never has a respectful gesture by an Echuca family soured as much as one this week. The family who discovered the head of a Turkish soldier among the belongings of a World War One digger have remained in hiding for the fear of what the wider community would do', the paper reported.

Yet looking over the cuttings, I couldn't see any anyone condemning, let alone threatening, the family of the soldier. Altintas was widely reported offering his thanks. He'd said he didn't blame anyone, explained repeatedly that he simply wanted more information about the souvenir. What, then, was the source of the family's fear?

Perhaps it was to do with changes in how the Anzac experience was remembered. Twenty years ago, Anzac Day ceremonies seemed to be in terminal decline. The prolonged brutality of the Vietnam War chilled enthusiasm for military parades, and through the late seventies and early eighties, attendances at marches dwindled. By 1984, feminists protesting against rape in wartime attracted nearly as much media attention as the veterans themselves. But in 2005, Anzac Day basked in a renewed popularity. Tens of thousands of Australians, many of them tousle-haired backpackers, slept out on Gallipoli beach, while thousands more attended the dawn ceremony at Melbourne's Shrine of Remembrance. It was a change in more than just numbers. The events had become boisterous rather than subdued: as part of a festival that seemed less a commemoration than an unapologetic celebration, a huge screen on Gallipoli beach showed Eric Clapton and the Bee Gees. Somehow, the occasion had become detached not only from the violence of war but also from history itself. Each year, school children explained to nodding reporters that the diggers kept Australia free, almost as though the Anzac contingent had repelled Turks invading Sydney Harbour.

Perhaps that was why the family feared that they'd be blamed: not so much for their ancestor's deed but because they themselves had, by drawing attention to the reality of war, marred the increasingly obligatory veneration of Anzac. A severed head did not, after all, lend itself to jingoism.

Then, somewhere else in the library, I came across some research on trophy skulls, and was stunned by how common the souveniring of body parts had been, especially during the Second World War. In June 2003, roughly a year or so after the Echuca head came to light, US police conducting a drug raid in Colorado uncovered a trunk engraved with the words 'Guadalcanal' and the date 'November 11 1942'. Inside they found a human skull. It had been lacquered and engraved with the words 'This is a good Jap. Guadalcanal S. I. 11 Nov 42. Oscar MG J. Papas USMC'. The skull had been auto-graphed by two or three dozen other soldiers. Their willingness to record their identity suggests that it didn't even cross their minds that using a human head in that way might be inappropriate. The aviator Charles Lindbergh, returning from a visit to the Pacific Front in 1944, recorded the customs officer in Hawaii asking whether he was carry-ing any bones, a question made necessary by the quantity of human souvenirs coming through. In 1984, the team excavating and repatri-ating wartime Japanese corpses from the Mariana Islands estimated that an astonishing 60 per cent of the bodies lacked skulls.

The Japanese also committed hideous atrocities: the rape of Nanking, the abuse of prisoners of war, the forced prostitution of women. But the souveniring of corpses seemed to have been more prevalent among Allied soldiers—Australians as well as Americans. Private Jake Kovco, the Australian soldier killed in Iraq, belonged, for instance, to a battalion that possessed, in its officers' mess, a pen stand made from a human femur.

In my research, one particular story about a skull struck me as uncannily similar to the scenario Altintas had imagined. In 1993, a veteran, ageing and remorseful, asked a relative for help in returning a trophy skull to Japan. The relative contacted a journalist and told him the story. The soldier's platoon had captured a Japanese sniper at Guadalcanal. They had no facilities to hold a prisoner, so later that night they shot him. They cut his head off, boiled away the flesh and placed the skull on a pole. Then they all signed it and inscribed the bone with 'One Dead Jap' and 'Shot at Guadalcanal'.

Most of the stories of souvenired body parts come from the Second World War or Vietnam, rather than the Great War. The explanation for this was possibly a practical one. Conditions for soldiers in the Second World War were better than they had been twenty years earlier. With the primitive accommodation and transport provided to soldiers of the Great War, it might simply not have been possible to smuggle an object as bulky as a skull without being caught.

This was another point Altintas had raised. He'd wondered how an object as bulky as a skull could have been brought back on a Great War troopship. Perhaps, he'd suggested, it had been carried by an officer, someone of importance and standing in the community. Perhaps that explained the family's reaction to the publicity. Perhaps the reputation of a historical figure was at stake. He hadn't thought that uncovering the truth would be difficult though: 'You see, at the police station, they were definite. They told me that the young man who found the head had just gone, walked out of the station just before I arrived. They must know who it was.' He'd suggested looking at obituaries. The skull, it was said, had been found by a family cleaning up after a relative's death. If I found a death notice of someone the right age, a week or two earlier, that would be a good place to start.

I tried to put the plan into operation, absently noting, when the Echuca papers flashed up on the catalogue, how I seemed to have committed myself to the search without ever making a conscious decision. But when the staff brought out the bound editions of the *Riverine Herald* from the stacks, the problems became evident. Echuca wasn't a huge town, but people died there with sufficient regularity to keep the obituary pages full. I assumed I was looking for a deceased who had children, since it sounded like someone from a younger generation handed the head in. But that didn't narrow things down much. How far back did I need to scrutinise? It could have been months before the house was tidied up, and even more months before the family came to a decision about what to do with the head.

I tried to cross-reference with a list of Echuca soldiers who'd served at Gallipoli. But that was hopeless, too, since so many of the names were extremely common Anglo-Celtic ones. The war seemed to have been largely fought by men named 'Jones' and 'Smith' and 'Roberts', surnames too prosaic to match against obituaries. In any case, just because a man enlisted from a certain area, it didn't follow that his son would die there seventy years later. If the Gallipoli veteran had moved to Echuca after the war, the place of recruitment was entirely irrelevant.

Seeing my desultory scratchings of names and dates, one of the librarians asked directly what I was searching for. I explained. She looked at me and made the obvious suggestion. Had I tried the coroner's report? I hadn't. Who knew that you could telephone the coronial staff and ask directly about records pertaining to mummified human heads? I'd half expected to be asked the reason for the enquiry ('What are you: some kind of monster?'), but the polite woman taking the call, entirely unruffled, asked me to hold while she went off to rummage through whatever diabolical cabinet contained details of the myriad ways people in Victoria hurt themselves and each other. Minutes later, a PDF of the coroner's report arrived by email.

It was a fascinating document. On 15 November 2002, Deputy State Coroner Iain West conducted an investigation into 'the death of an unknown adult male' at Echuca. West could not identify the deceased, but he attributed the cause of death to a 'gunshot injury to the head' received at an 'unknown date at the Gallipoli Peninsula, Turkey'.

The identification of the head as a genuine relic rested in part on an investigation conducted by the forensic pathologist Malcolm Dodd and the forensic anthropologist Christopher Briggs. Briggs provided an 'osteological report' that concluded ('from the size of the mastoid processes, the shape of the chin and the overall robusticity of the skull') that the head was definitely male. It was Caucasian and possessed characteristics (such as high cheekbones) which, he said, were 'noted in individuals of Central European descent'. The fusion of the plates in one part of the skull indicated that the head belonged to a teenager. Other evidence, including the wear of the teeth, suggested an age between the late twenties and the early thirties, and it was this second age band that he eventually settled on. Dodd's report concluded that the two holes in the skull were an entry and exit wound, consistent with a .303 bullet used by Australian troops during the Gallipoli invasion. 'The single gunshot wound described would', he said, 'be sufficient to cause death'.

Coroner West also asked Dodd whether, in his opinion, it was possible to exclude 'suicide or any other mode by which [the deceased] may have been shot'. The euphemistic 'any other mode' seemed a reference to Altintas's speculation about cold-blooded murder. In response, Dodd first ruled out suicide. He discussed 'the usual sites of election' for people bent on self-harm, a phrase in which you glimpsed the daily tragedies to which a coroner necessarily habituated himself. People shot themselves, he explained, in the temple, the forehead or the roof of the mouth; no one deliberately fired a gun at the top of their own head. He also rejected the execution scenario. Had the bullet been fired from close range, he said,

> it would be highly likely that the back of the head would have been blown away by the severity of the blast given the proposed calibre of the projectile. In this case, both entry and exit sites of the skull comprise well-defined circular areas of bone deficiency with radiating fractures, indicating a 'distant range' shot. A contact shot from a heavy calibre handgun or indeed a combat rifle would … literally have blown the head apart.

The coroner pressed further, and Dodd acknowledged that 'the entry wound through the upper left frontoparietal area and accompanying exit near the mid of the occiput is an odd angle' but suggested 'a sniper may have shot at the deceased while his head was peering out of a trench'.

It still didn't make sense. The trenches of the Great War were constructed so that soldiers stepped up onto a duckboard to fire at the enemy. Peering out of a trench exposed your head, but not the *top* of your head. Nevertheless, Dodd's reference to a sniper made me think. What if the dead man were a sniper too? In that case, he could well have been lying down when he died, since the Turkish sharpshooters often left the trenches to hide in the shrub. If the victim were prone, the bullet angle became more logical. Say he was stretched out behind cover and, while loading his rifle, looked down for an instant—just as an Australian sniper fired. In that case, a wound in the top of the head became perfectly logical.

The scenario of a sniper duel seemed especially plausible, since the marksmen of the Great War did, indeed, take keepsakes from men they killed. The New South Wales farmer Archie Barwick wrote from Gallipoli in April 1915, 'I shot 3 snipers dead today, they were picking off our poor fellows who were hobbling down to the dressing stations, the first one I killed I took his belt off to keep as a souvenir of my first kill with the rifle, the other two I laid out beautifully'.

Was that what happened with the Turkish head? Did a rifleman seek a trophy of a piece of smart shooting? Dodd made clear that the heavy-calibre bullet would have killed the Turkish soldier instantly as it crashed through his brain. If, like many of the snipers at Gallipoli, he was hiding in No Man's Land, his body may have lain unattended for some time. Dodd couldn't identify any chemical agent on the remaining flesh and suggested the mummification was probably natural, the result of a corpse drying in the sun. Perhaps the Australian sniper couldn't—or didn't—reach the body of his victim for months. Perhaps he stood over the remains of the man he'd killed after they'd become desiccated and only then decided to take a reminder of how beautifully the man had been 'laid out'.

Under those circumstances, the removal of a preserved head would not necessarily have been a gory business. It was possible that the successful mummification of the skull might itself have spurred the idea of a souvenir, in the way recorded by Australian soldier John Adlard in his diary of Ypres. 'Picked up a skull today', he wrote, 'with strips of dangling skin and hair. It looks very comic.' It was certainly possible, but still only speculation.

When it came to the head's origin, West recorded only that Sergeant Kennedy of the Echuca Criminal Investigation Unit had taken 'possession of a lidded wooden box containing a mummified human head, after he had received a report of its existence from a local resident'. According to West, Kennedy then explained how 'further inquiries' had revealed that 'for approximately thirty years, the head had been in the possession of Mr Noel Tunks, a retired art teacher who had obtained it on loan from Mr Joel Elenberg, a Melbourne painter and sculptor'. When Noel Tunks was duly called to the inquest, he said that Elenberg had told him that the head was that of a Turkish soldier killed at Gallipoli, but hadn't given any more information about how it had come to Australia or where he'd originally obtained it.

The repetition of the second narrative before the coroner quelled some of the suspicions I'd inherited from Altintas. One could easily imagine a local community hiding the truth from a prying big city media, especially given the feelings of betrayal that Kennedy and the *Riverine Herald* had voiced. But would it be worth lying to a coroner—a reasonably serious business—over events that happened so long ago? I doubted it. Still, I needed to speak to this Noel Tunks. If anyone could shed more light on the two stories and how they'd come to change, he would be the man.

The unusual name made finding an address easy enough. Composing the letter was the difficult part. Asking a stranger about his relationship to a piece of a mummified corpse was a delicate business. It was hard to find the right words. And how could I politely ask him to clarify the difference between two flatly contradictory stories without accusing him of lying? I did my best, tearing up one draft after another, until I had something that could be sent. The letter explained that I was interested primarily in the origins of the head and had wondered if Noel Tunks could suggest anyone who could tell me more than had appeared in the newspapers or the coroner's report. Did Joel Elenberg have any relatives, for instance? If so, would they speak with me? My interest was in the past, I said: I did not seek to embarrass the living and would be happy to preserve the anonymity of anyone involved.

Weeks passed with no reply, and in a last rush to finish the thesis, I'd given up on the head when the mail eventually brought a response. The letter politely but firmly reiterated the story from the coroner's report. Noel Tunks had received the head from Joel Elenberg. Elenberg collected unusual objects for his art. Elenberg died without disclosing how he originally came across the head. No one else knew anything about it. What's more, it quashed, in a way that seemed quite conscious, any hopes of further investigations via Elenberg's relatives. 'Some enquiries have been made regarding some input from his wife and family', it said, 'and I am told that the wife does not want to be involved in any discussions regarding the skull or other matters regarding Joel. So it would be a waste of time contemplating such a move.' As to the discrepancies in the stories, the email explained that Noel had given the head 'to a friend to deliver to Melbourne University for safe keeping. This friend gave it to a friend who gave it to a friend. This person concocted a story that his grandfather brought it back from the war etc. etc., all of which was not the truth.'

The letter fanned the embers of my suspicion to a new heat. Aside from the tone of the correspondence, which clearly implied a desire that I desist, the narrative just seemed too neat: a story diverting attention from anyone living and sealing off all avenues of investigation into the dead. Was it credible that the police had initially been taken in by the inventions of an unnamed fantasist, the friend of a friend of Noel Tunks? Would so many different people really have passed a mummified human head around so casually, handing it from acquaintance to acquaintance like an unwanted holiday souvenir?

The letter was signed N Tunks but directed any future correspondence to an email address under a different name. After further hesitations and equivocations, I sent a message asking more directly about the details Altintas had provided. He'd told me, I explained, that, when he arrived at the station, the police had told him that the relative of the Gallipoli veteran had only just left. They'd spoken of the man as someone they knew, not a random prankster. How did Tunks explain that?

This time the reply came almost immediately. The writer took no offence at my implied disbelief; instead, he politely offered to do anything he could to help with my research:

> I think I told you at the time it was given to the police in Echuca there were many lies and cover-ups associated with the event. The skull really played no part in the city of Echuca. It was taken there by Noel's friend unbeknown to Noel. Noel's instructions to his friend were to drop it off at a university but the friend had other ideas. The person to whom the skull was delivered lied about its origin. Prior to the skull being taken to Echuca it was stored in Noel's home both in Maryborough and Avoca.

Then there was a final detail, one that left me feeling both guilty and embarrassed. My correspondence, the email explained, hadn't been with Noel Tunks himself but with his legal guardian. Tunks suffered from dementia. He could not tell anything else. That, presumably, explained the cease-and-desist tone. The letter hadn't been meant to suppress a historical investigation so much as to dissuade, quite reasonably, a stranger bothering an old and sick man.

Perhaps Altintas was wrong. Perhaps there'd been no attempt to shield the head's owner; perhaps the 'lies and cover-ups' had simply stemmed from a silly prank. I didn't know, and I didn't think I'd be able to find out—certainly not by plaguing any further the carers and relatives of a dementia sufferer. I looked at the folder of clippings, those scribbles from the library. The research created its own momentum. You took one step, which then led to another, and before you knew it, you'd embarked on a journey without ever really knowing where it would lead you.

The Turkish soldier had been a human being. He deserved the dignity of having his name recorded, to be remembered as something other than the shrunken object in that box. Realistically, however, the prospects of so definite an outcome had never been good. In none of the cases of souveniring from the Second World War had the identity of the trophy victim been determined. Acts of desecration invariably targeted anonymous bodies, since, almost by definition, a corpse with a name was far harder to treat as an object. Even if the research had proved successful, what exactly would I have found: the name of the killer? the unit in which he served? a particular engagement—perhaps even a date he saw action? And then what? What would any of that have actually told me?

The head had emerged from wartime violence. But that in itself didn't guarantee insight into the heart of things, into the sudden fury of a wartime killing. No, violence had flared for an instant, back in 1915, and someone had died with a bullet in the head. That was true; that was what we knew. But the moment had passed. The head was a husk, its eye sockets empty and sightless. It was as real—or as unreal—as another headline from Baghdad.

When the site nowthatsfuckedup.com was eventually closed down, Chris Wilson was arrested on the grounds of obscenity. But the charges against him pertained exclusively to sexual images, not to his death photos. Sex was a familiar taboo, and the anxieties about it could be more easily assuaged. Killing was different, especially in an epoch of permanent war. The authorities could not deem Wilson's war porn legally obscene without making a judgement about the

soldiers who'd sent them—and ultimately about the wars that produce such men.

I looked again at the email from Tunks's guardian. It didn't
matter, I decided. I'd been approaching the whole business from
entirely the wrong direction. The head from Gallipoli couldn't explain
killing. I needed to understand killing to appreciate the head, and that
meant trying something very different.

2

NOT EVERYONE'S CUP OF TEA

'Have you got some other clothes?' Demetri asked, looking up from his knife grinder. 'You'll get blood all over that nice shirt.' I shrugged, tried for nonchalance. The shirt was old and ugly—and the blood was the point. We were in a little bush town in Queensland. Demetri was a professional roo-shooter. He killed for a living, and he was going to show me how.

'I was awfully excited', wrote Private WR Guest to his family from Gallipoli in 1915. He'd killed his first Turk. 'It is just like potting kangaroos in the bush.' The comparison stood out again and again in the letters and the diaries of Australian servicemen in the Great War. Kangaroos were man-sized; they stood upright; you shot them dead with a rifle. Billy Sing, the Australian sniper credited with hundreds of personal kills at Gallipoli, specifically attributed his deadly accuracy to his experiences shooting kangaroos—and so did scores of other soldiers. Private Guest and his peers wrote their letters, casually assuming that friends and relations back home would understand the comparison. For men of the era, the killing of animals was a regular chore. Whether roos in the bush or chickens in the backyard, previous generations took for granted that meat meant blood and death.

But the Great War was a long time ago, and potting kangaroos in 2007 was nearly as foreign to inner-city Australians as potting Turks. David Hicks was a roo-shooter; the people I knew weren't. We didn't kill kangaroos, or chickens or sheep. We didn't kill anything much at all. Did this contribute to our inability to understand Iraq and Afghanistan? Initially, it was just an idle question, a residue of the energy spent on my fruitless research. But then I started wondering, as much about practicalities as anything else: was it possible simply to tag along with a shooter? Was the killing of animals secret—or, at least, discreet—or could anyone find out how it was done? Was it just that people from the inner suburbs of the big cities—people like me—chose not to know?

Eventually, with the thesis finished, I emailed the Kangaroo Industry Association of Australia about the possibility of interviewing a kangaroo-shooter, explaining how it might help my research. The association remained, however, stubbornly silent. The industry was engaged in its own desperate counterinsurgency against animal liberationists and their allies, and in that campaign, a proposal to compare its activities to the battlefields of the Great War was, one presumed, not immediately appealing, no matter what Private Guest might have said about kangaroos and Gallipoli.

I turned instead to a man named John Weaver. Weaver maintained a personal website that featured a cornucopia of roos, pigs and goats in various stages of disassembly sufficiently gory to suggest that its proprietor might discuss shooting without worrying too much about the impression he created. So it proved. John was heading overseas, but he recommended phoning a man called Demetri in rural Queensland: 'The nicest bloke you'll ever meet—a real character'.

Once I'd been given Demetri's number, and once I knew the trip was viable, it slowly became impossible not to go. Roo-shooting would be bloody, it would be violent and it would be upsetting—I knew all of that. But to let my own distress stand in the way seemed a piece of miserable cowardice. Kangaroos were shot every day. It happened and I didn't do anything to prevent it; in fact, most of the time, I gave it no thought whatsoever. Refusing to gaze upon an activity you tacitly condoned—or at least did nothing to oppose—seemed entirely craven, a moral abnegation.

I tried to be practical. Queensland was a tremendous distance to travel for such a half-formed scheme. There was no guarantee that the experience would convey anything useful about killing or the Gallipoli head—indeed it seemed more likely than not that it wouldn't—but the idea had taken hold and wouldn't be uprooted. If I despaired about the ease with which foreign wars were assimilated into daily life, so that the details of the atrocities emerging daily from Iraq and Afghanistan became exclusively the concern of news junkies or policy wonks, then wasn't my own revulsion at the thought of animal slaughter a warning sign? Wasn't it, in fact, exactly the kind of conduct that kept aspects of the War on Terror in the shadows? We all knew, at some level, the cruelty done in our names, yet no one probed the recesses of Afghanistan's Bagram Air Base too closely, for fear that the details of enhanced interrogation might distress our tender feelings. If you didn't want to look, didn't that suggest that there was a reason to open your eyes?

It was an inability to answer this question that eventually brought me to the passenger seat of an old ute in Queensland, with evening falling, an ice-cream container of bullets perched near the gearstick, and a battered rifle resting uncomfortably on my knees.

Demetri was in his late sixties, with the leather skin of an outdoorsman and the alert gaze of a magpie. When I first came into his sports shop on the main street of the town, I sensed him silently weighing me in the scales of his own experience and finding me distinctly wanting. He was born in a poor Greek village near Delphi and, after the civil war, arrived in Queensland, at the other end of the known universe. He taught himself English while working in a Greek café and cutting hair, and he won the acceptance of locals suspicious of European ways by knocking them unconscious—the manner in which, it seemed, disagreements in postwar Queensland were routinely settled. He was, I concluded, a tough old guy; yet he was, at the same time, the nice bloke that John had promised.

Demetri had never been to school, and it was that lack of education that allowed him to flourish as a roo-shooter: 'I used to watch my grandfather and my father when they were skinning hides. Like youngsters here, if they live out in the bush, they know all about it. You take the kids from the city, they know nothing—like yourself.' The baleful effects of formal schooling, particularly as manifested in my own example, provided a running conversational theme throughout the evening. But Demetri delivered his assessments so genially that they never seemed rude—particularly since, on the rattling train ride from New South Wales to Queensland, my lack of knowledge gnawed at me. What did I know about violence? What did I know about war?

The military literature was haunted by this curious epistemological anxiety. John Keegan, the doyen of British war writing, begins his classic book *The Face of Battle* with a strange confession:

> I have not been in a battle; not near one, nor heard one from afar, nor seen the aftermath. I have questioned people who have been in battle—my father and father-in-law among them; have walked over battlefields … I have read about battles, of course, have talked about battles, have been lectured about battles and, in the last four or five years, have watched battles in progress, or apparently in progress, on the television screen … But I have never been in a battle.

Keegan knew battle, much better than any front-line soldier, but he would never understand it, not in the way that soldiers did. The problem was killing—the aspect of war that peacetime could never replicate. Keegan could train as a soldier; he could experience hardship and danger and camaraderie, but unlike those about whom he wrote, he could never kill, and thus he felt he could never grasp war like they did.

There was, it seemed to me, a faint echo of this sentiment in the contemporary contrast between rural battlers and the urban elites. For decades, politicians and pundits had hammered the theme relentlessly: those on the land were the real Australians, possessed of a folk wisdom more valuable than the book smarts of inner-city sophisticates. The sophisticates themselves often promulgated the argument, partly, perhaps, because they felt alienated from the timeless cycles of birth and death enacted daily on a farm. In the country, they nurtured life and they ended life and, to a keyboard jockey living in the artificial light of an office cubicle, that experience seemed inherently profound. The distinction was largely bullshit, of course. Yes, Demetri knew things that I didn't—of course he did!—but that was hardly an argument against education, and while Keegan's confession was understandable, it was also deeply neurotic.

But here I was bouncing across country roads in a roo-shooter's ute, and the university seemed a long, long way away. Demetri ran a distinctly low-tech operation—defiantly so. The truck carried a GPS locator, but he regarded the machine with amused contempt. In his day, he explained, you needed to use the stars, and once you could navigate with the heavens, satellites were superfluous. I nodded, in a studied imitation of indifference. I was more or less lost as soon as we left town, and by the time we headed off road and into a paddock, I had not the vaguest idea where we were.

We stopped somewhere in the twilight and unwrapped the steak sandwiches Demetri had bought, waiting for the darkness to gather. While we ate, he told me more about his early life in Australia, about his brief stint as a boxer and the houses he'd built in the town. Whatever else he'd done, roo-shooting had always been part of his life: 'You shoot a kangaroo: you got to skin it or you got to gut it. Yes, it's a bloody game. But with cattle, it's the same, but the educated people don't think about that because they don't see it. I can clean and gut kangaroos, and it doesn't worry me. But if I'm watching TV and I see a medical operation, I can't stand it. If I see someone give someone a needle, I can't stand it.'

He didn't really know why that was the case, why it was that human blood bothered him and animal blood didn't: 'I wouldn't like to shoot a kangaroo just for the fun of it, but when you're doing it for bread and butter it's different. A lot of people—educated people—talk about the poor kangaroos. But when you go kangaroo-shooting, when you shoot that kangaroo, the bullet is there before the sound. They don't even know what happened. But think about what happens to sheep and cattle. The men go out with motorbikes, four wheel drives, horses and all this, muster them for kilometres, put them in the motor yards, load them on the truck, take them to the saleyards, no water, no food, and from there to the abattoir— what a punishment that is compared to what happens to the kanga-roo!' Fair enough, but it didn't make me feel better about what we were about to do. The steak tasted particularly fleshy, and I noted absently that I could still swallow. I wanted the shooting to start; I didn't want it ever to start.

I'd been a vegetarian for a long time—until, in fact, I'd lived for six months in the Philippines. On that trip, I'd stayed with commu-nity activists who'd ushered us into an impoverished barrio to meet with peasant organisers. The villagers entertained us in the traditional way: they killed and cooked one of their pigs, so they could serve its meat with rice. With the greasy flesh on a plate, I hesitated—but only for an instant. People had sacrificed a major portion of their worldly goods in the name of hospitality. I could hardly admit a concern for pigs when most children here never received adequate protein, and the necks of the women swelled with obscene goitres brought on by iodine deficiencies.

That was all years ago, and since then I'd reverted, without much thought, to a traditionally carnivorous diet. But John had casually explained that friends of his who'd come shooting had often spent their first evening vomiting. And even though he'd been a shooter since childhood, the kind of butchering he'd needed to per-form as a professional had shocked him at first: 'You know, seeing an animal slit open and all its guts fall out. But that only lasted a short time. I have carcassed thousands and thousands and thousands of kangaroos and pigs since then, and it just becomes a job. You don't even think about it. Chopping off its head, cutting off its forearms, gutting it and turning it into pure meat, seeing all that blood and guts: I don't turn a hair.' He didn't turn a hair, but how I'd respond to the head-chopping and forearm-hacking he described seemed much less clear.

The idea that killing animals might, in some way, prepare you to kill people was an old one. Even the Mongols, not known for delicate sensibilities, had seasoned their young men for battle through great slaughters on horseback. More recently, in the Second World War, the British Army had tried inoculating its (increasingly urban) recruits against battle failure by taking them into an abattoir and showering them with sheep's blood as they stuck dummies with bayonets. The Vietnam veteran R Wayne Eisenhart recalled an even more graphic version of the same training. He and his fellow recruits were brought before a staff sergeant. The sergeant was holding a rabbit, which he caressed and petted until, without warning, he crushed in its head with a rock and tore its carcass into fragments with his hands and teeth: 'As we left the clearing he stood there with fur all around his mouth and blood running down his throat. The intended message was that one was going into a war and civilisation and all its emotional vestiges must be left behind. One must be violent and unmerciful.' Violent and unmerciful, I repeated to myself. That was how we would be.

Demetri finished his meal and wiped the grease from his fingers clean on the paper bag. 'Probably dark enough.' Off we went, rattling across the paddock. He drove with one hand; with the other, he twirled a pole coming down through the truck's roof, rotating the electric lamp so that spindly fingers of light probed out across the scrub. For a long time, I couldn't see anything—or rather I saw herds of objects that looked convincingly animal-shaped until the truck drew closer and they resolved into trees and bushes and shadows.

We drove for fifteen minutes or so in a slow semicircle, and the only kangaroos visible were hopping safely away in the distance, with part of me silently willing them on. Don't you understand? We're coming to kill! Flee! Go! Go! Perhaps we'd get through the whole night without troubling the wildlife at all.

But then Demetri's lamp fastened onto a large roo and pinned it with the brightness. In a sudden, graceful move, he swung the truck in a semicircle so he could aim out the window, and he killed the ignition. The kangaroo stood still, its head upright, staring at us not in fear but in wonderment, an Old Testament patriarch confronting an awful angel of fire and light. Demetri put his rifle to his shoulder and pulled the trigger, and the animal jerked backwards and disappeared, as if a rope attached to its legs had been savagely yanked. The cabin filled with the smell of cordite and my ears rang from the noise before it was swallowed by the expanse of the paddock. Demetri started the engine and the truck hurtled forwards over the scrub. It was all so sudden.

'You hit it.'

'Of course I hit it.' An instant later, he'd stopped the motor again. We jumped down from the truck, into the chilly night air, and there it was, a medium-sized kangaroo splayed on the dirt. Dead. Spectacularly, bloodily dead. The bullet had smacked into it so hard that its eyes oozed from their sockets and most of the top of its skull had been shredded. The transformation was so comprehensive and irrevocable, the distance so great from the alert animal in the spotlight to this broken thing lying at our feet.

I was analysing my emotions; Demetri was getting to work. He took out his newly sharpened knives and, with a couple of cuts, he removed what remained of the head. The blade split flesh with the wet sound of a cut cabbage. 'Sometimes, the bullet will do your work for you', he said, conversationally, throwing the lump into the darkness over his shoulder. He sawed off the tail, leaving it coiled on the ground like the trunk from a small, grey elephant. A kindling-snapping crack and the forearms came away, and then he used the knife to slice open a slit in the hind leg, just below the joint.

'Your job', he said. 'Put your fingers through here'—he gestured to the cut he'd made—'and your thumb here and then lift it up onto the truck and set it up onto the hook'. I tried to follow what he said, but I couldn't get my hands into quite the right place and I staggered slightly, holding the gamey, still-warm carcass next to my chest, while I tried to insert the hook. The kangaroo was heavier than I expected, but even though I couldn't manage the grip Demetri wanted, I compensated with brute force until eventually the hook went into the joint, leaving the body hanging from the side of the ute. My shirt was bloody already. Demetri plunged his knife into the midsection of the animal dangling from the truck. The guts splitting sounded like canvas tearing, and the intestines flowed wetly onto the dirt. There was something obscene about how they glistened in the truck's lights, reddy-purple as coral and rippling unnaturally.

And we were in the truck and moving again. 'What about all of that?' I asked, gesturing back where the fragments of kangaroo were disappearing into the darkness behind us.

'The foxes take care of it. Look.' He rotated his light and I could see the pairs of eyes moving over the field.

So the night went. We drove in slow, bumpy circuits around paddocks that seemed in the darkness impossibly vast. In the distance, mobs of roos would appear and sometimes bound alongside us, keeping pace with the truck, while Demetri casually identified the vague shapes as blues and greys, bucks and does, running the light back and forth to choose a target. Sometimes his lamp would pin two animals at a time and the second would remain transfixed even as Demetri fired at the first, almost as if the noise of the gun only added to whatever otherworldly power the spotlight exerted.

By law, the abattoir couldn't accept animals unless they'd been shot in the head. It was a regulation Demetri hated: 'Bloody government doesn't know anything. You shoot it in the body, it dies instantly. You shoot for the head, it turns at the last minute, and then …' Later,

I saw what he meant. Most of the time, the roos were dead when the truck reached them and I got out to drag them to the hooks: soft, rag-doll limp, a trickle of blood trailing behind them. But it wasn't always so easy. On one occasion, the roo twitched at the moment Demetri fired, and the shot exploded its muzzle rather than its brain. When we got to it, the animal was lying in the dirt, whimpering and clawing at the earth. Demetri chopped with a machete until it fell still. 'Bloody thing', he said, meaning, I think, the bullet more than the animal.

In the trenches, according to the poet Charles Sorley, death involved a three-stage transformation: a man suddenly became an animal, screaming and writhing in inarticulate, brutish pain, and then a thing, an empty insensate object. These were already animals, but I could still see something of what Sorley meant, for the shuddering death throes were so primal that they seemed to wrack a species different in kind from the dignified creature staring back from the spotlight.

I felt slightly sick then, and again later, when we killed the first joey. About half the roos Demetri shot were female, and inevitably some carried their babies in their pouches. The joeys couldn't survive without the mother, and shooters killed them, usually by cracking their heads against the ground. I didn't understand what was happening until Demetri reached down and pulled something from the pouch, a thin cry ending abruptly as he smacked the screaming, little body onto the earth and threw it over his shoulder into the paddock.

John had told me a story in response to my initial questions about the psychological effects of roo-shooting: 'This was years ago, before you needed to be licensed. This guy bought a new rifle and went out and shot a roo. Anyway, the roo had a joey, and this little thing hopped out of the pouch. The guy burst into tears, threw his gun into the bushes—a two-thousand-dollar rifle, mind you. He picked up the joey and insisted that they all went to the vet. It just emotionally wrecked him; he was crying all the way to the animal shelter.'

The anecdote had niggled at me, and it was only later, after I put the phone down, that I recalled the description by an American Green Beret of the young soldier he encountered during an ambush in Vietnam. 'I froze', the commando recalled,

> 'cos it was a boy, I would say between the ages of twelve and fourteen. When he turned at me and looked, all of a sudden he turned his whole body and pointed his automatic weapon at me, I just opened up, fired the whole twenty rounds right at the kid, and he just laid there. I dropped my weapon and cried.

The structural similarities were obvious: both roo-shooter and soldier came undone when confronted by the individuality of their victims, by details that spoke to them of the lives they'd destroyed.

For John, the story was simply an anomaly: 'It's not everyone's cup of tea. Not everyone could do it or would do it. A lot of people just can't do it; I mean, they physically can't. On the other hand, I've seen people who are initially completely anti–roo-shooter, completely put off by the process, and after a week or so, they were having a ball.'

I wasn't having a ball, but the more roos we killed, the less any of it—the killing, the hauling, the gutting—bothered me. I became acclimatised to activities that nauseated me simply by doing them; since my attitudes conflicted with my behaviour, I adjusted my attitudes. I am a fundamentally good person, I told myself, and, by and large, I do good things. Yet here I was in the midst of blood and gore. Did this mean that I was a bad person? No, it meant that the blood and gore must be OK.

That was part of what happened that night, but there was more to it than that. Demetri, quite reasonably, expected me to contribute. The tasks he gave me seemed simple enough. I was to open and close the gates as we steered from paddock to paddock, and to pull the dead roos over to the truck and hoist them up onto the hooks so he could gut them. Demetri moved at the clean, unhurried pace of the craftsman, and shamed by his calm efficiency, I found myself worrying less about the fate of the roos and more about whether I could perform my allocated duties with the same grace. Because almost everything went wrong.

Over and over, Demetri showed me a particular grip for hoisting the carcasses smoothly and effectively, and each time I nodded my understanding. But really I never quite grasped what he meant and instead persisted in lifting in a clumsy, fumbling fashion, relying on strength and nervous energy, and covering myself with blood and the musky stink of dead roos. Even the gates defeated me. The truck would stop and I'd get out and realise with a sinking feeling that this particular farmer secured his paddock with a peculiar, jerry-rigged wire arrangement that differed entirely from the peculiar, jerry-rigged wire arrangement used by the previous farmer at the previous gate. I'd tug anxiously at the tangled metal in the spotlight, feeling more and more hopeless, until eventually Demetri would come out from the cabin and, with a few simple twists, swing the gate open.

My preoccupation with measuring my performance against Demetri's effortless competence meant that I lost sight of the meaning of our shared work, since I judged events largely in terms of what they physically required of me. I watched, in the spotlight, the head of a large male roo fly off in a splash of blood and brain, and I absently acknowledged that something rather gruesome had taken place. But that realisation exerted no emotional force because I was silently calculating how much such a big animal might weigh, and whether or not I'd be able to lift it without feeling Demetri's silent disapproval of my educated, cack-handed clumsiness.

One famous study of Israeli soldiers preparing for combat discovered that, more than death or injury, the men were worrying, in the final minutes before battle, about whether or not they'd be found wanting by their peers. Men at war killed and died because they were embarrassed not to. Nothing—neither taking a life nor being shot—mattered more than letting down peers. 'As usual,' wrote

Siegfried Sassoon about some particularly torrid battle, 'my main fear was that I should make a fool of myself'. That was my fear, too, and with good reason.

The shock of watching something die came from an instinctive empathy, a recognition that the terrible transition creeping over the animal in the dirt would eventually afflict me and the people I knew. Their limbs would twitch and spasm just like that; threads of spittle would bubble from their mouths as their central nervous systems went catastrophically awry; they would whimper and then be no more.

Yet as more roos were killed, their deaths became less a premonition of our common fate than a peculiar affliction besetting kangaroos and kangaroos alone—almost a part of their nature, like an ability to hop. Dying once more became foreign, abstract, something happening to them, rather than to me or to anyone I knew. 'One forgets quickly', wrote the novelist Frederick Manning about the trenches.

> The mind is averted as well as the eyes. It reassures itself after the first despairing cry: 'It is I!'
> 'No, it is not I. I shall not be like that.' And one moves on, leaving the mauled and bloody thing.

Both John and Demetri emphasised the independence that roo-shooting fostered. John, in particular, had taken up shooting in mid-life after a successful career as a teacher. He'd moved into a strange town and learnt a new and very different set of skills at a time when many people would have been thinking about retirement: 'I found myself changing over a whole range of areas. You physically get stronger; your shoulders get broader; your muscles get stronger because you are just lifting 30-kilo roos all night and unloading them in the morning. Learning how to fix my car, rewiring blown circuits in the middle of the night out in the midst of nowhere, getting bogged and getting out again by myself—you just get used to doing that sort of stuff all the time. You just don't worry about anything, and it toughens you. I'm not boasting or anything, but I could go out into the night right now, walk 10 kilometres in the dark, and I wouldn't turn a hair. It just wouldn't bother me—that's the sort of confidence it gives you.'

I could see what he meant. As the ute bounced and shuddered through the scrub, the possibility of an accident or mechanical failure occasionally occurred to me. What would we do? Nobody would or could help us here—not for hours, at least. When the truck engine died, and I lurched out to drag back the warm kangaroos, it felt like we were the last men on earth, abandoned out here with the night birds and the other mysterious creatures that called to each other under stars undimmed by artificial light.

Demetri had told me, before we set out, that when he arrived in Australia, he'd been forced to study what he called 'nature's laws'. This was what he was talking about. You would not want to be out in this paddock without an appreciation of the bush and how it worked. You'd need to know the weather; you'd need to know the terrain; you'd need to understand the geography.

Yet, if we were following nature's laws, we were doing so in an Adamic sense: understanding the natural world through conquering it. 'Let us make man in our image, after our likeness', says Genesis, 'and let them have dominion over the fish of the sea, and over the fowl of the air, and over the cattle, and over all the earth, and over every creeping thing that creepeth upon the earth'. When we encountered a fowl of the air—or at least of the scrub—Demetri shot that, too. 'Beautiful eating', he said, holding the feathery carcass of a bush turkey. Like the roos, it was strangely shrunken in death. With its eyes glittering in the light, it was huge; now, as Demetri tore its feathers out in great handfuls, it was nothing more than the puckered carcass you found in the poultry freezer.

Each time we came upon a mob of roos, Demetri expertly classified their moonlit silhouettes by gender, age and species. He was choosing which one would die and which one would live, a selection that involved a power extending way beyond that which most people exercised in their working lives. Yes, I could see why roo-shooting would give you confidence.

The kangaroos, after we'd killed twenty or more, weren't even animals. Demetri's rifle seemed to possess an almost magical power, transforming, with a sharp crack, the flitting, ephemeral shadow at the edge of my vision into a very real, very solid lump of meat and fur to be hauled up and put onto hooks when the truck stopped beside it. More and more animals died, and time seemed to be measured only through the number of carcasses resting on the hooks. The corpses on the ute slowly accumulated; I began to develop a rude competence in my simple tasks. Demetri showed me how to hoist the big bucks by grabbing hold of their testicles ('Like a handle', he said). I did as I was shown, and lo, lifting them became much easier, a tiny success that left me oddly elated. Demetri's rare words of praise warmed me unexpectedly, so much so that it didn't occur to me until afterwards how odd it was to be tugging on the testicles of an animal that only seconds earlier had bounded freely across the paddocks.

Eventually, the ute held its fill of gutted, headless and armless kangaroos, swaying on the hooks where I'd impaled them. 'That's enough', said Demetri. 'Time to go home.' He effortlessly navigated us through paddocks and gates and tracks until we were on the road heading back into town. 'Be back here early tomorrow', he told me. 'We've got to get these unloaded.'

I didn't sleep much that night. When the tide of adrenalin ebbed out, it left in its wake a nagging complicity. We had killed many animals, and something had happened that couldn't be undone. I lay awake on a lumpy bed in my little room, listening, through the thin walls, to the brawling in the pub opposite, the raucous fury of very drunk men, and concluding, with the existential despair of the insomniac, that violence was the currency in which the whole world preferred to trade.

The next day—the blue skies, sunshine and fresh air—was easier. I went back to Demetri's house, and we drove our load of stiffening roos out to the abattoir, just out of town. It was a rough and ready place: a basic structure under a tin roof, with a ramp against which the trucks could back up to unload into a refrigerated container. Our job was to lift the carcasses from the ute's rack onto the hooks on which they could be weighed and registered. It was heavy work, but simple enough and fairly untraumatic, too, for although the truck was still splattered with blood, the roos had become slabs of furry meat rather than wild creatures.

Periodically, other utes drove in, each spiked with a greater or lesser number of bodies. An air of country informality presided. Yes, it was a business, with money at stake, but it took place at a sufficiently leisurely pace for the other shooters to josh with Demetri about how he'd cook the turkey he'd shot, its carcass still hooked anomalously beside the roos. I remained on the edges of every conversation, wanting to join in but without quite knowing how. Most of the men—and they were all men—had been up all night, but though they were obviously tired and wanted to get their weight and go home, they were friendly. They showed a polite, weary curiosity about who I was and what I wanted; they encouraged me as I occasionally stumbled with a particularly large or awkward corpse. Yet the encounter still felt uncomfortable, and our conversations stalled and trailed off. Their jokes went past me; the easy banter they exchanged fell flat when I tried to join in, until I just shut up and lugged the carcasses.

Demetri belonged to a much earlier generation and had been born into the unimaginably different culture of rural Greece in wartime. But these men were my age or younger. We lived in the same country and spoke the same language, but our lifestyles were so very different that it was hard for us to connect. Here I was, on an excursion, a field trip; here they were, working, just like they had done the day before and just like they would do the day after. For them, none of this was mysterious or secret. It was simply how people in this place, at this time, made a living.

But it had always been like that, hadn't it? As the killing of animals had become more taboo, the task had been allocated almost exclusively to that segment of the population who had always done the jobs we hadn't want to think about, the people who, in different circumstances, would have been sent to kill humans. In Australia, in 2007, the gulf between those who killed and those who vaguely wondered what killing might be like was just as great as it had ever been.

I lifted the roos in the cold morning air, until I was tired and stiff, and then we washed the gore off the truck and went back to Demetri's place. I thanked Demetri for his time and assistance; he replied with another friendly warning about the pernicious consequences of education, and then I made my thankful way back home.

3

THE KILL FLOOR

It wasn't enough. Back in Melbourne, the sickening realisation dawned upon me: all those dead roos, and it still wasn't enough.

I'd been thinking a lot about my initial conversation with John. He hadn't been particularly surprised to be asked about war, because, he said, he'd often thought of roo-shooters as a potential asset for the Australian Army. They were good shooters; they were fit; they were tough. But, most of all, they were independent. Out in the bush with Demetri, I'd seen exactly what that meant.

But now that I was home, now that I could reflect more clearly, independence no longer seemed a good reason to compare roo-shooting to war. In fact, it seemed more a reason why the comparison didn't stand. Contemporary soldiers served in enormous organisations. They did not drive around in the night, making their own decisions about when and where to fire. From the moment of enlistment, they learnt to follow orders, not to think for themselves. Independence had nothing to do with it.

The makeshift abattoir where Demetri weighed his harvest had crystallised a thought that should have been there from the start. Roos were a marginal, fringe element of the meat industry in Australia. That was the only reason kangaroos could be harvested by individuals with rifles and utes: the business was insufficiently developed to enforce greater efficiencies. Modern wars were entirely different. They mobilised men on a mass scale, and thus required a level of organisational complexity that did not allow, other than in a few exceptional circumstances, independence or self-reliance. The Lee Enfield rifle, the weapon by which that Turkish skull had most likely been perforated, contained 131 separate parts, so its provision to millions of men necessarily entailed an advanced system of production and distribution. With the Great War in mind, no less an authority than Winston Churchill explained that modern armies were 'gigantic agencies for the slaughter of men by machinery'. Killing was not about individual initiative: war had been, he said, 'reduced to a business like the stock-yards of Chicago'.

Stockyards: that was what I needed to see. Not an atavistic business in which one man shot one animal, but a modern abattoir, a facility organised with the same mass logic as a modern war. After all, in Australia, each and every year, eight million cows, five million pigs and 437 million chickens perished at our hands; in the USA, the deaths grew so large as to dissolve any mental picture into an impossible abstraction. That was industrial killing, and it seemed reasonable to assume that such quantities made the business qualitatively different from what Demetri had shown me.

The visit took a little while to organise, not least because I didn't want to go. Kangaroo killing had been bearable, but only just, and this, I sensed, would be considerably worse. There was a friend of a friend who worked in an abattoir; there were phone calls made; there were arrangements put in place, but, even after that, I prevaricated for days.

Again, the same impulse propelled me forward. I cooked meat every day, wore leather, used the pieces of dead animal as casually as everyone else. To grill the sausage but avert your eyes from the fate of the pig: there was something vile about that. I'd been a vegetarian, and now I was not. This was what I accepted—I could at least look upon it. Besides, if the experience of roo-shooting was to mean anything, be something more than an exercise in voyeurism, I needed to push on, if only because of a Macbethian logic: I was already in animal blood stepped in so far that wading further made more sense than returning.

A man named Kevin answered my call. He had, he said, been expecting me. He gave me a date and a time; he said he was looking forward to our meeting. The address was disconcertingly close to Footscray, where I worked for the literary journal *Overland*. Melbourne's inner west had contained, at one time, the largest cattle yards in the Southern Hemisphere. At its height, the place must have been rather like the Chicago of Upton Sinclair's famous novel *The Jungle*, filled with 'a sound made up of ten thousand little sounds ... the distant lowing of ten thousand cattle, the distant grunting of ten thousand swine'.

On this day, though, the lowing and grunting had ceased. Like the industrial working class itself, the abattoirs had retreated from the urban centres, pushed into more discreet locations in the suburbs. This was an international trend: animal advocates noted, with a certain bitterness, that the United Nations building, a monument to the rights of humans, had been constructed directly on top of the old New York stockyards, where the absence of rights for animals had been so repeatedly demonstrated. In the Middle Ages, butchers had converted live animals into dead meat on every city street, with passers-by dodging the arterial blood from a stuck calf as reflexively as they ducked the contents of chamber pots thrown from a window. The establishment of discreet facilities for killing reflected a new sensitivity to the sights and sounds of animal life. In London, in the early nineteenth century, for example, campaigners fretted that the Smithfield livestock market posed a moral threat to the working class, since the freely copulating animals encouraged loose sexual practices among the impressionable poor.

In 2007, the wooden railings of Victoria's old stock route lent historical colour to the new housing developments in Flemington. Yet pockets of industry had evidently survived. Only minutes away were the meatworks: a flat expanse like a university campus with an array of buildings protected by a guard in a little booth near the boom gate. In the car park, on the day of my visit, I wondered why I'd never noticed. There was a procession of huge cattle trucks driving in and out. Was I really so inattentive, or was this something I'd chosen not to see?

At the mention of Kevin's name, the guard ducked back into her little sentry box to make a phone call. I could hear her talking to someone but couldn't make out the words. I watched a truck full of bones navigating the gate, and I breathed in the acrid chemical air and tried to stay calm. It took about ten minutes before Kevin arrived, sufficient time for me to work myself into a state of high anxiety, thinking about how I would cope.

He came walking towards me, wearing white meatworker's pants and a smock, rubber boots and a hairnet. His was a pleasant, gentle face: he smiled easily; he was one of those people who immediately put you at ease. Which was fortunate, because after he greeted me and we shook hands, he said, 'You want to see the kill floor, do you?' Put like that, it seemed odd, even perverse. The kill floor, the floor for killing—and you wanted just to come and look at it.

'Yes', I said. 'If that's all right.'

He nodded and explained that they received lots of visitors. The universities, for instance, often sent out students, trainee vets, to see how the industry really worked. 'Occasionally, they faint.' He was matter of fact. 'Are you squeamish?'

I told him I'd just been kangaroo-shooting, so no, I didn't think I was squeamish. Which was true and not true: I'd coped with shooting with Demetri, but when I was a vegetarian, I'd often felt nausea just looking at meat. On one occasion, I'd looked in a butcher's window and seen a whole pig's head with the faintest trace of dried blood trickling from its nostril, and the pathos of that almost-human nosebleed had haunted me for months. Another time, I'd walked past the multiple meat stalls of the Queen Victoria Market and had nearly vomited. The loamy scent, only a few degrees from overt putrescence—a reminder, it had seemed to me, that here was a charnel house, and that the shoppers jostling for bargains filled their trolleys from a selection of corpses already starting to rot. Still, squeamishness had always seemed despicable, a repulsion not at the thing itself but the confrontation with it, as if the act would be perfectly acceptable so long as there were no witnesses.

I signed a visitors' register; they gave me a special pass, and we walked towards a building as big and as functional as an aircraft hangar. The chemical smell grew stronger the closer we came, and the acrid air ate away at my courage. I cleared my throat. 'Like ... I'm not going to be sick or anything, am I?'

'Nah.' Kevin had been born into the industry. His father worked with meat; he'd first come to the plant when he was thirteen or fourteen, and had become acclimatised to the slaughter he saw then. He'd started as a labourer in the mutton kill, and he'd worked his way up over twenty-three years. He spoke reassuringly, without patronage or sneer, and with none of the insider's scorn for the unini- tiated. 'You'll be right.'

We went inside and walked through doors and corridors, up and down stairways, with a muffled mechanical throb always some- where in the background. The place was institutional, with clean utilitarian floors and surfaces. We ducked into a little room, where someone allocated me rubber boots, a uniform and a hairnet. It's all for the blood, I realised. *We're going to be sloshing through blood.* Kevin stood patiently as I fumbled into my industrial outfit. Then he led me through a door, into a room fitted out with something like a urinal with a hose attached. He hosed down his boots; he washed his hands. 'You get so used to doing this here that you don't even think about it.' I copied him, wiping my hands clean on paper towels.

Then we climbed up to the control room, an eyrie with glass walls perched above the factory floor, a room of computers and filing cabinets and telephones and the assorted bric-a-brac of white-collar life, all of it familiar and mundane except for the view from the big windows of white-clad shapes cutting and tearing and stabbing at lumps of flesh twisting on chains. Kevin introduced me to his work-mates, and I smiled and gave some kind of frozen greeting, trying not to let dissonance overwhelm me. The fluorescent banality of an office, each workspace individualised with the usual homey touches: the personalised screen saver, the family photo stuck to the monitor, the footy tip sheet and the rest of it. But behind the glass was a demonic landscape irrigated with arterial blood.

'Oh, yes,' said Bruce, shaking my hand, 'Kevin told me about your research. It sounds really interesting.' I nodded weakly, thinking, Christ, I'm about to go down there. I wondered if I could physically do it. Bruce, like Kevin, seemed friendly, though with a less laconic, more talkative personality. He'd been quality assurance manager for seven years. Before that he'd worked in banking, but he'd moved into the meat industry after his ex-brother-in-law told him about the pay. 'The job was dirty but the money was clean', he joked. The view through the windows, down onto the production floor, however, had grabbed and held me, and I struggled to concentrate. Realising that Bruce was still talking, I tore my gaze away from the man sawing at a dangling corpse somewhere below us. 'We'll go down to the kill floor', said Kevin. 'Bruce, are you free later? Want to come and talk with Jeff?'

'I'd be happy to.' He shook my hand again.

More corridors, more stairs, another room at which we washed and scrubbed, and then a door was opening and we walked out into that landscape. Blood, so much blood: a thick red flow along the floor, crimson smeared on the coats of the workers fixed at their sta-tions, drops falling from the flayed cattle that hung from the ceiling and swayed past us at various stages of dissection. The unstopping, purposeful activity amid the jarring, shaking, shuddering sounds of a factory in operation overwhelmed me and, without thinking, I found myself focused on minutiae rather than totality: the faded blue tattoo on the wrist of the man over there, the one pulling the skin off the carcass; the tongues extruding thickly from the cows that had not yet lost their heads. We'd entered a Bruegel canvas, the

Triumph of Death reconceived in a twenty-first-century setting: a universe dedicated to the punishment of flesh by knives and chains and clanking machines.

John Weaver had described a shooter's ute as a miniature, mobile abattoir, but here the difference in scale resulted in a difference in quality, with the factory infinitely more confronting. For the first minutes, I was utterly numb. What steadied me in the midst of sights and sounds that felt so intuitively and gut-churningly wrong was, oddly enough, etiquette—a consciousness that I was a visitor to this place, a worksite where so many people laboured eight hours a day most days of the week, and if I were to display my shock or, worse still, any horror, it would seem an unbearably patronising judgement upon them and the things they did for a living.

We walked down the assembly line, past each worker standing at his post labouring over an enormous carcass, and I imagined everyone surreptitiously watching, almost daring me to show emotion. *Yes, this is our work; this is what we do. So, go on then, disapprove of us.* In fact, the men—burly white blokes mixed in with slender Sudanese and Ethiopians—showed only a faint curiosity: not the hostility I think that I'd harbour towards an outsider watching me carve newly dead animals, but the kind of mild attention that you'd devote to any novelty during long hours on a monotonous task.

My initial sensory overload was diminishing, leaving in its wake a more controlled state of low-level horror, in which I could function and pay some attention to the surroundings. The abattoir was far more efficient, far more open, than I thought it would be. Many of my expectations of a slaughter yard had come from *The Jungle*, in which the meat industry of the 1890s was depicted as an enormous swindle, grinding up any putrid scraps of flesh to serve up to unsuspecting consumers. I'd read animal rights' texts that were more up to date, but they still described grimy, antiquated facilities, crammed with drugged-up men casually stabbing at the animals and each other. This place, on the other hand, was very new, and though you couldn't really describe a facility so awash with blood as clean, it was sterile and antiseptic, and full of space and light. Delinquency seemed unimaginable here: the factory was too controlled, too efficient. It did what it was supposed to do; it didn't do anything else.

I wondered, then, how much my response reflected an instinctive revulsion at blood, and how much it was related to an equally automatic response to the industrial setting. In white-collar jobs, there were systems to monitor your productivity, but they were less obvious, less intrusive. But there's nothing subtle about an assembly line. It sets a pace, and that is the speed at which everyone works. Abattoirs were, after all, the primal factories, the cradle from which modern production had grown. The explosion of urban living created an insatiable market for meat, and the huge abattoirs servicing it developed efficiencies that were later adopted elsewhere. Henry Ford, for instance, modelled his car plants on the systems already in place in the Chicago meatworks. Kevin, when we talked later, also used the auto industry for comparison. 'We could be at Toyota', he said, 'manufacturing a car. The difference is that we're a destructive industry: we start with a unit and end up with multiple units, meat, hide, what have you. But basically we are a processing line.'

Thus the further we walked, the more intact the cattle carcasses hanging above us became. We were tracing an evolutionary chart, except in reverse: at the other side of the factory, all was pure, formless meat, and as you worked back, the bodies developed more and more features—skins, heads, entrails—until you reached a corner from around which the line emerged, swinging complete and obviously newly dead animals.

Kevin moved along the gory floor with the grace of long familiarity, delicately pushing aside a carcass so I could wriggle past without blood dripping on me. 'Death yawns at me as I walk up and down in this abode of skulls', wrote Bronson Alcott after one visit to a butcher. 'Murder and blood are written on its stalls ... I tread amidst carcasses. I am in the presence of the slain. The death-set eyes of beasts peer at me and accuse me of belonging to the race of the murderers.' Bronson Alcott would not have liked this place.

Kevin tried to tell me something but I lost his words in the machine racket. He leaned closer and shouted. 'We'll start down to the kill floor. This way.' Cows in a field seem pliant and manageable, almost physically diminished by captivity. In this place, they were awesome: tremendous walls of meat suspended from the ceiling. If a carcass fell, it killed the person it landed upon. I could hear the animals now, their bellows blending with the shrieking machines. 'Down here', said Kevin. We walked through another door and we were there watching the killing.

A cow came up a covered ramp and into an enclosed space where a machine pressed down upon it and gripped its head tightly. A worker reached over and gently touched its skull with a tool that looked something like an electric drill. A sound like a staple gun firing, and the animal fell, as if its life had been turned off with a switch. Another man ran the edge of a knife along its throat, opening up a huge gushing wound, before the carcass tumbled down rollers onto a platform near the floor, legs splaying and spasming.

Afterwards, I couldn't reconstruct the sequence, even though we stood without speaking and watched animal after animal die. It was as though sensory overload had broken down the experience into isolated images. I remembered the cow's head pinned for the stunning, the animal somehow so immobile and so helpless that its death seemed inevitable, almost preordained. I remembered the sounds of the cows as they came up the ramp, their roars more indignant than fearful. I remembered my shock at the physicality of the process: the size of the animals, their weight and solidity, the power with which they kicked their legs as they flopped down the rollers and were hoisted up into the line.

At the time, I thought the gun killed each animal, since, when it pulled back from their skulls, they fell, entirely still. But actually it was intended simply to stun, and death came only when the knife split the throat: a two-part process that, some writers suggested, served an important psychological function, since the first man could think of himself only as anaesthetising a live animal, while the second person cut a beast already inert and lifeless. The moral responsibility lay with neither: one stunned and the other bled, but neither actually killed. Of course, the blank cartridge in the firing squad soothed the executioner, but it didn't signify much to the witnesses, and from where we stood, what registered was the undeniable fact of a killing taking place.

The process was clinical, much more so than you might have expected. I'd read horror stories about the stickers toying with animals before they despatched them, about cows that took minutes to die. Nothing like that happened here, and it was hard to see how it could. The killing systems were so carefully planned and calibrated to allow very little divergence from the approved method. The cows came up the ramp and within minutes they were dead. The slaughter was quick and efficient and by-the-book. 'The death cries of the animals whose jugular veins have been opened are confused with the rumbling of the great drums, the whirring of gears, and the shrilling sound of steam ... What is truly startling in this mass transition from life to death is the complete neutrality of the act. One does not experience, one does not feel; one merely observes.' This account of an abattoir from the 1940s entirely matched my experience sixty years later.

We stood for a while, watching the killing, and then we moved on. I had seen the worst of it, and from then on, blood-soaked men cutting at carcasses seemed entirely unexceptional. That was part of the abattoir's function: to concentrate acts that would have seemed abhorrent anywhere else into a place where they became ordinary, normal. The workers sawed through bones and flesh, and the line rattled and moved forward, with man and machine locked together into a natural process, an inevitable motion. The great military theorist Carl von Clausewitz remarked that those watching their first battle will conclude that 'the light of reason does not move here in the same medium, that it is not refracted in the same manner'. So it was in the abattoir.

The rest of the plant was almost anticlimactic. Down the line, we contemplated the ripping off of skins and the removal of heads and the cutting out of entrails, and it all just seemed efficient, even a little dull. At one station, Kevin introduced me to a man inspecting the lungs and hearts and the other internal organs as they flowed towards him on an assembly line. Again, I went through that same process of initial shock and eventual familiarisation. A cow's lung looks like a man's lung, and the person pawing at it at first seems utterly depraved, a predator toying with eviscerated prey. Watch him long enough and his task dissolves back into the repetition of the factory. Then, when he talks to you and outlines what he's doing, the meat changes again and you're looking at a fleshy abstraction on which certain lumps and certain marks allow, as he explains, the identification of pleurisy and other diseases.

We came to a room entirely dedicated to entrails, where very tall and very black African men methodically hosed down offal, removing the traces of fodder and dung from horridly pale and gleaming piles of cow's stomach. Blood no longer bothered me, but the white gizzards somehow did, with their pallor clearly not meant for the light. Kevin pointed to the different chambers that comprised the bovine digestive system. 'This is called blanket tripe; this one here is book or bible—you see how it looks like an old book—and over there, that's what we call honeycomb.' The quaint terminology, recalling thrifty peasants constructing their meals from every scrap of the animal, reassured me. This was not perverse. It was traditional.

'A big market for tripe, is there?'

He nodded. 'Some people eat it. But it ends up in all kinds of places. Ever had chicken nuggets?'

Of course.

'That's from here. Fish fingers, that sort of thing, as well as toothpaste and cosmetics.'

The factory processed sheep as well. Another assembly line, another row of workers gradually taking the flesh apart, and again the chute from which the live animals emerged. By then, though, something of the factory had already entered me, so I watched the slow and bloody disintegration of a flock of sheep without emotion. The small woolly bodies kicked and convulsed as they bled out on hooks, but they lacked the heft of the cattle and, perhaps because of that, the import. They seemed more like twitching toys than living animals, and their death throes didn't produce the same emotional resonance.

More women worked in this part of the factory, precisely because the carcasses were smaller, and as elsewhere, you couldn't help noticing the proportion of non-white workers. In the cattle kill room, one of the stickers had seemed to be talking while he cut the cows' throats. I'd looked towards Kevin.

'He's praying.'

The workers on the killing floor were Muslims. The abattoir, like most abattoirs in Australia, was designed to allow the production of halal meat, since most of the customers were in the Middle East. This, apparently, had been the case for a long time, and it struck me as an odd irony. Cattle was a traditional Australian industry, centred in socially conservative rural Australia. Yet the kinds of Islamic customs that so stirred tabloid columnists had been quietly adopted here, simply because it made economic sense. And why not? Nobody was going to enquire too closely about the exact details of procedures amid the blood and the entrails.

After peering at more ribs as they were split, skins as they were ripped, and guts as they were graded, we went back to find Bruce. In a little nondescript room, up above the assembly line, we sat down and we talked about killing.

Did either of them go through any psychological adjustment when it came to working in the industry?

Kevin simply shook his head, but Bruce nodded. 'My dad was from the bush and his dad had a butcher shop', he explained. 'My experience prior to coming into the industry was seeing dad killing chickens in the backyard and feeling a bit squeamish about it. But when I came into the meat industry, the thing that hit me was the smell more than anything. That was the thing that really stood out for me. The first month or two, I was still a little bit funny—probably the first four weeks ...'

'The thing with the smell', Kevin interrupted, 'is that it's more outside. When you get on the floor, it's hardly there.' I understood, at that point, what should have been obvious: for all his easygoing manner, Kevin was a senior manager of a huge plant. He knew what was at stake in these questions; he was choosing his answers carefully. Which wasn't to suggest any dishonesty. I'd noticed how the smell had changed too. Walking towards the plant, the odour from the yards and the rendering seemed almost a physical presence, but once I got inside, the ventilation pushed it away. Besides, next to the sight, smells barely registered.

'These days, either of you have any sensations when you go to the kill floor? Does it affect you at all what takes place there?'

'No', said Kevin.

Bruce was more expansive. 'It has affected me', he said, 'if I've seen an inhumane slaughter …'

Quickly Kevin agreed. 'Oh, yeah, that side, yeah.'

'We slaughter animals; we don't torture animals', Bruce continued. 'Sometimes, I've seen when the stunning apparatus has malfunctioned and the animal has been stuck without being stunned, and I don't like that. Outside that I don't have any problems.'

How long did it take new workers to get acclimatised to what happened in an abattoir?

'It varies', said Kevin. 'Some people just go bang, straight into the system.'

'For me,' said Bruce, 'I think it took about four weeks before I was comfortable'.

Kevin continued. 'Some just love it from day one. It might be four weeks; it might be a couple of days. Depending on the job they're put into, I think. Some of the boning room people probably wouldn't handle the kill floor.'

Was there a formal program to get new employees used to the work?

Bruce nodded. 'About five, six, seven years ago, nothing. You rocked up at the gate. You want a job on the floor? Yeah, no worries.

No pre-screening, nothing. Now, we have a lot of training programs. There's a TAFE course where you go through OHS, get an overview of the meat industry and what have you, so you can come into the work already briefed up.'

'The induction process at the moment,' said Kevin, 'they'll go through hygiene practice in the room and then they'll take them for a tour around the factory, similar to yourself, but not as in depth. They'll look through the viewing areas, and you'll usually be able to tell whether they can handle it or not handle it.'

'So you do get people who can't handle it?'

He shook his head. 'I haven't seen a great number. I know some people who can't handle the temperatures of the boning room or the chillers, or we might find a bloke who can't handle the smell of the intestines. But I haven't seen too many that don't like it because of the smell or because of how horrific it might be. We do have a few who do a runner after the first smoko break. But I think that's more that they've come off the dole and said, oh, I'll give it a go and then I'll piss off. As I said, we get a lot of uni students come through— and they're the only ones who I've seen bite the dust or feel like they have to leave straight away.'

Bruce told a story about his younger brother, who had been studying accountancy and, after an unhappy first year, came to work at the abattoir over the school break. He'd asked for a job where he wouldn't get too dirty. 'So I put him on something that I perceived as being pretty good.'

'What was that?' I asked, interested in the hierarchy of tasks in an abattoir.

'Washing heads.' Then, perhaps realising that washing heads didn't sound altogether appealing, he explained. 'You've always got water, you see. You can wash yourself down.'

I nodded.

'Anyway,' Bruce continued, 'I went to check on him after the first hour and I thought he was going to pass out. But, at the end of the day, he got a cash payment and he looked at it and said, Jesus, I'm coming back tomorrow. He got over that hump by reason of the money, which is really good. Like I told you, when I went from working at the NAB to working here, my pay and conditions improved immensely.'

'Does the good money relate to the stigma?'

'Yeah,' said Kevin, 'I think so'.

Bruce nodded. 'But it was also that, at that time—and no pun intended—the industry was making a killing with exports, which were so lucrative that the wages could be inflated. Now we're being brought back to a level playing field, and we struggle to get skilled people as we once did. There's not as many abattoirs as there once were. There used to be nine in this area. Now we're the only survivor.'

I'd been hedging around this question and finally I just blurted it out. 'Do you think, if people kill animals all day long, it affects how they relate to other people?'

Kevin remained as unflappable as ever. 'Look, I don't think so. You'd walk past people on the street and you'd never know they worked in the job. We've got an old bloke there who's been involved in the industry for fifty years, and you just wouldn't know. He's just the nicest old guy.'

Bruce agreed. 'People say, yeah, I can picture a meatworker: rough-edged, covered in tats, loves getting blood on himself. But it's not like that at all. The last time I saw an inhumane slaughter was about five years ago, and part of my job is to make sure that doesn't happen. The easiest way for a plant to lose its licence is through the RSPCA for inhumane slaughter.' He repeated his formulation: 'We slaughter animals; we don't torture them'.

'I tell you,' said Kevin, 'when those medical shows come on TV, I just can't watch them. With animal blood, it's no problem. But for people, I just can't look. Even though the intestines and all that stuff looks exactly the same, there's something … My wife watches it, but I just can't. At the end of the day, I think you just have a sense that these are animals and those are humans.'

I wondered about that, after I'd said goodbye to them both and walked out to the car park, my hairnet still in place (I only noticed it when I came home, its surface finely sprinkled with arterial blood). Backing out, I made way for a huge cattle truck as it swayed and bounced out onto the road. The animals it had carried were, I supposed, about to roar their way up the ramps, where they'd encounter the stun gun and their stickers, a realisation that seemed, at that instant, truly terrible—but only for a moment, until the everyday sights and sounds of an ordinary western-suburbs highway provided a reassurance that the planet continued to turn and the heavens weren't moved by the kill floor and its business.

Was the killing in the abattoir different from what Demetri did? It was and it wasn't. The main similarity was the repetition. Demetri wasn't on an assembly line, but he was still working commercially, which meant he needed an efficiency beyond that of a recreational shooter. He killed automatically, with careful, practised movements, and the more he did so, the more I came to accept it, as the routine, the repetition, abstracted the nausea and made the death manageable.

The abattoir took that process to another level. It was a killing factory, and repetition was built into it, removing, as much as possible, the idiosyncrasies that might mar the pattern of the work. Industrial killing was ordered; it left nothing to chance, and that was the reason for the numbness of the kill floor. There would be no joeys there, no roos shot in the face, just one cow after another cow, until all the cows merged into the general category of cattle. To put it another way, my distress at the roos' deaths dimmed when natural empathy—the extrapolation from their suffering to the suffering of others—gave way to an acceptance of inevitability. After the killing of the twentieth kangaroo, dying from bullet wounds seemed something that roos just did, a peculiar characteristic of the species. The abattoir massively intensified that process. The cattle were presented in one way and one way only. They were there as meat, and the whole construction of the place made you feel their deaths to be preordained and unstoppable.

Demetri's operation depended upon a recognition of kangaroos' animality. He related to them as wild creatures, entwined with a certain ecosystem. During our session he'd noticed the wind picking up and conversationally explained how the breeze made the roos skittish. His observation wasn't the result of formal study or the dreaded education; he simply needed that kind of knowledge— nature's laws, as he'd put it—to do his work.

On the kill floor, the workers knew nothing about the natural instincts of cows—or, more accurately, the cows there had no natural instincts, not just because they'd spent their lives in captivity, but because the abattoir was designed so that they behaved in one way and one way only. They weren't cows; they were machines designed to die. They came up the ramp; they were immobilised; they died. That was what happened. That was all that could happen. The concentration of the killing made the abattoir seem initially much more overwhelming—there was far more blood, for one thing. But the numbness came sooner, too, and that seemed to me to be the direct result of the industrial processes.

Yet if killing roos seemed more emotionally draining, it also had its compensations. John, after all, had consciously retrained himself as a shooter, not for the money but for the lifestyle. 'It made me more self-sufficient,' he'd said, 'more comfortable with people, more confident with unusual situations'. Nobody would make a similar claim about working on an abattoir assembly line. The whole point of factory-style production was to break the work down into simple steps so that the workers never encountered unusual situations. In fact, in the course of our discussion, Bruce and Kevin had explained how the kind of self-sufficiency John described had been banished from their industry. 'In the old days,' Bruce said, 'the butchers took a great deal of pride in their work. They started at one end [and worked their way] to the other, and the end product was all theirs, whereas here it's going through fifty hands.'

Kevin agreed. 'They were what we call master butchers. They really took pride in their work; they did everything themselves. "This is my product, this is what I've done."' It was a classic description of how industrialisation deskilled an artisanal tradition. The factory might make the mechanics of a particular task easier, but the price was the loss of any sense of control, self-reliance or ownership—in short, everything that John and Demetri enjoyed about what they did. What did that mean for the work?

There was, however, a more important question. What was the relationship between killing animals and killing people? A cow was not a human, and maybe it was entirely possible to think about cattle in the abstract, without seeing the individual animal in front of you. Surely killing people would be entirely different, wouldn't it?

4

HUMANE AND PRACTICAL

Fred Leuchter was among the ghosts. Well, 'ghost's', actually, with the greengrocers' apostrophe in the title inevitable amid the website's general shoddiness. The page showcased amateur spirit photos, snaps compiled by suburban Americans in which ectoplasmic figures of one variety or another frolicked casually in the background: here, in the bare trees behind a grinning holiday-maker, a splotch of fuzz identified confidently as 'a man in a wagon with a horse pulling him'; there, a ring of lights near the refrigerator where, apparently, grandfather died only a few weeks earlier.

Among these spectacularly unterrifying phantasms, one image genuinely chilled. The photo showed a high-backed, wooden-slatted chair, of a design that seemed merely slightly eccentric until you recognised the leather straps and electrodes and realised the exact function this piece of furniture performed. 'I enclose this photo of Tennessee's Electric Chair', explained the photographer, 'with unknown things photographed in the chair. I am an execution technologist and replaced the Tennessee Chair. This photo was taken in complete darkness and flashed with room light. It has been authenticated by Kodak.' The 'unknown things'—visual distortions which vaguely resembled a snarling face or even, perhaps, faces—were less interesting, despite Kodak's 'authentication', than their contributor. 'This ghost photo was submitted by Fred Leuchter', explained the site—and then, best of all, it provided an email address for him.

After the abattoir, I knew I was committed. I might have stumbled into this, but now I would see it through. I wasn't sure how the kill floor related to Iraq, but the evisceration of cattle had provided a palette with which the imagination could colour the scraps we learnt from that war. If people bled like that—and presumably they did—then the euphemisms of occupation (the insurgents 'taken out', the enemy positions 'neutralised' and so on) lost their comforting blandness amid the images of the cows' paroxysms and their streaming blood.

It made sense, then, to approach the Australian military directly. The slaughter of animals was one thing, but the army was an institution that deliberately and systematically trained in killing humans. What research had it performed on the topic? What conclusions had been reached? How did Australian soldiers prepare to kill their enemies? How were they expected to feel afterwards?

But an official perspective on killing was not so straightforwardly obtained. The Department of Defence maintained a Co-ordination and Public Affairs Division, to which one could apply for interviews with military trainers, but the official protocol required the completion of a 'Request for Defence Support' form, a document on which the petitioner needed to provide, among other information, an explanation of how the particular project would 'enhance Defence's image or assist Defence in furthering its objectives'. An investigation of war's resemblance to an abattoir did not, despite my best literary efforts, lend itself to either of these.

After the request was officially declined, in the early part of 2007, researching military killing seemed well-nigh impossible. If the military bureaucracy was inaccessible, then Australian veterans probably would be, too. Most of the soldiers with recent combat experience served with elite units. In all probability, they'd make their own unofficial assessment of whether discussing killing would enhance Defence's image—and then they'd say no.

Uncertain about how to proceed, I turned to whatever literature I could find. There were, it seemed, two distinct schools in relation to the experience of killing in war and its effects. In her 1999 book *An Intimate History of Killing*, Joanna Bourke looks at documents from US, British and Australian soldiers of the First, Second and Vietnam wars, and argues that ordinary, well-adjusted people kill remarkably easily—enthusiastically, even. She quotes the poet and Great War officer Julian Grenfell: 'It is all the most wonderful fun, better fun than one could ever imagine. I hope it goes on a nice long time; but pigsticking will be the only tolerable pursuit after this one or one will die of sheer ennui.' More soldiers suffered mental collapses behind the lines than at the front because, she says, they found not being allowed to kill more stressful than killing itself. The majority of people asked to kill did so—and many of them became enthusiastic about it.

A few years before Bourke published her history, Lieutenant Colonel Dave Grossman wrote a book called *On Killing*. Grossman's background as a former long-serving officer in the US Army made his basic contention seem even more powerful. He argues that people who would kill must overcome a hard-wired aversion, a resistance so strong that, throughout history, the vast majority of soldiers have baulked at it. It's not that they've found killing difficult or that they've hesitated before pulling the trigger; it's that they've physically been unable to kill. They've either fired in the air or not fired at all, even with their own lives at risk.

After the Battle of Gettysburg, nearly 30 000 muskets were collected from the field. Given the rigmarole involved in stuffing charge into a muzzle-loading weapon, you would expect that a fully loaded musket would have been a rare find. Yet an astonishing 24 000 of the salvaged firearms had been loaded—and many had been loaded multiple times. The combatants had been, apparently, desperate to avoid shooting anyone, so when they'd stood shoulder-to-shoulder with the other soldiers, they'd carefully loaded their muskets and then pretended to fire. More recently, studies of US soldiers in the Second World War presented evidence that only about 15 per cent even attempted to kill anyone. The rest, despite themselves and the wishes of their officers, proved to be unconscious pacifists: they could not overcome their natural resistance to killing.

Killing was easy; killing was hard. Here were the two canonical studies, by the two acknowledged experts in the field—and they had arrived at fundamentally different conclusions. How did one account for that?

Soldiers in the American Civil War described battle as 'seeing the elephant'. The origins of the phrase were obscure, but it recalled the fable of the blind men who groped at a strange beast and variously characterised it as a rope, a pillar and a wall. Battle took place in the mud, in the heat, in the dark, in the dawn, amid explosions or gas clouds or collapsing buildings. Its essence was chaos; it was a toxic environment, one of the worst places humans could be. J Glenn Gray, the American philosopher who wrote on his own experience of the Second World War, famously noted how 'the great god Mars tries to blind us when we enter his realm, and when we leave he gives us a generous cup of the waters of Lethe to drink'. Men kill other men in war, dosed up on a mix of fear, exhaustion and adrenalin, a cocktail that necessarily hindered any normal process of recollection. It also made the study of wartime killing inherently problematic. Obviously, you couldn't re-create a battle in a laboratory, much less one in which people actually died. So, for the most part, researchers relied on interviews, memoirs and letters, in which men who had killed tried to peer back into the dark chaos of combat and make sense of what they'd done. Naturally, the accounts were contradictory. Naturally, you could prove almost anything you wanted.

That was what made the death penalty suddenly seem so relevant. A modern execution was one of the few occasions in which a human being was deliberately killed in an antiseptic, dispassionate fashion, with every stage of the death logged and recorded. If ever the act of killing could be analytically isolated from its surrounding fog, it would be in the scrupulously monitored death chamber of a contemporary prison, where the conditions were as controlled as any laboratory experiment. Obviously, an execution wasn't the same as a battle, but the comparison would surely provide some useful insights.

At first, the idea was purely hypothetical—or, rather, historical. I'd been studying at RMIT University, and each time I went to a seminar I walked down Bowen Lane, past the spot where Melbourne's public executions had been conducted. In the early settlement, the natural rise made the location ideal for the gallows. When Jack Napoleon Tunermenerwail and Robert Smallboy were hanged in 1842, a crowd of six thousand people, a massive assemblage for the small colony, gathered around the hill to hoot and jeer and laugh. That execution had been a chaotic, shambolic affair (in which one of the men slowly strangled to death), but less than forty years later, when Ned Kelly died, only a hundred metres or so away, the prison staff documented every aspect of the killing. We knew what Kelly weighed; we knew what he ate; we knew his remarks on the way to the scaffold, admiring the prison flowers—an array of verifiable detail never available in accounts of combat. The problem, for me, was that Kelly's executioner, Elijah Upjohn, had been dead for more than a century—and contemporary execution technologists were hard to come by, especially in Australia. That was why Leuchter mattered.

Fred Leuchter stars in the extraordinary Errol Morris film *Mr Death: The Rise and Fall of Fred Leuchter*, much of which consists of its mild-mannered, nerdishly bespectacled subject talking directly to camera about his life and his work constructing gas chambers, lethal-injection machines and electric chairs. Leuchter seems, to put it mildly, decidedly odd, though in the first portion of the film he is perhaps more awkward than unlikeable. Chain-smoking and drinking endless cups of a drink that, with his nasal Boston accent, he calls 'cawfee', he calculates the precise weight-to-length ratio for a hangman's rope to cleanly break the neck, tests the current on a ninety-year-old electric chair and describes the chemicals necessary to poison someone lethally in the shortest time possible. With thick glasses, a white shirt and neat tie, Leuchter might be taken for an accountant from the 1950s, a Norman Rockwell subject, albeit with a boyish enthusiasm for ghoulish machines. Yet the grimly comic mood of the early sequences is misleading, and just when *Mr Death* seems to have settled into a lightweight exploration of eccentricity, its real power emerges.

The Morris film had first screened in 1999, and Leuchter had kept, it seemed, a very low profile since then. As soon as I started thinking about executions, I launched a desultory search for his contact details on the Internet, not really expecting to find anything. Almost all of the results dated from the 1990s, and I'd more or less abandoned the effort when the ghost pictures materialised on my screen. Even then, the listed email address was, I calculated, nearly a decade old. Given the changes in web technology, it seemed most unlikely to be current. Without thinking too much, I typed a quick message, explaining my project and enquiring whether the address still reached Fred Leuchter. I turned back to the Internet ghosts, and I was idly sniggering at a fearsome spectre someone had detected behind Ted Danson during the filming of *Three Men and a Baby* when my computer signalled new mail. 'Dear Jeff,' the message read, 'you have reached Fred Leuchter. How can I help you?' The email sat there blinking on the desktop. Suddenly, a whole new problem presented itself. I could contact Leuchter, but did I actually want to? This was, after all, a man as famous for denying the Holocaust as for designing killing machines.

The story went like this. In 1988, a Canadian neo-Nazi activist named Ernst Zündel faced the unusual charge of 'spreading false news' after publishing a pamphlet called *Did Six Million Really Die?* Zündel didn't believe the Holocaust had occurred; he did, however, consider it quite likely that UFOs emanated from Neuschwabenland (a German-claimed part of Antarctica), under the control of a reconstituted Third Reich. He was, in other words, a nutter, but a dangerous one, whose publishing house served as one of the biggest outlets of Nazi memorabilia, spewing forth fascist propaganda and periodicals to be disseminated throughout the world. Zündel, in consultation with the British Holocaust-denier David Irving, resolved that his trial would publicise his cause. He contacted American prison wardens, looking for someone with expertise on gas chambers. They directed him to Fred Leuchter, to whom Zündel put the following proposition: would he travel to Poland, investigate Auschwitz and, using his professional experience, testify as to whether Jews had been gassed there? Leuchter agreed. Later, he explained that he felt a responsibility— a man faced serious charges, after all. Critics suggested that the $35 000 he received for his troubles might also have been a factor.

The second half of *Mr Death* concerns Leuchter's Holocaust-denying career. We see him in Poland, all myopic grin as he scrapes the ruined chambers of Auschwitz for cyanide crystal. He is, one might think, engaged in a tremendous adventure; he displays no consciousness of the desecration involved in his amateur sleuthing. Upon his return to the USA, Leuchter produced the document Zündel wanted. It argued that no extermination facilities had existed at Auschwitz: the ventilation systems were inadequate; the chambers were too small; most crucially, the walls did not, Leuchter claimed, manifest the chemical residue produced by an operating death chamber.

The 'Leuchter Report' didn't help Zündel's legal difficulties (he was sentenced to fifteen months' gaol), but then, exoneration was never really his aim. The report—and its author—became a *cause célèbre* in fascist circles in the USA and throughout the world. *Mr Death* shows Leuchter flashing his awkward, toothy grin at a conference of right-wing extremists and neo-Nazi thugs, and nearly twenty years later, you could still find Fred Leuchter quoted about the 'Holocaust hoax' on Nazi websites—which was why, in its review of *Mr Death*, the *Miami Herald* described him as the 'face of evil'.

Chatting with such a man wasn't an appealing prospect, but what choice did I have? I was researching killing, after all. One couldn't expect to speak with Mother Teresa. This was where the trail led; this was where I had to go. 'Hi Fred', I typed, 'Thanks for getting back to me so promptly ...' I explained my research and requested an interview, but then hesitated. Should one be polite in such a message? One thing to contact the face of evil; another to *thank* it. I deleted the passage about his promptness. Then, deciding this was entirely childish, I replaced it and pressed send.

Over the next weeks, Leuchter and I corresponded. The emails were short and businesslike, with Fred reiterating his willingness to help. He was busy right at the moment, but he would happily do an interview as soon as some spare time arose. 'I'll get back to you later this week', he wrote. 'I have been in touch with the Tennessee Governor's Office trying to stop an execution which will result in a torture session!' He was referring to the scheduled electrocution of Daryl Keith Holton, in a chair that Leuchter had designed but which had subsequently been modified by his replacement, an engineer named Jay Wiechert, for whom Leuchter felt utter contempt. Leuchter thought Wiechert incompetent and blamed him for a number of gruesomely botched executions.

His reference in the email to a 'torture session' was particularly striking. The odd expression recalled *Mr Death* and the segment in which Leuchter explains his attitude to executions. He supports capital punishment, he says in the film, but he doesn't approve of what he calls 'capital torture'—in fact, he is determined to stamp it out. That is why he doesn't feel any moral pangs about his work and considers himself a humanitarian. By manufacturing high-quality execution equipment, he ensures that people whom the judicial process has condemned to death die without suffering. He is not responsible for their sentences. It is the courts that send them to die, not him. He simply makes sure that the process takes place humanely. Bruce, I remembered, had said something similar about the slaughter yard: they killed cattle, he'd said, but they didn't torture them.

While I waited for Leuchter to conclude his business in Tennessee, I telephoned Deborah Denno, Professor of Law at Fordham University in New York City. Denno was the pre-eminent legal scholar on issues arising from execution techniques, and her name featured prominently in the literature on the death penalty. I knew she'd written on Leuchter, and I wanted to ask her specifically about him, but I also wanted to get more of a general background on capital punishment in the USA.

Her interest in capital punishment began, she explained, when she wrote an article on the Eighth Amendment to the US Constitution, the famous section that outlawed cruel and unusual punishment: 'There were only nine Supreme Court cases before 1962 that actually analysed the Eighth Amendment or used it. One of the most significant, the most critical, was *Kemmler*, and in the research, I really focused on it. But when I was doing this, I said, I wonder what really happened to Kemmler himself. The court kept on talking about him, but I never knew what happened to him. But then I read ... and it was just awful.'

Kemmler was William Kemmler, a fruit-seller who, in 1890, killed his lover with an axe and duly became the first man scheduled to die in a new invention called the electric chair. Naturally, he appealed his pending execution, relying on the Eighth Amendment, and the case that bore his name duly set a crucial precedent for capital cases. After the failure of his appeal, Kemmler was ushered into the death chamber by a prison staff unsure what protocol applied to the new procedure. Twenty-five official witnesses had been invited; fourteen of them were doctors. Eventually, the warden introduced the prisoner with a conversational 'Gentlemen, this is William Kemmler'. The condemned man gave a polite nod and made a statement expressing his belief in a hereafter. He took off his coat, and calmly sat down in the chair, while the prison staff fussed with the electrode they attached to his head. The warden placed a black mask over his face and Kemmler said goodbye.

Then the switch was pulled. Kemmler snapped rigid, as the current overstimulated all his nerves, and then after ten seconds, the machine turned off and he fell back limp against the straps. The chair had done its work. Or at least, so it seemed—until the witnesses realised Kemmler's chest was still moving. Someone yelled for more power. Again the switch; again the body went taut, and this time the current stayed live for seventy seconds or so, with blood beginning to form on Kemmler's face and the rich, fatty smell of burning flesh permeating the chamber. The second jolt proved more successful, and Kemmler was adjudged lawfully dead.

As Denno said, the whole business was just awful. Yet on 4 May 1990, a hundred years after Kemmler, a man named Jesse Tafero was also put to death in Florida's electric chair, and he, too, died heaving and gurgling, with flames and smoke coming off his uncontrollably spasming head. Tafero was another case that Denno had studied: 'I knew electrocution was used in this country, and I read modern accounts of it and I thought, there's just something not right about this. So I wrote an article. But when you write on the death penalty, there are so many death-row attorneys who need the stuff. They are overworked and underpaid, and I could see immediately how useful the information was to people. So I wrote another article, and it was even more widely used ... there was a constant demand for information. As an academic, you have the luxury to pull this information together in a way that these attorneys don't. You can see the effect, and it's rewarding—though I'd love to work on other areas, I always get hauled back into this.'

I was interested in Denno's perspective on the rationale behind the introduction of the electric chair in the USA. Given the awful mess it made of William Kemmler, why did it continue to be used? 'In the 1880s,' she explained, 'the Governor of New York was appalled by the hangings taking place in America—these public events attended by thousands of people. They were becoming so horrific that he was concerned that, unless something happened, the death penalty would be abolished. That was the context in which the chair was invented.'

In its early days, the USA conducted old-style European executions, scarcely updated from the grisly festivals of cruelty of the

Middle Ages—events at which crowds were expected, even encouraged, to watch as the executioner presided over an elaborate ritual. But by the second half of the nineteenth century, public executions were falling out of favour in the industrialised countries. The gatherings around the Tyburn Tree were supposed to draw ordinary folk into a reaffirmation of the existing order and its codes, but governments became less keen to see the masses congregate, particularly at events that stirred such dangerous passions. If, in the past, gratuitous cruelty had stirred awe, in a democratic era it was just as likely to provoke disgust. The two sets of executions in Melbourne thus illustrated a worldwide trend: in 1842, the hangings were chaotic and public; Kelly's execution was orderly, measured and private.

In New York, the evolution of capital punishment took a peculiarly scientific turn. There, Governor David B Hill decided to bring the resources of modern science to bear, establishing a special commission to identify the best way for the state to kill. In three years, his commissioners compiled an exhaustive, alphabetised catalogue of potential techniques. Under the letter 'B', the investigators explored 'beheading', 'blowing with cannon', 'boiling', 'breaking on the wheel' and 'burying alive'; 'S' included 'shooting', 'stabbing', 'stoning', 'strangling' and 'suffocation'. Eventually, however, the Report of the Commission to Investigate and Report the Most Humane and Practical Method of Carrying into Effect the Sentence of Death in Capital Cases rejected dismemberment and crucifixion (both on the list), choosing instead an entirely novel technique, something so different and new as to require the coining of its own neologism: electrocution.

'The electric chair was seen as very modern', Denno said. 'But most of all, it was supposed to be humane.' The chair emerged from the glorious era of applied science, in whose golden aura it basked. The electrification of America's convicts followed, more or less immediately, from the electrification of America's cities, a process that pitted the famous inventor Thomas Edison and his direct current against George Westinghouse and alternating current. The chair became a grisly battleground for these two technological giants, since Edison's rearguard action against AC rested on its supposed greater deadliness. Philosophically, Edison disapproved of capital punishment; practically, he recognised the soundness of associating Westinghouse with what he called the 'executioner's current'. The perfection of the electrical execution therefore involved a series of public demonstrations by Edison's supporters in which they successfully put to death various animals, including an unfortunate elephant known as Topsy. Yet these stunts were not perceived as ghoulish so much as thrilling, a demonstration of mankind's new power over life and death. Science could despatch the 4-tonne Topsy with the flick of a switch, while the chair itself was showcased, wires and straps and all, among the technological exhibits on display at the Chicago World's Fair.

That open-mouthed wonderment at science's advances had long since dissipated, yet as Denno explained, the assumptions about what made an execution successful had remained largely unchanged since the 1890s. It was still thought that the capital sentence should be inflicted quickly, efficiently and with the minimum of pain, and that the achievement of this 'humane execution' was largely a technical problem. Despite odd localisms (the Mormon doctrine of blood atonement enabled Utah, at one time, to overcome Anglo-Saxon squeamishness and allow the condemned the chance to meet the headsman rather than the hangman), there was a general pattern in the conduct of executions throughout the twentieth century, with new technologies emerging to counter the problems produced by the old technologies.

Thus, after thirty years or so of electrocutions going wrong, DA Turner, inspired by the efficacy with which poisonous chemicals despatched soldiers during the Great War, engineered the first gas chamber. Like Governor Hill, Turner saw himself as a humanitarian, and just as electricity had been hailed as a technical solution to the agonies of the noose, gas was promoted by Turner as promising clean, scientific deaths in place of Kemmler-like burnings. Unfortunately, the gas chamber possessed all the chair's failings and few of its advantages. You could turn an electric current on and off with a switch, but wardens quickly discovered that poisonous fumes required careful management if the guards weren't to asphyxiate each other alongside the inmate. And even with the best preparation, the prisoners still died slowly and in agony. The 1992 gas execution of Donald Harding was, Denno explained, so protracted and grisly that one of the witnessing journalists couldn't stop crying, the attorney-general vomited, and the prison warden threatened to resign rather than use the chamber again.

'Gas is the most problematic method of execution', said Denno. 'It's horrific when you read these accounts. They were all horrific. People would watch someone dying in excruciating pain, and even though states were still changing to lethal gas until 1955, after that point, it ended. The gas chambers were just having too many problems.'

Such problems mattered to the state—and not simply because of the awful publicity a botched job produced. By the second half of the twentieth century, the ideal of the civilised, scientific killing had become so well established that inmates who could argue that their execution might not be humane stood a real chance of achieving a stay. That was one reason why death-row attorneys found Denno's articles so useful: appeals often rested on whether the state could demonstrate its ability to execute the appellant cleanly and efficiently. This, of course, led to some particularly macabre arguments. Denno told me about the grotesque courtroom dialogues she'd seen: 'I was in Florida when an inmate had to witness the testing of an electric chair. The judge wanted him to see that the chair worked! Another time, in Texas, during the evidentiary hearing, they had a doctor actually step down from the stand and look at the inmate's veins to testify that he had viable veins and that, because he wasn't a drug-user, they weren't going to have the kinds of problems they've had with other inmates. The inmates are just sitting there and we're talking about what's going to happen to them.'

I tried to imagine what that would be like: standing in court, while the experts learnedly argued about how best to kill you. 'What happened to the inmates in those cases?'

'They were both executed.'

'Jesus.'

I'd not meant to mutter aloud, but Denno must have heard me, because she continued, with more animation. 'It's perverse. It really is. We're showing you that it's not a cruel or unusual punishment. How? By letting you watch the electric chair, or having a doctor look at your veins in a courtroom setting with twenty people watching. I mean, how cruel could you get!'

The state of the prisoner's veins had become a particularly fraught question with the introduction of lethal injection, trialled from the late 1970s and now the predominant method in most US jurisdictions. Confronted by some particularly ghoulish death chamber failures, Ronald Reagan, as Governor of California, famously lent his imprimatur to lethal injection with a folksy recollection of humanely putting sick horses to sleep out on his ranch. If the gas chamber utilised industrial technology, lethal injection mirrored a prosperous, medicalised era in which even animals deserved the ministrations of a vet. In a society where death usually took place in a hospital rather than at home or in the street, the paraphernalia of lethal injection (the gurney, the IV line, the needle, the antiseptic room) seemed instinctively appropriate for ending a life, far more so than a Hitleresque gas chamber or an electrical device straight from the set of a B-movie.

Once again, though, the humanity of the procedure was more apparent than real. Research by Denno and others revealed that, with the American Medical Association forbidding doctors to assist, the state lethal-injection protocols were often devised quickly and carelessly by people who didn't really know what they were doing. There were no 'experts' in humane killing, and the patina of efficiency in the supposedly clinical process disguised procedures sometimes designed, almost literally, on the back of an envelope. One of the significant documents in the evolution of lethal injection was a 1977 letter from Dr Stanley Deutsch of the Oklahoma Medical School's Anaesthesiology Department to a senator who enquired as to what drugs might be used. The drugs Deutsch recommended, in a casual paragraph or two, became, almost by default, standard, despite the reservations of other experts. Elsewhere, Fred Leuchter played a role in the adoption of potassium chloride in executions, even though he'd extrapolated the lethal doses for the New Jersey protocols from the quantities used for killing pigs.

'A detailed investigation of lethal injection's creation and history', Denno writes, 'shows that at no point was the procedure medically or scientifically studied on human beings'. This remarkable fact had particularly disturbing ramifications in light of one of lethal injection's peculiar innovations: the inclusion of a paralytic agent to stifle any moaning or choking from the condemned until a different chemical stopped their hearts.

'What's the point of that? How does paralysing the inmate make the process more humane?' Then I understood. 'Oh. It's for the witnesses, isn't it? It makes it easier to watch.'

'With lethal injection,' Denno agreed, 'that's definitely an issue. It's a method of execution created as much for the observers as for the inmate, which is also a way to perpetuate the death penalty. That's the way the death penalty remains in this country. If people are assured that people are being executed humanely, then it all seems less problematic.' Thus, a macabre irony: the transformation of the execution into a peaceful spectacle might have ensured that the inmates died in utter agony. They were paralysed, after all, and if the second drug didn't render them unconscious before the third drug stopped their hearts, they couldn't reveal the pain of chemicals slowly destroying their internal organs. The spectators saw only a person drifting off as gently as Ronald Reagan's old horses, not knowing that the reality was closer to something from Edgar Allan Poe.

In the context of the history Denno described, Leuchter's slogan 'capital punishment, not capital torture' didn't seem so ridiculous.

That was, essentially, the official motto under which executions had been conducted since the 1890s. The difference was that Leuchter took it seriously.

When Denno spoke with Leuchter, not long after his exposure as a Holocaust-denier, he'd made more or less that point. The system needed him, he said. 'When we talked,' Denno explained, 'he'd lost his business and he was very bitter about it. He said that wardens were still calling him but begging him to not to tell anyone, because they had nowhere else to go. You have to remember that until 1990, Leuchter was the creator of most of this country's execution machinery. To this day, directly or indirectly, he is responsible for how the great majority of inmates in this country have been executed and how they will be executed.'

The publication of the 'Leuchter Report' led—inevitably and quite understandably—to sustained attacks on Leuchter's credibility. Though Leuchter produced his report as an expert witness, under cross-examination at Zündel's trial, the prosecution forced an acknowledgement that his only academic qualification was in history and that he lacked any particular expertise in chemistry, toxicology or incineration—all topics canvassed by the 'Leuchter Report'. Quite clearly, Leuchter didn't possess the skills necessary to 'investigate' the Holocaust, as his report demonstrated in and of itself. Once Leuchter had become notorious, anti-racist campaigners seized on his court-room admissions and pressured the prison system to sever its association with him. His lack of formal engineering training, it was suggested, meant that he wasn't a bona fide 'execution technician' but someone who had insinuated himself onto death row without proper accreditation.

In the USA, senior prison wardens are political appointees. The employment of Fred Leuchter—a man seen by audiences all over the world merrily scraping away at the Auschwitz gas chambers—would not help a warden's prospects for career advancement. More fundamentally, if Leuchter remained the public face of capital punishment, the perception that the institution was itself ghoulish and abhorrent would only grow. It was much easier to sever all official connection with Leuchter and his company, and to accept the characterisation of him as a maverick, a fraud and an impostor. That was what the wardens did.

Yet Leuchter wasn't a fraud—or, at least, no more so than anyone else. Yes, he lacked formal qualifications. But so did most of the people responsible for the death penalty. As for certification, what degree would really qualify an execution technologist? To which institution would you go to complete a course in capital punishment? Leuchter might have been self-trained, but he knew as much about what he was doing as anyone in the USA. When he decided to launch a business manufacturing execution equipment in the mid-1980s, he'd researched more or less everything known about the field. He dug out the old protocols from prisons; he read early journal articles about the workings of electric chairs; he studied the drop tables used to ensure successful hangings; he examined the autopsies of executed men and looked at reports of executions that had gone wrong. That's why, at the height of his success, he consulted, to a greater or lesser degree, for every death-penalty state in the USA.

'So when you saw him,' I asked Denno, 'he was still giving advice?'

'Yes, but only unofficially. It was a Catch 22, since by taking him away, the methods of execution became even worse—he told me that would happen. He said there were a lot of problems in a lot of states and that he was a necessary tool. In a certain sense, that was true. He was necessary. How many other people knew as much as he did?'

What about the obvious question: was there any relationship between his work and his political evolution, his views on the Holocaust?

'It's an interesting one. You know, I actually got really obsessed with that whole Zündel case, and I phoned the place that tested the bricks from Auschwitz, and the person who testified in that case explained how Leuchter had got it wrong. I wrote a very long footnote about it for one of my articles, before I had to leave it alone.'

She thought for a moment. 'Leuchter pitched himself to me as some-one who was speaking for these neo-Nazi groups not because he really believed what they said ideologically but just because he was an expert on gas chambers, and he was just reporting what he'd found. Now I found that a little bit hard to swallow. We all have an expertise, but most of us are going to be selective as to who we talk to. I don't think he was as innocent as he said, but as to whether Leuchter's ideas were affected by his work, it's difficult to say. He's a complicated guy, and whether it's cause and effect from the work, or whether that's just his character, I couldn't really tell.'

I ended that conversation more convinced than ever that Leuchter mattered. His own profound strangeness seemed a unique reflection of the paradoxes of capital punishment itself, like the fair-ground mirror that grotesquely distorted individuals' distinctive characteristics, thus, in its own way, revealing the truth about them. There was no one more qualified to explain the trauma or otherwise of taking a human life. It was Leuchter whom I needed now.

5

THE RIGHT LEG

Despite Leuchter's fears about the efficacy of the Tennessee chair, Daryl Holton's execution had proceeded according to plan. 'No blood or bodily fluids could be seen leaving Holton's body', explained the Tennessee *City Paper* with an unseemly civic pride. 'No smell from the electrocution process could be discerned in the witness room.'

I sent Leuchter an email asking whether, now that his business with Tennessee was over, he was ready for the interview. A day passed and then another and then a week, and there was still no response. It wasn't a problem, not at first. Everyone got inundated with mail sometimes, and it was easy for messages to bank up unnoticed. So I re-sent the email. No reply.

After a fortnight without an answer, I went back and read his earlier messages. Was there a nuance I missed? No, the emails were all friendly enough. He was willing to help, he said, even if he'd never committed to a specific time for an interview. His emails contained an electronic signature, with an address, telephone number and fax. Thinking that he'd perhaps changed email addresses, I called his telephone. It was disconnected. The fax still seemed to work, so I sent through a document explaining how keen I was for the interview to go ahead and giving him my telephone details. A week passed and no response.

It seemed obvious, by that stage, what had happened. This was the age of the Internet, when nothing was secret and everything was knowable. You could discover a remarkable amount about anyone through simple Google searches. That was presumably what Fred Leuchter had done. There was plenty of my stuff online. It wouldn't take much to get an idea of my politics, and if you were chummy with the world's leading neo-Nazis, you'd scarcely want to assist someone identified with the Left. So much for that, then.

In place of Leuchter, I contacted the American academic Robert Johnson. His book *Death Work* was a close observation of the execution team in Virginia as they prepared for and carried out a number of capital sentences, including detailed interviews with the staff members about what they had done and how it affected them. It was a text almost unique in the literature of the death penalty, since very few books examined so closely the impact of capital punishment on executioners, and none did so through the kind of qualitative research Johnson employed.

Johnson had worked with Denno, and proved as easy to talk with as she'd been. He was affable, intelligent and friendly, and, apart from his gentle Southern accent, there was nothing, really, to distinguish him from the people with whom I interacted on a daily basis, even as he discussed an entirely different reality. 'Let me tell you,' he said, early in our conversation, 'the first night when I observed this team carry out this electrocution and then went with them to the morgue with the body and then out for a drink afterwards, I thought my life was never going to be the same again. It was profoundly depressing; it took about six months for me to get reoriented and move on.'

Johnson's PhD had been in criminal justice, and he'd first been interested in studying suicidal inmates. From that, he'd researched the effects of solitary confinement, before working on an ethnography of death row, later published as *Condemned to Die*. 'About ten years later, I was a consultant for the Virginia correctional system, and they were carrying out executions, and the warden simply asked me if I had any opinions on this. I told him that I really hadn't observed executions and didn't have much insight into them. And he invited me to observe them, which I did. Then the men were very comfortable with me and were willing to talk, so I interviewed them and they invited me to follow them around during two executions, which was where *Death Work* came from.'

At that time, the prison took no real responsibility for the mental health of the people carrying out the executions, and any measures the staff took to protect themselves were entirely informal. In fact, Johnson later speculated that one of the reasons they were willing to allow him to accompany them was, perhaps, because he'd inadvertently provided moral support: 'That was something that occurred to me afterwards. Here's this bearded guy, looks like an academic, sounds like an academic, observing us, talking to us. It adds some normalcy and credibility to what's taking place, perhaps. You have to remember, these were just regular working-class guys—the kind of people I grew up with.'

They might have been regular guys, but they were also conscious of themselves as a team, a tight unit of eight seasoned men. The prison only invited its best officers to the execution squad—people who had proven themselves able to handle difficult situations—and they were all free to decline. 'They had bonded very tightly,' Johnson told me, 'almost like an elite combat team, like a band of brothers, even across racial lines. They thought of themselves as a family, and they took pride in that connection and their competence. There was also a sense that because the execution was a team effort, no one of them was solely culpable. In that sense, they didn't need dummy switches on the electric chair. Even though only one of them pulled the switch, they saw it as done by the team so that the responsibility was somehow diffused.'

The reference to a combat team was particularly interesting. The argument about the difficulty of wartime killing originated in the work of SLA Marshall, the famous American military writer. Marshall interviewed troops in the aftermath of bloody Second World War battles and was shocked by the percentage who never even tried to discharge their weapons. But he noted that, even as individual riflemen failed to fire, crewed weapons such as heavy machine guns continued to kill effectively. That success seemed to be the result of a twofold process: on the one hand, the teamwork necessary to operate the gun broke down responsibility, precisely as Johnson described in the prison; on the other, peer pressure was exerted on each man to perform his task effectively.

Even in the absence of a crewed weapon, a similar process could be observed among tight-knit groups of soldiers. The nineteenth-century military theorist Ardant du Picq put it like this: 'Four brave men who do not know each other will not dare to attack a lion. Four less brave, but knowing each other well, sure of their reliability and consequently of mutual aid, will attack resolutely.' The argument that men fight neither for their country nor for any great cause, but for the people immediately around them, had become almost a cliché of military theory.

Johnson's comparison with an elite combat team was, then, quite exact. The men he'd studied kept up their own morale through their strong identification with each other and used, almost consciously, the kind of collective diffusion employed by soldiers in combat. All their procedures in the chamber were broken down into tiny, discrete components, as though they'd been subjected to a time-and-motion study. They killed the convicts according to a predetermined schedule: there was a certain time allocated for every part of the execution, and everything unfolded according to that timing. Johnson had asked a member of the team what he did. 'He answered, "the right leg", and just stood there looking at me as if that were an answer. And in some senses, it was. That was how they broke what they did down into small parts. This man's job was simply to strap down the inmate's right leg, and that's what he rehearsed doing, as they ran through procedures for the execution over and over again. I think, from a

psychological point of view, the breaking it into small parts—
focusing on it, rehearsing it, making it mechanical—is, again, a way
you protect yourself. You are not just staying in the moment; you are
staying in the task, concentrating on the one simple thing you have
to do, rather than thinking about what's happening overall.'

That kind of rehearsal was crucial to the military's response to
Marshall's research. Since the Second World War, Western militaries
had assiduously worked at training soldiers to overcome their inhi-
bitions, to teach them how to kill in battle. In the Second World War,
only 15 per cent of soldiers fired, but by Vietnam the figure was said
to be closer to 95 per cent. Today there was almost total participation. Traditional military training had taught men to fire on a range,
separating the technical skill of shooting from any context. They
learnt physically how to operate their weapons, and it was simply
assumed that they'd put that knowledge to use by killing the enemy
when the time came. In contrast, the newer training provided a simulation of battle conditions that was as accurate as possible. The
trainees practised in full battle dress, in terrain similar to that in
which they'd deploy. Instead of a bullseye target, they fired at human
silhouettes, which popped up for a few seconds and then collapsed
like stricken soldiers when shot. The process worked by conditioning an automatic response that would, in battle conditions, override
the instinctive reluctance to kill. Presented with a target, the soldier
aimed and fired, just like he'd done so often in training. The similarity between the battlefield and the training ground allowed troops to
maintain a 'denial defence': at one level, they could believe that the
people they shot in combat were simply animated targets, like those
they'd shot so many times before.

The careful rehearsals Johnson described to me seem to involve
something similar. But he also emphasised the importance of the
prison structure. By definition, a death sentence precluded any rehabilitation, and Johnson thus suggested that death row necessarily
transmuted the prisoner from person into thing, a piece of living meat
to be kept in storage until the execution date arrived. The process

intensified in the final period before the sentence was carried out, when, a few days before his execution, the condemned man was moved to a twenty-four-hour death watch. The guards with whom Johnson spoke made the same point repeatedly and in different ways: by the time the inmates were taken to the chair, they were already dead, both to themselves and to others. The inexorable bureaucratic protocol that prepared them, step by step, for execution methodically stripped them of humanity, so that, when they were escorted to their electrocution, with heads shaved and property reallocated and funerals pre-planned, they no longer seemed of the world of the living. Inmates occasionally assured each other that they would attack the guards in the chamber, but in reality, when the final moments arrived, no one ever struggled and no one ever fought. Resistance simply wasn't possible: when they shuffled into the chamber, the injection or the lethal jolt merely concluded a progression that had begun long ago, a journey largely completed while their hearts were still beating.

The comparison with the abattoir seemed irresistible. There, the kill floor was less affecting than shooting with Demetri precisely because of a process like the one Johnson described: repetition, abstraction and a relentless mechanical pace. But Johnson took the argument even further. If death row transformed the inmates, he suggested, then it also did something similar to the staff. A maximum-security prison was an inherently dangerous setting, with the safety of the officers resting upon inflexible security procedures. The protocols necessary for daily security stripped guards of their individuality, since personality became largely irrelevant to the predetermined tasks. The execution team were, on one level, an elite, but the rigidity of their duties in the death chamber suggested that their status didn't provide any more room for personal autonomy; on the contrary, the significance of their task only made doing the job 'by the book' even more important. The execution itself had thus evolved into a process that unfolds not only without human agency but almost without relation to human beings at all. At a certain time, under certain circumstances, a sequence was initiated, and executioners and the condemned were moved through their paces according to its dictates, like a car progressing through the Ford factory—or a carcass moving through a slaughterhouse.

The abattoir, too, seemed to be all about controlling animals, shepherding them on a journey of destruction from the gate at which the cattle truck unloads to the exit through which meat emerges for sale. But the control exercised over animals was also a means of managing the workforce, with the assembly line transforming the old master butchers into mere labourers, who performed a specific cut at a specific time.

In that sense, executioners, too, had been deskilled. Once upon a time, the executioner had been, in his own cruel way, a craftsman. In the grisly rites of the Middle Ages, he'd featured as a figure of ceremonial importance—a ringmaster in a circus of pain—since the complicated brutalities he was called upon to inflict (breaking on the wheel, say, or hanging, drawing and quartering) required a certain measure of skill. Overseeing such procedures had been a specialised trade possessing its mysteries, vocabulary and techniques, handed from master to apprentice, and often from father to son.

What Johnson was discussing, by contrast, was a mechanical process broken down into Taylorised components. Obviously, in most respects, that made killing easier. When asked how they felt, the interviewees could talk about doing a job, about following protocol, about making sure everything went according to plan. But they could never totally escape from what they were doing. 'I don't think anyone completely ever gets the mechanisation of the process right', Johnson explained. 'For instance, one of the officers I spoke to talked about inadvertently catching the eye of the inmate as they strapped him in the chair. And afterwards that was what stayed with him: the memory of his eyes.' To block such encounters, the team members talked among themselves about the inmate and the crimes he'd committed, even going to old newspapers to draw out the horrific details. 'Back then, this was really before the DNA exonerations, and I don't think people seriously thought about innocent people. I didn't, and

I'm very liberal—I just didn't think about it. I assumed everyone on death row was guilty. And one of the things that my team did was play up the cruelty of the crime to get psyched. Us versus them. We're the good family; he's the bad guy—that was key.'

At the time, all of the interviewed executioners seemed to be coping. But twenty years later, the team leader—the man who seemed most in control—contacted Johnson of his own accord. 'I did this work in the late eighties, and about a year ago, the guy who headed the execution team and went on to carry out about sixty-five executions—I only observed three—called me up and said, "Would you like me to come up and talk to your class?" I said, well, certainly. Back when I was with this team, no one wanted to be identified, nobody wanted to say they were from an execution team. This was in Richmond, Virginia. It's a small town. Half of these guys were from the inner city, half of them were rural, and they didn't really want to be known for their job at the time. Anyway, he'd subsequently retired and has become opposed to the death penalty and now favours life without parole. He came up to my class and talked, and it was pretty remarkable to see how, once he got out of the culture of the death house, his basic religiosity came fully into play. I think it has something to do with the sentiment that came up with the team members: several of them were concerned that the deadening of emotions that they had to develop in order to do this job was seeping out into their lives.'

'So he was worried about the effect on his personality?'

'I think that he has some concerns both for his personality but also for his soul. I mean, he's a pretty religious guy.' Johnson stopped. 'I've got his number somewhere, I think. Would you like to talk to him?'

I drew a breath. Losing the interview with Leuchter had been a blow, but in another respect it had been a relief, since it excused me from the moral problems he represented. Yet here was an opportunity to speak directly with an executioner. How could I say no?

Johnson emailed me a few days later with a name and number. The executioner was called Jerry Givens; he lived in Virginia. That was really all I knew about him, other than his anonymous participation in the interviews that led to Johnson's book. With stomach aflutter, I phoned in the early evening, Melbourne time.

It is easy to downplay the craft of journalism. Interviewing seems simple, intuitive—everyone can ask questions. But, of course, a good reporter marshals considerable skill to draw out the subject, to keep the conversation on track, to know when to wait and when to probe. I was not a good reporter—I was not a reporter at all— and of all the bad interviews I've ever conducted, that phone conversation with Jerry Givens was the worst. My anxiety was rising even as the international dial tone skittered in the earpiece. An executioner seemed a semi-mythical creature, a figure from a Tarot card rather than someone you could call on his mobile phone.

'Hello? Is that Jerry Givens? It's Jeff calling from Australia. I'm doing some research about the death penalty. Robert Johnson gave me your details and suggested I should speak with you.' Already, my voice came too fast, dousing any silence with a torrent of superfluous words.

'Oh. From Australia, right? Yes, he said that. What you want to talk about?'

The accent: that was the first problem. Johnson came from the South and talked like a southerner, but his regional intonation sat lightly over a standard English, and there was no problem comprehending him. Jerry Givens, by contrast, used an entirely different grammar and lexicon. He spoke in an extended drawl, with the words stretched and slurred, so that it took a beat or two to even understand his greeting, especially as the phone line stripped away any visual cues. It quickly became apparent that the phonetic barrier was equally impenetrable from the other side, too.

'What you say your last name was? I'm gonna write that down.'
'Sparrow. It's Sparrow.'

'How you spell that?'

'S—P—A ...'

He repeated. 'S—T—I ...' The nasal Australian intonation: to anyone raised on American English, the 'A' sounds like an 'I'.

'A', I tried to enunciate, feeling increasingly ridiculous. 'For apple. Sparrow. It's like the bird.'

'You say Dird? D—I—R—D ...'

'No, not Dird. The bird. Sparrow. It's Sparrow.' The more flustered I grew, the more Australian my pronunciation became. He couldn't understand my questions; I couldn't understand his answers—and the Abbott and Costello routine continued. 'Perhaps I could start by asking you to describe your experience of the death penalty?'

A pause. 'Describe the death penalty?' The thousands of kilometres of intercontinental cable transmitted in perfect definition his growing understanding that he was speaking with a halfwit, a whiny-toned stranger from across the world phoning to ask what capital punishment was.

'No, no, no', I gabbled. 'If you could tell me about your background. What kind of work you did.'

'Oh, OK. Well, I was the executioner.' Of course he was—that was the reason for the call—but his frankness was still somehow disconcerting. Official discussions of capital punishment stressed the institution rather than the individual, consciously avoiding terms that recalled hooded men with axes. You anticipated a euphemism, a generic correctional title, with the exact nature of the work becoming clearer only through a longer discussion. Thrown off guard by such a matter-of-fact acknowledgement, I responded as if he'd simply said that he worked for a prison.

'So ... um ... how did you get into that?' At this point, replaying the recording becomes almost physically unbearable. Even now, it's difficult to think that I actually asked a man how he 'got into' executions, as if we were discussing his enthusiasm for yoga or stamp collecting.

He didn't seem impressed, either. 'You know, it's a long story, man. I can't tell you all at once, particularly on the phone. If I'm gone tell you, it's gonna be kinda rough, you know what I'm saying? When I talk on the phone, I can't see your face. Better you come here and we talk face to face.'

The interview was not going to work. That was clear—and it was almost with relief that I realised he'd reached the same conclusion. 'Well, I do think I will need to come to the US at some time. Perhaps when I do I can give you a call, and we can talk then.'

'Yeah', he said, with what sounded rather like sarcasm. 'You do that.'

6

CLOSE TO THE FIRE

In the wake of the Givens fiasco, killing seemed more impenetrable a mystery than ever before. People wouldn't talk to me, and then when they did, I couldn't talk to them. There was an obvious political impediment to convincing the military—or, for that matter, Fred Leuchter—to speak, but the difficulty went deeper than that. The kangaroo abattoir had illustrated the social gulf between those who worked with violence and those who didn't, a chasm that had yawned open again with the Givens interview. The taboo on killing meant that the shedding of blood brought otherwise hidden class relations to the surface. The Sudanese immigrants labouring in the slaughterhouse fostered in me a sense of guilt, deep in the gut, a knowledge that, at some level, I was the cause, that their work hosing lungs followed logically from the fine meal I'd eaten last night. In essence, they lived the way they did so that I need never personally slit the throat of a calf.

That was also part of the problem with my call to Virginia. I was not responsible—of course I wasn't—for however many poor wretches had been guided into electric chairs by Jerry Givens. Yet my own insulation from violence contrasted so sharply with his exposure to it, and the difference formed a barrier between us far greater than difficulties of regional intonation.

But perhaps I was just brooding too much. The subject preyed on the mind, weighed me down, took over my thoughts. If I'd begun by feeling ambivalent about the difference between Dave Grossman and Joanna Bourke, that had long since changed. I'd been reading both their work obsessively, and had found Grossman's tight structure far more compelling than Bourke's more anecdotal research. More than that, though, if she said killing was easy and he said killing was hard, I knew which side I was on. I wanted Grossman's argument to be true; I wanted it badly. I didn't need to hear about happy killers, didn't want to think about slaughter without trauma. The conclusion of the American soldier-poet Brian Turner in his poem 'Sadiq' felt right, on all kinds of levels:

> It should make you shake and sweat,
> nightmare you, strand you in a desert
> of irrevocable desolation, the consequences
> seared into the vein, no matter what adrenaline
> feeds the muscle its courage, no matter
> what god shines down on you, no matter
> what crackling pain and anger
> you carry in your fists, my friend,
> it should break your heart to kill.

A few months earlier, Opinion Research Business, a British polling agency, had released a fresh estimate of deaths in Iraq since the US invasion. More than a million, it suggested: an astonishing, unthinkable number, but one more or less consistent with an earlier study published in the medical journal *Lancet*. This was not some ancient atrocity, a jerky newsreel from a far-off land; this was happening now, in our time, on our watch. Yes, it should break your heart to kill. But did it?

Grossman said that it did. His theory went like this. Most animals readily used deadly force against prey or for protection against predators, but in contests with others of their own kind for territory or for mates, they defeated rivals with ritualised posturing instead of claws or fangs. When rattlesnakes fought, they wrestled rather than bit, just as piranhas chose not to devour. Animals instinctively knew that in struggles with others of their species, their own safety depended not on escalating the violence but on restraining it, allowing the weaker to submit ostentatiously and then slink away unharmed.

Humans were the same. It was easier to kill from a distance (which was why in modern wars the bulk of casualties were caused by artillery and bombs) or when the victim fled (thus initiating a chase reflex). But in face-to-face encounters, the instinctive reaction was not to kill but to avoid killing. Instinct guided terrified soldiers not to escalate the conflict beyond ritual. A small minority killed, but until the advent of modern training, the rest either discharged their weapons loudly but harmlessly into the air (to posture) or refused to fire at all (to submit).

Grossman was a soldier, not a pacifist. The resistance to killing could, he said, be overcome, and in his book he discussed the techniques that the army had employed to successfully train its men. Nonetheless, the point remained: there was a pain attached to killing, a debt to be paid.

Wanting that to be true had brought me back to the death penalty. If Grossman's argument held, an execution—the deliberate, close-range killing of a powerless individual—should be particularly difficult, particularly traumatic. On the web, I saw a snippet of video in which Ron McAndrew, a former Florida prison warden, talked about the executions over which he'd presided, and he seemed to illustrate Grossman's point entirely.

McAndrew was easy to track down, and this time, the interview went much more smoothly, partly because I felt more determined

and partly because Ron McAndrew was a campaigner for abolitionism, who had told his tales many times before. There was no need
to ask questions, no need to say much of anything; the words just
tumbled out of him, almost of their own accord.

He'd loved his time in the prison system, he said, in his slow,
thoughtful way, and he still missed it today. It was a job he'd come to
late in life, after he'd taken early retirement from a business career and
then moved to Florida. Needing health insurance, he accepted a prison
job as a temporary expedient—and then discovered a zest for it: 'It
was just so challenging. When you step from the parking lot into a
prison, it's like going to another planet. It's a whole different social
structure. It's where two cigarettes represent what 50 dollars would
mean to you. It's a place where a metal spoon that you can sharpen
down and turn into a knife is a valuable, valuable thing. It was just ...'
His voice trailed off for a minute, a ghost of that former enthusiasm
briefly audible. 'I'd never seen anything like this in my life. This was
really my first experience with a prison. And it just stuck on me. All
of a sudden, I found myself hitting the floor in the morning, running,
couldn't get to work fast enough. I couldn't learn enough.'

He set out to advance through the ranks in corrections, enrolling
in a part-time degree in criminal justice administration, and taking
jobs from one end of Florida to another. But the death penalty
changed everything. 'A position in Florida State Prison, in North
Florida, opened up. I was the eleventh applicant and the last one
interviewed. And I got the job. And, of course, I hadn't been there
more than two weeks and I had to do my first execution.' He paused,
and enunciated the name slowly: 'John Bush'.

This was 1996. John Bush had robbed a convenience store and,
with two accomplices, kidnapped the eighteen-year-old woman
working there. The three men drove her to an isolated area, where
Bush stabbed her and another man shot her, all for a predictably
miserable sum. Bush was convicted of first-degree murder, armed
robbery and kidnapping.

McAndrew had gone into the North Florida position conscious of what he had to do. It didn't bother him. 'The head of the Florida Department of Corrections, a fellow named Harry K Singletary, called me up. He knew me as a person, he knew me to be stable. He said, "Ron, Florida State Prison—I understand that they want you to be the man to go there. I'm willing to sign the papers but I have to ask you a very sensitive question."

'I said, "What's that?"

'"Are you going to be able to handle those executions?"

'I said, "Yessir! I would not have applied if I could not handle it."

'He said, "I can tell you I don't want the job. I would never go to Florida State Prison. I support the death penalty and so on and so forth, but that's some real dirty work there. You think you up to it?"

'I said, "Yessir, I'm up to it."'

Telling the story, McAndrew was openly scornful of that initial confidence. 'Those were just words. You know, I thought I was up to it. I wasn't. I don't think anybody is.'

I asked him if he'd thought about the death penalty at that stage and, if so, if he'd had a position on it.

'Oh, yes. I was very pro–death penalty. There were two murders in my own family, twenty years apart. My sister-in-law and my cousin were both murdered. I thought that anyone who would pre-meditatingly carry out murder deserved to be put to death.'

But as a warden, his perspective changed. 'The warden is in charge of absolutely every detail of an execution. This isn't something he passes on to other people. He is the man who selects the executioner; he is the person who appoints a team of nine people; he is the person who takes them to the death chamber. You practise an execution dozens and dozens of times before you actually carry it out. You use a correctional officer volunteer to sit in the electric chair and you go through the routine.' There was no mirth in that laugh. 'It's like a little theatre: you are putting on an act for the governor. And I used to joshingly call it the governor's theatre: OK, it's the governor's show and we have to put on a good show for him today, so everyone make this look as pretty as you can. That was the whole idea: we were supposed to make a person's death look pretty for the press.'

He spat out the word *pretty*—and no wonder. It was exactly the wrong word to describe the death of Pedro Medina in 1997, an execution over which McAndrew had also presided. Medina had been convicted of murdering his former teacher. He denied the crime, and the execution proceeded despite mercy pleas from the Pope and the daughter of the victim. His last words in the chair were 'I am still innocent'.

It went terribly wrong. 'When Pedro Medina was executed, I believe that I was set up', McAndrew said. 'I saw the man squeeze all the water out of the sponge and I asked him at the time, is there enough saline in that sponge? And he said, yeah boss, we got plenty of water. When we turned on the electricity to kill this guy, flames shot out from underneath the helmet and we burned his head badly. There was steam going down the side of his face and coming out of his eyes, and his nose burned as well. It was horrifying. The chamber filled up with smoke. We could hardly see each other, it was so dark. The sponge let off a lot of smoke and a terrible smell. But you could still smell the burning flesh.'

The botch caused something of a scandal, though Florida's attorney-general, Bob Butterworth, tried to laugh it off. 'People who wish to commit murder,' he said, 'they better not do it in the state of Florida, because we may have a problem with our electric chair'. McAndrew didn't see the humour: 'It doesn't take you long to realise that killing people who killed other people doesn't make you a kind or gentle person. It leaves scars that are there forever.'

After that, he went to Texas on three separate occasions to assist with lethal injections. He knew that in the wake of the Medina fiasco, the Florida legislature would lean towards a different method, and he wanted to prepare. I wondered whether it was the particularly gruesome nature of the Medina electrocution that affected him. Was lethal injection easier?

He answered with another anecdote: 'There was a previous warden at Florida State Prison, who, during a press interview after an execution, was asked what would happen if he switched over to lethal injection. "Don't you think that it would be less traumatic?" they said. And his response—and I'll never forget it—was just two words: "Dead's dead" … If you are killing somebody, you are killing them. You know, when the person has been executed, you tell the witnesses that he's been pronounced dead. That's all you say, and then you close the curtains so they don't see anything else. But you've got to stay there. You've got the body. You got to take all this apparatus off of them and you've got to pull the needles out of their arms if it's a lethal injection, and you've got to stuff their body into a body bag. If they were electrocuted, their eyes are wide open— I mean, frozen in position wide open. You've got to put them into the back of a hearse and take them to the medical examiner's office.' He broke off. 'Do you know what it says on the death certificate for anyone who is executed? When they say cause of death, do you know what the word is? It's homicide. Homicide!' Again, that distilled contempt, a bitterness boiled down to its essence.

'You've also got to realise that most of these guys on death row are also ex–drug addicts—heroin addicts and what have you—and they don't have any veins. Their veins are flat. In order to get an IV you've got to do what's called a cut-down. You know what that is?' I did. An IV cut-down was a painful and difficult procedure, using a scalpel to part subcutaneous tissues to expose an artery. 'Well, the only guy we had to do this was a guy with a little bit of medical training in Vietnam, back during the war. He was a medic, but he'd never actually done it on anyone—he just knew the procedure. You've got to get two IVs in, since you gotta have them in each arm in case one blows out, especially with someone who's got flat veins. Then you've got to switch the pipes and pump it into the other arm.

'This last guy they executed up there, it took them thirty-four minutes. And he could still move his head on the table and he's looking around—I've talked to some of the guys involved in this—and he's saying, "What in the hell's going on? What are you guys doing? Jesus Christ, man, this is hurting! Give me a shot! Do something! Stop the pain! Put me to death." Four minutes later, finally, he was pronounced dead. They couldn't get the stuff to go through the veins. They had the needles ... one went straight through the artery: completely through and out the other side. It's a horrible thing; it's ghastly.

'Then there's the time you've got to spend with this guy, the thirty days before he's executed. He's moved to a holding cell and he's put on what's called death watch, which means you have a correctional officer sitting in front of his cell around the clock. This is to prevent the person who is going to be executed from committing suicide. We can't cheat the governor out of his execution, because it's the biggest political toy in the United States.'

I asked whether, as warden, he developed any kind of relationship with the prisoner, whether he got to know the man in any way.

'Get to know him? You visit with him every single day for those thirty days. You go down; you have cell-front conversations; you help him out with his family and his friends. The family's in your office, just sitting there. I never forget the second guy that I executed; name was Mills.'

Mills was John Mills Jnr. His crime was reminiscent of Bush's—perhaps not surprisingly, given that those who progress to the chair usually originate in the same sad substratum of poverty and criminality. Mills tried to rob a trailer home and, when he encountered the owner, took him down to an airstrip, beat him with a tyre iron and shot him to death.

'Now Mills had two sisters, a brother and a mother,' McAndrew continued, 'and they came numerous times to my office. And these folks are sitting there looking at me, knowing I'm the person that's going to turn around and tell the executioner, "Give him the juice". You're helping them with their woes and what have you, and of course they hold out hope until the last minute, because the attorneys are all working overtime, faxing things to the Supreme Court, and naturally the families are all hepped up about this. They always figure there's a chance, you know. I've had them stop and hold hands and pray in my office—and even pray for me.'

The long-distance phone line was too thin, too flimsy, to bear this conversation.

Could he say, in general, how people he'd known who had been involved in performing executions had been affected afterwards?

He hesitated for a moment. 'There's many cases where I don't know what has happened to the folks who were involved, but I do know in a few cases. There was a warden who was there prior to my time, who had carried out numerous executions, and I know he is deeply troubled by it. It has affected his whole life. A man who was never religious, in any way, shape or form, has become a devout Christian, trying to get away from the nightmares of all these faces that he sees on a regular basis. Another guy who was an assistant warden there—we talk a lot about executions and what's happened in the past, and it's therapeutic for the two of us. He was my boss in another prison, and today he's an Episcopal priest. I think he found a certain sense of solace in the pulpit.

'Some of the others? Some of them are dead from what I would say are stress-related diseases and ...' He paused again to rethink his sentence. 'I don't know of a person in there that, if I were to meet on the street tomorrow, they would be happy about all the executions they'd carried out. Just about anyone who was involved, if I said to them, listen, they're going to have a vote on whether we're going to continue with executions or not, most all of them would say to me, well, I'd vote to stop executions.

'As for me, it really brought me down; it left me in a mental quandary that I just couldn't get out of, after I left Florida State Prison. Seven years ago, I reached out and said, I've got to have some help. I talked to my doctor and he sent me to an interview with a mental-health specialist, but they told me that they didn't think they had anything to offer me. They said, I'd recognised what the problem was but I was just troubled by it, and they thought I was doing the right thing by just talking about it. So I reached out to my priest, and it was through him and my church that I renewed my faith, and in a process of a year or so I found the old Ron again and improved upon him.'

Before we said goodbye, I apologised for making him relive the events he described. 'It doesn't bother me to talk about it now', he said. 'I talk about it all the time; I talk about it as much as I can. My job now, in my semi-retired years, is to bring people close to the death penalty—bring them up so close to the fire that it will heat their britches up.'

When the digital recorder clicked off, I was still thinking about that heat. Suddenly it was obvious. Jerry Givens had said he'd speak face to face. Very well: we would speak face to face. There was a US passport in my cupboard; I had a little bit of money saved. With the last issue of *Overland* finished for the year, taking time off work was possible. So why not go? In the USA, Givens would tell his story. McAndrew had supervised executions; Givens was the executioner. Theirs was the perspective I needed—and it was an American one. Perhaps I could track down Fred Leuchter, too. He lived in Boston and his email signature contained his address. Ignoring messages was one thing, but my physical arrival at his doorstep would be harder to brush off. All that was necessary was a certain chutzpah, and I'd interview him yet.

I needed a holiday, anyway, and I hadn't been to the USA since I was five. With luck, in between the interviews, I'd get to do some tourist stuff, see a little bit of the country. It might, I thought, even be fun.

Of course, it wasn't.

7

THE EXECUTIONER'S PARADOX

Eleven years of conservative government in Australia fell apart on 24 November 2007, as I was flying across the Pacific to find Fred Leuchter.

The queue at the polling station in the morning felt far livelier, more expectant, than the line of holiday-makers at the airport baggage check. The gentle-faced woman in the window seat still wore her Kevin 07 T-shirt and, somewhere over the ocean, when the flight officer announced the election results, she let out an involuntary shriek of joy and disbelief.

The parties that night became legendary: the singing and the drunken conga lines a celebration not so much of new government but of the end of a low and dishonest decade, an edifice of lies and war starting to crack.

On the Qantas flight to Los Angeles, it was different. The Kevin 07 woman did her best to celebrate, but we were jammed too tightly together, and the imaginary drumsticks she banged against the seat in front knocked my carry-on bag onto the floor so that my reading material fell out with a thump. Kevin 07 looked down at the titles— *On Killing*, Theodore Nadelson's *Trained to Kill*, Trombley's *The Execution Protocol*, and a photocopied article by the neurologist

Harold Hillman entitled 'The possible pain experienced during exe-cution by different methods'—and her eyes widened. She looked back at me and I started to say something. Then she turned stiffly to the window—and didn't speak for fourteen hours. In those security conscious times, no one wanted to sit next to someone unhealthily interested in death. Too bad: I needed the time to read more about what death row actually did to prison staff.

Robert Johnson's work was largely qualitative, but I had also read a number of analytical papers by psychologist Michael J Osofsky, who took a particular interest in the disengagement techniques employed by execution staff. Survey responses suggested that execu-tioners used a combination of techniques to wriggle free of moral agency: they used euphemisms and rehearsed various ethical, eco-nomic and social justifications for the death penalty; they ascribed subhuman qualities to condemned inmates; they disavowed any per-sonal responsibility for the taking of life, blaming either the prison-ers themselves or the criminal justice system as a whole. 'We have a job to do,' one man explained, 'and that job isn't to be a cold-hearted individual. It is simply to carry out the order of the state.'

'It's not up to me to say yea or nay', said another. 'That's for the judges and juries. I'm not a part of the deal-making process. I'm here to do the job. I'm assigned to do it and have the job to do.'

Respondents observed that the more executions they performed, the easier killing became, with their focus shifting from the rights and wrongs of the death penalty to the workaday details of render-ing the prisoner dead. Studies of soldiers had shown the same thing: when combat became familiar, the participants worried more about efficiency than anything else.

Within the death house, that abstract concern about process was best exemplified by the medical technicians who delivered the lethal IV—and then swabbed the inmate's arm to prevent infection. While the distress produced by executions seemed to decrease as the job became more routine, the moral disengagement of people who had carried out just one execution was just as high as that experienced by those involved with many. Disengagement seemed, in other words, to be a technique to facilitate executions rather than a consequence of familiarity. For prison staff who didn't participate directly but supported the execution process, the pattern was quite different. The men and women who counselled the families of inmates and victims on execution day commenced their work with a high degree of engagement, which then eroded over time as they participated in more and more executions.

But as I thought about this, there was something else, something about the way the executioners disengaged, that seemed both familiar and maddeningly elusive. The staff on the death teams used multiple techniques simultaneously. For instance, they accepted moral justifications for capital punishment; they dehumanised the inmates, and they placed the responsibility for the execution elsewhere. You could summarise the contradictory logic like this: 'It's right for us to kill people; those who we kill are not really people; it's not us who kills them'. Phrased that way, the reasoning became distressingly familiar. Here was the logic of Holocaust-denial, the logic of Ernst Zündel and his website: 'The Jews didn't die in the gas chambers; the Jews deserved what they got'. By then, I was too exhausted to think through the implications for Leuchter and my interview, and instead sunk back into that twilight zone of intercontinental travel: a fug of exhaustion, cramp and artificial light, in which minutes drag and hours slip past without trace.

The descent into Los Angeles woke me abruptly, with an inelegant trickle of saliva still dribbling onto my shirt collar, a detail that I failed to notice as we stumbled, bleary-eyed and cramped, out into LAX, and my final apologetic smile to Kevin 07 seemed, judging from her horrified response, rather like Jeffrey Dahmer's drool-flecked leer. Another flight, another five hours, and there was Boston. From Logan airport, it was a bus trip to Cambridge, where I was staying. That night, I fell at once into an exhausted sleep, only to wake before dawn and lie for hours with teeth grinding.

In the morning, Boston felt both vaguely familiar and entirely fantastical, as if at any moment someone would wink and the landscape would shift and rearrange like a stage set and the people would drop out of character like actors breaking for cigarettes. The crispness of the winter day made Melbourne not just distant but imaginary, with the memory of heat, only forty-eight hours earlier, now entirely improbable against the permanence of the snow frozen onto the pavement.

Until now, all the research had been oddly distant. One thing led to another: you started reading about a head from Gallipoli and the next thing you were telephoning executioners. Even talking to Ron McAndrew had seemed unreal, since the experiences he discussed were so far from my own that his voice came from the receiver like a strange whisper from another time and another place. Here—slipping on the icy concrete, passing a panhandler with a misspelt cardboard sign, watching everyday Americans doing everyday American things— reality suddenly hit me. I was walking the streets of Boston, looking for an execution technologist, with almost no sense of what I'd do when I found him. How, exactly, had this seemed a good idea?

Google Maps had provided a guide to the Leuchter house. Unfortunately, I'd confused miles and kilometres, and very quickly, the expedition became decidedly unpleasant, with a route that had seemed entirely manageable on the computer screen actually stretching on forever. The light winter drizzle settled into a steady soaking that eventually pulped the Googlised instructions into a sodden mass.

The trail led through an industrial area and out the other side into a neighbourhood that was wide and tree-lined and crammed with distinctive Bostonian wooden two- and three-storey houses. It was all undeniably picturesque, not a word that you associated with the neighbourhood of an execution technologist. Peering around in the rain for a street number, I remembered the plane trip and was suddenly struck by the thought that, among these well-tended houses, I might be the intimidating one: an intruder in a respectable suburb, red-eyed from jet lag, dishevelled, soaking wet and babbling about electric chairs.

Nevertheless, here was the house; here was the door. I hesitated, knocked and then knocked again. No answer. A lamp burned in one of the windows, and a dog seemed to be barking inside, but there was no one at the door.

My imagination had been busily conjuring all kinds of unlikely scenarios about Leuchter, scenes in which he appeared brandishing mementoes of past executions or holding court before an array of tattooed boot-boys. That he might simply be out doing something else seemed implausibly prosaic. Still, there it was. I took out pad and paper and scribbled a note: my mobile number; I was in the country, still keen to talk. It would be very much appreciated if he could call.

In a nearby Starbucks, I drank espresso macchiato, feeling slightly ill. I hadn't necessarily expected the Leuchter interview to come off, but even had he slammed the door, it would have been more useful than a simple absence. After coming all this way, the man remained just as obscure as when he'd been solely a presence on the Internet. Should I stay in Boston and try at another time? But I didn't know how long I might need to wait. My funds were so limited that, sitting here doing nothing, I could almost hear the money ticking away, like a taxi meter stuck in traffic.

I had to try something, and that rising feeling of desperation made calling Jerry Givens much easier. This time, the conversation was entirely anticlimactic. 'How you doing there? Good to hear from you again.' He sounded genuinely pleased, almost touched that I'd come so far to talk. Even better, over the domestic line, he was much easier to understand, so that we actually managed something approaching a normal conversation. Yes, he said, he'd be happy to meet. He was about to attend a conference at a Holiday Inn Express in Richmond, Virginia. He suggested I meet him there. Could I be there at about 10 a.m., when the event began? I could, though it would involve a certain amount of scrambling. I'd go straight to

Virginia and then come back to Boston. While inconvenient, it was better, psychologically, than simply waiting.

The plan meant catching a Delta flight into Richmond the next day. From the airport, the taxi boomed hip hop all the way to the hotel Jerry had nominated: a monstrous Buddha of a building, squatting beside a freeway in an industrial suburb, where a night's accommodation cost about twice my budget.

That night, I dreamt, inevitably, of executions. There were dark shapes bent over a gurney, a death-row team at their work, but the peculiar horror lay not in the act itself but in its aftermath. As in McAndrew's story, the men tried and failed, in the gluey motion of the unconscious, to untangle their apparatus from the warm body they'd just killed. That was the point at which I woke, dreaming of tubes and needles that clung, like a black spider, to a corpse strapped to a table.

In the morning, the hotel buffet proffered an array of sausages and grits and other deep-fried objects, all of which I consumed with a grim determination to recoup some of my costs. In the foyer, I sat with my laptop to await Jerry and the other conference-goers.

I was unsure what the event was about. Somehow—probably because Robert Johnson had told me of Jerry's religious convictions—I'd assumed that this was some kind of revival meeting, but there was nothing in the hotel indicating any special spiritual fervour. Instead, the sign on the door welcomed participants to a 'safety forum', which seemed a distinctly unlikely topic for a man who'd specialised in putting people to death. They started dribbling in at about 10.45—all men, mostly large, arriving singly or in small knots. I was trying not to stare when I heard someone call my name and found a man standing by my table. He wasn't hooded; there was no axe, and he didn't look sinister at all: a solid black man, in his fifties, perhaps, with a bald head and a thin moustache and little wire glasses. 'Jerry?'

He smiled, and when I extended a hand, he enfolded me in a bear hug. 'Good to see you, man. You find it here all right?' Jerry now worked on the roads, driving out to repair the metal barriers on the side of the highway. The conference was a refresher course in occupational health and safety, and most of the participants were also drivers: a mixture of black and white working-class guys. As they milled around, Jerry introduced me to his workmates. I'd come all the way from Australia, he said. I was working on a book, and I was going to interview him. We shook hands, and as we made small talk, I wondered if they knew what the book was about or, more specifically, why I was interviewing Jerry. Later, he explained that his workmates knew about his previous occupation: 'The guys joke around some. Call me "Killer" and things like that. But it don't bother me.'

Jerry's boss, a fellow with sandy hair and a red face and a pugnacious John Bolton moustache, picked up on my nationality. 'What y'all doing electing a socialist down there?' He didn't expect an answer but shook my hand and then ushered his employees back into the theatre. The conference was starting; we would do the interview at lunch time.

Jerry duly emerged, a few hours later, carrying a box of pizza slices. Almost before I asked anything, he explained what I later came to call the executioner's paradox: 'If you going to take a life— a human life—but this person hasn't done anything to you, well, if it don't affect you, something's wrong with you and you should get out. But if it do affect you, you should get out, too. You see?'

Chatting with him about the forum and listening to him joke about his workmates, what struck me about Jerry was how normal he seemed. He had a sense of humour; he smiled easily. I mentioned the phone interview, and we both laughed about the difficulty we'd had understanding each other. He was good company, fun to be around, and early on in our conversation, I found myself saying, you know Jerry, you don't seem like an executioner.

What was his background?

'I came up in the projects', he said, and then explained: 'The housing projects—here in Richmond, Virginia. I have one brother, two sisters, and my mother—she worked and raised us. Sent us to school. All of us finished school. None of us really get into trouble.

Basically, we all live in the same area. I get to see them each and every day. My mother's still living.' He described his family as neither rich nor poor but something in the middle, but that seemed largely a matter of modesty. 'What I consider poor, I look at South Africa and I see how people live, and then I appreciate life more: the things I have; my blessings.'

Certainly, his background was that of an ordinary worker. He'd originally been employed by a company processing tobacco, a major industry in Virginia. 'The guys on Friday would go out into the parking lot and drink and get high and come back and act stupid. I was working in there one day and I had a big fan behind me. A guy threw some tobacco in the fan and told me to turn around and I turned around and the tobacco got in my eye. And before I knew it, I smacked him. And when I smacked him, the supervisor said, "Well, we don't tolerate no violence, no fighting. I'm going to have to dismiss you." But coming home, when I stopped at the red light, I saw a sign looking for places in the penitentiary. The sign said they were hiring. I went in there and met this guy, Mr Johnson ...'

Robert Johnson? The guy I'd been talking with? Capital punishment seemed to throw up strange ironies at every turn, but an executioner obtaining his first gaol position from a leading scholar of the death penalty seemed spectacularly peculiar. Jerry laughed. 'No, a different Mr Johnson. See, he gave me a form and I filled out an application. I was getting ready to get married, and I had to break the news to my wife that I'd lost my job, so when I got home I could say, well, I probably have another job now, working at the penitentiary. That July I was hired, in 1974.

'When I went there, I had on what they call a maxi coat, a long coat, and the gate closed—clink, clink—and I realised then that I just couldn't push my way out, that someone would have to physically let me out.' He leant back, suddenly pensive. 'Later, I thought about that moment a lot. Anyway, I went upstairs to be fingerprinted and went into the back, and the prisoners were hollering and cussing and calling me names. I took the physical and passed it, and the next two days they gave me a thing they called a stun gun. I was still in civilian clothes. Two inmates started fighting, and I tried to break them up, and the guy swung at me. I took the stun gun and popped him in the head. The captain of the guard escorted me down the front and put me inside the cage and said, "Cool down. We don't want to start no riot." I said, "That mean I lost my job?"

'He said, "Hell, no! That mean I got me a tough officer!" From that time on, the inmates called me "Stun Gun".'

The story strangely echoed Ron McAndrew's explanation of his enthusiasm for penal work: that same transition from ordinary life to the prison universe, with violence as the most obvious difference between the two. Jerry talked about a prisoner who had been burnt to a crisp inside his cell—how, when he tried to pick the man up, his hands went through the body. On another occasion, he'd intervened in a knife fight between two inmates, saving the life of a man stabbed twenty-seven times. 'That's the thing about working in a prison. One minute you're saving a life; the next minute, you're getting ready to take it.'

He'd gradually progressed through the prison hierarchy, rising up through a ranking system modelled after the army. 'I carried that name "Stun Gun" around for a while, and before I knew it I made corporal. Then I made sergeant. When I was sergeant, I was approached by a major, and he said, "Mr Givens, I need to talk to you, and see if you are interested in joining the death squad when they reinstate the death penalty". So I said, "Let me give it some thought". I thought about it and I said, "I don't think I can really tell my wife. I don't know what she would say or how she would react."'

Was that a difficult decision?

'Well, at that time, Jeff, we didn't have nobody there at death row, so I'm thinking, maybe we don't get nobody. Maybe it's never going to happen. You know what I'm saying? It's up to somebody else. So, I gave it some thought and called a meeting in the basement, where the old electric chair was, where the old death row was. Eight other guys met up with me down there. I didn't know all of them, but we introduced one another and we said, whatever we say down here stays down there—we don't talk about it to anyone else. And we stuck to that oath ever since.

'They were strong guys, you know, the type of guys I would carry into a cell distraction, a riot situation, and we could do battle. I knew they had my back and I had their back. I would talk to my team, if I had something on my mind; I would talk to one of them. We would sit around and chat and talk about different things. Whatever was bothering me, I knew I could go to those guys. I didn't drink; I didn't get high; I just tried to be strong. I prayed, and prayer helped me through this.

'But the first time I pressed that button, I had a new name: "Executioner". It brought a title. And, after that first one, I thought that it might affect me. One guy, after about the third execution, he left and never came back. I went by his house, and to this day, I never found out where he went. He couldn't deal with it.

'I tried to stop everything else, let myself be here now, let nothing worry me, as a way to cope with it. I prayed over a lot of stuff; I asked for forgiveness for a lot of things.'

I started to ask something, but the drivers were milling around and the meeting room door was open again. The lunch break was nearly over and I'd barely given Jerry a chance to eat. Still, he was happy to talk again. Before he went back to talk safety, we made another arrangement to talk about death. We'd meet again in about a week, in another part of Richmond near Jerry's home.

8

A TREMENDOUS SECRET

It took about eight hours for the Greyhound bus to haul its way from Richmond to Asheville, North Carolina, and most of those hours were very, very long.

Though the majority of passengers were older people—even elderly—the back seats were occupied by a clutch of young men in denim and neatly pressed T-shirts. At the men's room at the first rest stop, we all urinated on a white flyer carelessly dropped into the trough. You could still make out its spattered headline: 'Coping with life after prison'. The local gaol, it seemed, supplied newly released inmates with a ticket back home on the cheapest transport available, which inevitably meant they travelled Greyhound.

Jerry's stories about cell block battles and stun guns fostered a certain unease about ex-cons as travelling partners, but for the most part, they were entirely peaceable, concerned only with getting back to their loved ones. In fact, it was the older women passengers who dominated the trip. From the moment we departed, they compared notes about the most intimate aspects of their lives, talking across the aisles at a foghorn volume that made reading well-nigh impossible. By the time we reached Winston-Salem, the whole bus knew who'd been addicted to painkillers and who'd found Jesus and who'd lost their job. We learnt about the menfolk who'd left and the ones who should have left but didn't, the worthless daughters-in-law and the feckless sons. Exchanges about weight-loss and television, badinage about grocery prices and medical procedures: all voiced to carry from one end of the coach to another. It was maddening, at first—another symptom, I decided, putting down the book on which I couldn't concentrate, of a national propensity to assume the whole world cared about American problems. But then, when I started listening, the public conversation became at first fascinating and, eventually, strangely comforting, as though all of us, the entire coach, belonged to a huge dysfunctional family.

In Asheville, I was meeting Gail Eisnitz, an animal cruelty investigator whose book *Slaughterhouse* contains the only extended treatment I'd found of the effects of animal slaughter on workers in the meat industry. If the absence of research into the impact of executions on executioners was surprising, the paucity of information about animal slaughter was utterly astonishing. There weren't very many full-time executioners, but hundreds of thousands of people laboured in abattoirs around the world: was it really the case that nobody knew what that work did to them?

Intuitively, everyone sensed that animal slaughter was psychologically difficult. In Thomas More's *Utopia*, slaughter is allocated to slaves, since the Utopians conclude that butchering kills off mercy, 'the finest feeling of our human nature'. In the eighteenth century, an era much more neighbourly with death than our own, the brutalisation of butchery was proverbial, with John Gay advising his contemporaries:

> To shun the surly butcher's greasy tray,
> Butchers, whose hands are dyed with blood's foul stain,
> And always foremost in the hangman's train.

Even Bruce and Kevin had spoken about a four-week period of unease, the time it took employees to make a mental adjustment to the work.

Kevin had said something else, too, though I only realised the significance of it later. He'd mentioned his indifference to animal blood, comparing it with his nausea when confronted by bleeding people. Demetri had made exactly the same point about kangaroos, in almost the same words. And then I read a study of French abattoir workers, in which all the interviewed workers volunteered their sensitivity to human blood. What was going on? An obvious explanation was that killing animals involved sights, smells and sounds so naturally evocative of homicide that those who worked among them needed to react to human blood in an extreme way in order to reinforce the permissibility of the animal blood all around them. If that was the case, it didn't prove that workers had been psychologically damaged, but it did suggest an acclimatisation process of a certain complexity, which made the lack of academic study more remarkable.

In Melbourne, I'd been reading the British criminologist Piers Beirne. Beirne had written an overview of the research on the association between the abuse of animals and antisocial behaviour. That serial killers spent their childhoods tormenting cats and dogs was almost a cliché, but it seemed to be true nonetheless. Delinquent kids hurt animals; violent spouses vented their rage upon the pets of their partners. But, as Beirne pointed out, most such research defined 'abuse' as injurious behaviour towards living creatures exceeding socially mandated levels, a classification that immediately ruled out the day-to-day business of the meat industry. The psychological consequences of hurting animals in ways unacceptable to society had been widely discussed; the killing that society accepts hadn't.

I emailed Beirne at Maine University to check the point. Given the scale of the meat industry, its centrality to society and the number of people it employed, could it be true that no one knew what slitting hundreds of cattle throats each day did to you?

He replied the next day. 'You have travelled as far as I have with this question, and no further, I'm afraid. I've patiently waited for someone to do more but to my knowledge no one has.' It was Beirne who pointed me to Eisnitz's book *Slaughterhouse*. He quoted a passage in which an American meatworker directly linked his own violence and that of his colleagues with their work: 'Every sticker I know carries a gun, and every one of them would shoot you. Most stickers I know have been arrested for assault. A lot of them have problems with alcohol. They have to drink; they have no other way of dealing with killing live, kicking animals all day long.'

Eisnitz lived in Asheville. That was why I was here.

North Carolina in general—and Asheville in particular—seemed purpose-built for the contemplation of nature and humanity's relationship with it. By Australian standards, the woods by the highway grew impossibly lush: not brooding and foreboding like the forests of the Old World, but invitingly dappled, so that you expected to see apple-cheeked Boy Scouts hiking out from each path. The Blue Ridge Mountains gleamed on the horizon like a postcard; the air outside was so fresh as to hurt the throat.

She picked me up from my motel. *Slaughterhouse* had been so grim, so unrelenting, that I'd expected Eisnitz to be thoroughly hard-boiled: a wise-cracking, tough-talking animal detective. Instead, she seemed soft, quietly spoken, almost mournful. In the book she distinguished between her undercover identity and her real self: she preferred, she said, to spend 'my evenings at home with my cat, a cup of tea, and a good book'. That was exactly how she seemed in person: contemplative, bookish, gentle.

Her book had emerged from an undercover campaign inside the US meat industry of the mid-1990s. She'd often relied on unionists for access, so, though her primary focus was on the animals, the book contains shocking testimony from the meatworkers about what they do and how they feel about it. 'You don't care about people's pain any more', one sticker told her. 'I used to be very sensitive about people's problems—willing to listen. After a while, you become desensitised. And, as far as animals go, they're a lower life-form. They're maybe one step above a maggot.' Another explained, 'The worst thing, worse than the physical danger, is the emotional toll. If you work in that stick pit for any period of time, you develop an attitude that lets you kill things but doesn't let you care ... If you stop and think about it, you're killing several thousand beings a day.'

Eisnitz's apartment, where we talked, overlooked a pretty creek running down from the mountain. Sometimes, she said, deer drank there. There were pictures of animals all over the walls—zebras, foxes, cows. Though she'd studied natural resource conservation, she'd begun work as an animal illustrator before becoming a researcher. She'd certainly never expected to spend so much time contemplating the meat industry. 'I was working at the Humane Society, and I received a complaint from a worker who said that he was skinning cows alive. I couldn't believe it; I just said, no, that can't be. I knew how farm animals were raised and how bad that was. But in terms of slaughterhouses, I had no idea.'

The basic issue was that US slaughterhouses processed so many animals so quickly that the 'knockers'—the workers responsible for stunning—couldn't do their jobs properly and cattle often regained consciousness after they'd been hoisted onto the overhead rail. That meant the 'stickers', who were supposed to sever an artery so that the beast bled out, were confronted by hundreds of pounds of thrashing, writhing animal. They couldn't kill cleanly and they often just cut the spinal cord, allowing the workers further down the line to begin the dismemberment on a paralysed but live animal. It was tremendously cruel, but also incredibly dangerous, since a live cow twitching on the end of a chain was far more likely to fall on a worker.

With other animals, the details were different, but the causes were at root the same. Pork abattoirs, for instance, not only pro-cessed too many pigs but turned down the voltage on the electrical stun gun out of fear that the charge damaged the meat. Again, the workers dealt with live animals. 'When hogs end up in the catch pen alive,' an employee told Gail,

> the shackler beats them over the head with a lead pipe a couple
> of times—until they're dazed so he can get a chain around the

hog's leg—and then he hoists it up. By then they may have come back to life and be squealing their heads off. If there are a lot of hogs in the catch pen, the shackler doesn't have the time to use the hand stunner or pipe them. He'd hook them up, hang them alive, and I was expected to stick them.

I described the abattoir in Melbourne. It had seemed quite different from the places she described: well-run, clean and sufficiently open to let someone like me just wander in. So were these problems specific to the US industry?

'It's the management', she said at once. 'If the management doesn't care how it produces meat, then you are going to have an inhumane slaughter. If the line's too fast for the operation, for the workers to do their jobs properly, then that matters. When I was working on the book, I'd call someone in the UK and find that the average line speed there was something like 76 cattle per hour. Here it's 400 per hour. The production speeds are just too fast. Even in the modern plants—especially in the modern plants—workers can't keep up with the work: they just can't do it. It's the same thing with meat-cutting, the processing side. They can't even do that properly. The workers just can't keep up. In the past, they may have used a sledgehammer, but at least they gave each animal individual attention. Now they just pound on the head, pound on the head, pound on the head as the animals come by. Half the time the animals aren't stunned properly.'

She didn't blame the workforce. They were forced into it, she said. 'They don't want to be acting in violation of the law or to be intentionally cruel to animals, but they don't have a choice. And once they do it for a while, they become numb: they just don't see what they're doing any more. I had some workers in a slaughterhouse in Washington State where they were skinning and dismembering hundreds and thousands of cows alive. They said to the news media that they had no idea they were violating a law; they just

knew they had to keep going as fast as they could to keep the production line going, that if they stopped it or slowed it, they got a
ticket. And if they got a ticket, they risked losing their job.'

But what I specifically wanted to ask about—the reason I'd
come all this way—was how slaughterhouse workers had linked
cruelty at work to violence in their private life. In her book, Gail had
talked with a sticker called Tommy Vladak, who had been badly
injured by an unstunned hog. 'You're standing there night after
night,' he'd told her:

> digging that knife into these hogs, and they're fighting you,
> kicking at you, squealing, trying to bite you—doing whatever
> they can to try to get away from you—after a while you don't
> give a shit. You're just putting in your time. And then it gets to
> a point where you're in a daydream stage. Where you can think
> about everything else and still do your job. You become emo-
> tionally dead.

Later, he explained:

> The worst part, even worse than my accident, was what hap-
> pened to my family life. I'd come home, my wife would ask me
> how my night went, and instead of being happy to see her I'd
> say, 'What the hell do you care?' We'd get into arguments about
> stupid things. Or else I'd come in so drunk I'd wonder how in
> the hell I made it home. Then wake up the next morning and
> start all over again.

I asked Gail if she'd found any research confirming these
accounts of the psychological trauma from slaughter. She gave the
same answer as Beirne: 'There really isn't any. None that I've seen.
But the people I interviewed for the book—a lot of them, anyway—
said that they took it out on their wives and their families and their
children. They also talked of becoming numb to the brutality and

then going home to take it out on their families. But there isn't any research about it all.'

Why not? Kevin had said that vet students sometimes vomited when visiting the kill floor. That physical nausea surely suggested at least a possibility of psychological damage. Regardless of what you thought about eating meat, abattoirs were confronting places. Wouldn't management have concerns about the impact on employees, even if simply to avoid occupational health and safety issues?

Gail laughed. 'The management couldn't care less. Workers are so expendable in the industry here; workers and animals are almost the same in the slaughterhouse to management. Management couldn't care less if the animals are being dismembered or boiled alive; they don't care if workers are being injured, chewed up and spit out because there's just such a supply of workers willing to fill the job.'

That, presumably, was the basis for the difference between Australia and the USA. Both Bruce and Kevin had spoken of the relatively good wages in the Australian meat industry. The high demand reduced some of the pressure to achieve US-style production speeds. Without them, the factory could function as designed. When it didn't, as in the USA, the nature of the industry provided its own protection for exploitative managers. Precisely because what happened behind the slaughterhouse gates was such a taboo, no one was going to ask questions about working conditions.

Again, I came back to the strange paradox of a killing both ubiquitous and invisible. The USA was a carnivorous nation, perhaps even more so than Australia. Every highway, every mall, every tiny town sprouted its crop of Burger Kings and Taco Bells and KFCs, so that meat surrounded you everywhere—but only in its finished, most presentable form. There were no pigs' heads, no hooves, no purple entrails, just all beef patties and special sauces served in polystyrene boxes. Meat was everywhere but its production nowhere, like a tremendous secret at the heart of the culture.

I was thinking aloud, but Gail nodded emphatically. 'Yes, that's exactly right. It's a tremendous secret. It's just atrocious and appalling, and consumers just don't want to know. I did lots of radio shows, and people would tell me that they would hear it on the radio and just turn it off. Nobody wanted to publish the book; nobody wanted to know about it. People see the cover and they are just grossed out by it, and that's it. Consumers don't want to know what it's like for the animals or for the workers.'

As well as describing how animals are killed, *Slaughterhouse* tells of Gail's desperate struggle for publicity. That was the ghastly catch-22 when it came to confrontations with the meat industry: because animals died in their hundreds of thousands every day, unless there was evidence of something going spectacularly wrong there was no story—but footage of extreme cruelty was often too graphic, too upsetting, to show on television. Gail discovered, she said, that radio and print were actually more useful than television. Most people were too physically nauseated to watch footage of cows becoming meat; they could, on occasion, be persuaded to read or listen to descriptions.

Slaughterhouse created a stir when it was first published, and then, rather oddly, received a second round of publicity when its descriptions of animals bludgeoned with pipes found their way into Rory Freedman and Kim Barnouin's bestselling *Skinny Bitch*, a diet manual written by former models who had turned vegan. *Skinny Bitch*'s sales had spiked when Victoria Beckham had been photographed carrying a copy—a truly bizarre collision between celebrity culture and the kill floor.

But that popularisation didn't seem to have improved conditions. In 2005, eight years after *Slaughterhouse*'s original publication, Human Rights Watch released a report on the US meat industry. It observed that:

Nearly every worker interviewed for this report bore physical signs of a serious injury suffered from working in a meat or poultry plant. Their accounts of life in the factories graphically explain those injuries. Automated lines carrying dead animals and their parts for disassembly move too fast for worker safety. Repeating thousands of cutting motions during each work shift puts enormous traumatic stress on workers' hands, wrists, arms, shoulders and backs. They often work in close quarters creating additional dangers for themselves and co-workers. They often receive little training and are not always given the safety equipment they need. They are often forced to work long overtime hours under pain of dismissal if they refuse.

In Arkansas, the Human Rights Watch researchers interviewed a young man in a chicken-slaughtering facility. He said, 'I hung the live birds on the line. Grab, reach, lift, jerk. Without stopping for hours every day. Only young, strong guys can do it. But after a time, you see what happens. Your arms stick out and your hands are frozen. Look at me now. I'm twenty-two years old, and I feel like an old man.' The authors describe their interviewee as having 'swollen hands apparently fixed in [a] claw-like position'.

The physical injuries that the report documents were so extreme that you could understand why the investigators didn't even canvass the possibility of psychological trauma. The work was literally crippling people, even killing them; its effects upon their long-term mental health seemed, perhaps, much more secondary.

Yet Gail's respondents had specifically and repeatedly raised the issue with her. 'There was one night I'll never forget as long as I live', one of the workers in *Slaughterhouse* explained. 'A little female hog was coming through the chutes. She got away and the supervisor said, "Stick that bitch!" I grabbed her and flipped her over. She looked up at me. It was like she was saying, "Yeah, I know it's your job, do it." That was the first time I ever looked into a live hog's eyes. And I stuck her.' There it was again: the look in the eye, that same instant of recognition that John Weaver had described in the shooter who threw away his gun, and that Robert Johnson identified as a psychological stressor on death row.

I'd thought, at the abattoir I'd visited, that the mechanisation of the killing made that instant impossible. You could expect Demetri to miss occasionally with the head shot; you could expect kangaroos in the wild to manifest a certain individuality. But the kill floor had been designed to make slaughter simple and rhythmic and regular, so that deviations didn't happen. Of course, when I thought about it more, I realised how impossible that was. Killing could never be entirely routine, because life—any life—was necessarily unique and thus always individualised. The factory might operate as if animals were things, but they weren't, any more than the inmates on Virginia's death row were. That was why, after a visit to a goat abattoir near Brewarrina in outback New South Wales, the poet Coral Hull could write:

> There is always the goat who will penetrate you,
> who will look into you, glassy eyed, resilient,
> unresigned to the blade, to the breaking of the neck,
> & beside its stubborn terror,
> there is always the goat who will tremble inside,
> as its old knees buckle & scrape

The look, the acknowledgement of the sentience of the other, was accidental, but it was also inevitable. A study of Scottish livestock producers found that their relationship with their animals, their level of attachment or detachment, varied according to their position in the production process. Those working in jobs closer to the abattoir deliberately tried not to think of animals as in any way distinguishable. One dealer explained that he viewed sheep simply as money, specifically avoiding looking at them except at their torsos, since 'some have got attractive faces and look as though they are smiling'—and the implications of that were unthinkable.

But inevitably, a certain animal would act in some way that fostered individual recognition—and then the whole mental schema came crashing down. You could see the process in Gail's interviews. One man put it like this:

> You may look a hog in the eye that's walking around in the blood pit with you and think, God, that really isn't a bad look-ing animal. You may want to pet it. Pigs down on the kill floor have come up and nuzzled me like a puppy. Two minutes later I had to kill them—beat them to death with a pipe. I can't care.

Wasn't that exactly Ron McAndrew's problem? The executions he supervised depended upon procedure and rehearsal, during which the inmate remained undefined and nameless. But as warden, he related to the condemned men as distinct individuals: people with parents, friends, children and spouses. No wonder the tension had become intolerable.

But maybe I was moving too quickly. What did Gail think? Were the stresses in the meatworkers she'd interviewed—the domestic violence, the resort to alcohol and the rest of it—related specifically to killing? Or was it simply the result of working in a tedious, stress-ful and dangerous job?

'I think it's a combination', she said. 'Killing becomes mundane, just becomes something ordinary, because it's so fast and so repetitive. They become completely callous to it, and they take it out on the animals themselves. The repetitive nature of it is so overwhelming. Plus the fact that the animals are sometimes alive when they are sup-posed to be unconscious—it makes the workers feel even more pow-erless, having to do this terrible thing, with no way out of it. They just have to do it as best they can, kill as many animals as possible even if the animals are alive.'

Many of the workers in the US meat plants were, of course, immi-grants. 'They're just used to such a strong work ethic; they just think they're supposed to work, really, really hard, to do whatever they have to be able to do in order to send money back to their families in

Mexico. And they don't know that they have any rights, and they don't expect to have any rights.

'The jobs themselves are so dangerous and exhausting, and the people are pushed beyond their physical limits. They're so overworked, subject to such serious illnesses and injuries, like repetitive illnesses like carpal tunnel disorder and things like that. In some factories, workers aren't even allowed to take a bathroom break, or if they are allowed to, there are fifty women waiting to use the rest room. They actually told me that they wear pads in their underwear so that if they have to pee on the line they don't stain themselves. They just don't get any breaks.'

I couldn't think of any more questions. We sat in silence for a minute. It all seemed so horrible, so overwhelming. Then she asked whether I'd eaten. 'There's a nice Indian restaurant in town.' We drove into the main urban area, to a place called Mela. Gail ordered a vegetarian curry. I looked at the menu and hesitated at the lamb vindaloo, before choosing a vegetable dish, too. 'Don't feel that you should', she said. I didn't know what I felt, just that I didn't want to contemplate meat right then.

The veil shrouding the animal corpses with which we surround ourselves is perilously thin, and you need conscious and constant determination to avoid puncturing it. Viscera in the supermarket meat cabinets, rabbit fur on a coat, and the shapes of veins and capillaries in the leather of your boots: you can turn away, but if you think, even for a moment, about the nature of killing, these things still tug at the sleeves of your conscience.

We talked for a while about North Carolina and US politics. I explained some more about the book and asked her bluntly whether she saw any connection between the death penalty and her experiences in animal welfare. I meant in terms of killing, but she interpreted the question slightly differently.

'Yes, I do. Basically, it's the same population of people who are opposed to the death penalty who are striving for reform in the animal community. To give you an example, there's a veterinarian whose licence we're trying to get revoked because he testified at trial that hanging disabled pigs to kill them was an acceptable means to euthanise them. When we learnt that one of the members of the Veterinarian Licensing Board was a member of the ACLU and Planned Parenthood—that's in favour of abortion—we said, that's fantastic, she must be a good person. It's the same with the death penalty. We're all fighting for rights—of people or animals, but we're fighting for rights.'

I nodded. It was an attractive notion—that sense of a progressive community resistant to a ubiquitous culture of death. When the meals arrived, I sank into an unfamiliar American beer and the first decent food I'd eaten in days, and my previous despondency gave way to a comforting sense of self-righteousness. But that was entirely invalidated by what came next.

9

JUST SO MANY OF THEM

I'd found only one book that directly compared the killing of animals, capital punishment and military combat. It was called *Perpetration-Induced Traumatic Stress*. Its author, psychologist Rachel MacNair, lived in Kansas City: another bus out of Asheville and then a long, exhausting plane trip to Missouri.

We'd arranged via email to meet in the Plaza Library in the middle of town. There were Christmas decorations all around, and every shop piped 'Jingle Bell Rock' as you walked past. But I didn't feel the slightest bit festive, just exhausted and headachy and freezing, and inadequately dressed to walk across streets banked with snow.

MacNair had emailed me a photo, and I recognised her as soon as she walked into the foyer. She was small, with a pleasant, pixyish face; she greeted me with a slight Western twang. She'd been in the peace movement, I knew, but I would have sensed that anyway, for she spoke like an activist, with the almost pugnacious directness that comes from years of pushing meetings towards outcomes and decisions.

It was rare and not a little refreshing to find an agitator in a field so dominated by military men and social scientists. 'Activism runs in my family', she said. 'My one grandfather was a professor and was arrested for sit-ins in the South in Alabama—the only white man arrested with a bunch of black students, so he was alone in segregated gaols. My other grandfather was secretary of the Socialist Party at the time my mother was born. So I come from a background where activism in things like racial equality and peace and all that is just expected. When I became a Quaker at age fourteen, the entire reaction in the family was that it made perfect sense.'

The Australian activist milieu I'd known had been largely secular, and the distinction between the denominations of Christianity lay in a dusty heap in the recesses of my memory. The Quakers ... they made that austere wooden furniture, didn't they?

'That's the Shakers.'

'Oh. Well, I'm not sure that we have Quakers in Australia ...'

'Of course you do', she snapped. 'They're just not very numerous. We've never been very numerous anywhere. The places where we're most concentrated would be London, Philadelphia and the three-county area in North Carolina—and even there we're a minority.

'The Quakers are one of the traditional pacifist churches, along with the Mennonites and the Church of the Brethren. There is God in everyone, though in some people it's very hard to find, but it's there. From that follows pacifism and human equality, and therefore abolitionism. Abolitionism in the United States was a big deal. The Quakers were also a major force in founding abolitionism, very active in racial equality and opposing war.'

The description seemed more like a manifesto than the milk-and-water theology we'd been fed during religious instruction at school, and I began to grasp how her religion and her politics entwined.

'I was told that when I got to about thirteen or fourteen, I was to select my own church—but I wasn't happy with any of them. Our method of worship is one of sitting around in silence. We don't even have a minister. We do things; we pull together in committees; it's radically non-hierarchical. The Quakers met in the same place as the peace centre. I essentially got involved as soon as I was mature enough, and that was in the latter days of the Vietnam War.' She paused. 'Excuse me. Let me rephrase that: the American war in

Vietnam.' I nodded. In progressive circles, it was a distinction that mattered, a terminology that highlighted the millions of Vietnamese victims of a conflict usually remembered only for dead GIs.

'We did a lot of actions, and I learnt about non-violence. Eventually, I decided to go to Quaker College in Richmond, Indiana, where I got a major in peace and conflict studies. And then I spent many years in the field doing organising work, getting bread jobs to support myself while I was doing things for the peace movement: peace education, conflict resolution skills, opposing whatever war was happening, trying to lower the military budget, working against nuclear weapons and so on.'

We spoke the same language. My CV didn't look all that different: a decade or so working unskilled part-time jobs to give myself time for activism. I knew, I thought, exactly where she came from.

The book on perpetration-induced traumatic stress (PITS) arose from her PhD. As a peace activist, a pacifist, she'd wanted hard evidence on killing and its effects, something that, as I'd discovered, was extraordinarily hard to find. She came across a government study conducted during the 1980s, in which 1600 Vietnam veterans were surveyed about their wartime experiences and their health. Among a myriad of other questions, the study asked the men whether or not they'd killed anyone. Historically, governments had been very reluctant to enquire about killing. Here was a rare opportunity: a chance to statistically correlate data on wartime killing with other answers indicative of trauma.

When she crunched the figures, she found that post-traumatic stress disorder scored significantly higher among those who said they had killed compared with those who said they hadn't. Moreover, killing seemed to correspond with a distinct cluster of symptoms: violent outbursts, hyper-vigilance, alienation and so on. 'I'm looking at all these numbers and my hypotheses are being confirmed beautifully, and I went to my supervisor and I said, "Oh, look at this! Isn't it great!" And she said, "Rachel, that represents people's suffering—that's what those numbers mean!" Which was true—but I was still able to see how the patterns might be different for people who kill as opposed to people who don't.'

MacNair argued that PITS was a distinct subset of post-traumatic stress disorder. It resulted from killing and then also served as an enabler for it. Veterans who'd killed tended to suffer from emotional numbing, detachment from others, and an inability to control anger: PITS symptoms that made killing again easier and more probable.

'There's one and only one thing I was able to find through all my research that shields people from the aftermath of killing', she said.

'What was that?'

'Being psychotic before the killing takes place.'

While the quantitative data from Vietnam veterans constituted the core of her work, MacNair also gathered qualitative data to extend her argument. She looked at law-enforcement agencies; she also studied executioners. But, most of all, she read accounts of killing not just as grim narratives of harrowing experiences but as records of diagnosable trauma symptoms.

Donald Cabana, a warden at Mississippi State Penitentiary, had supervised two executions. One of them had been particularly disturbing, since, in the years he'd been working in the prison, he'd developed an intimate friendship with the man he was supposed to kill. Connie Ray Evans had murdered a man in the course of a robbery when he was twenty years old; by the time his execution date arrived, he'd become, Cabana believed, a very different person. Nonetheless, Cabana dutifully strapped Evans into the gas chamber and gave the signal for the execution to start.

MacNair read, in Cabana's memoir, his description of the minutes before and after Evans died. Cabana reports that he heard every sound on death row at a grotesquely magnified level; he struggled to walk, feeling, like a dreamer, that his legs wouldn't move properly; he says that the final seconds, watching Evans gasp for air in the chamber, stretched on endlessly. These perceptual distortions, MacNair suggests, should not be dismissed as literary flourishes. They are symptoms of peritraumatic dissociation: a psychiatric response to trauma, easily recognisable from the literature on post-traumatic stress disorder. Cabana writes how, after the execution, he plunged himself into work so as not to think about what he'd done. This, says MacNair, represents the classic relationship between avoidance and intrusive imagery, where a fear that repressed thoughts might re-impose themselves leads the traumatised person to occupy themselves relentlessly with other activity.

She found other accounts in which executioners diagnose them-selves as suffering from post-traumatic stress disorder. She quotes Fred Allen, who'd served on the tie-down team for a hundred execu-tions. Allen describes how he was at home, working in his garage, when he felt a peculiar sensation, a shifting, taking place somewhere inside him. Reeling, he stumbled into his house and, when his wife asked him what the matter was, burst into uncontrollable tears. The thoughts that overcame him were not only of the most recent execu-tion he'd conducted but also of all those that had come before. It was like a film projector, he says, showing the same sequence over and over again—the faces of the men he'd killed. 'You see,' he'd said to his wife, 'I can barely even talk because I'm thinking more and more of it, you know. There was just so many of them.'

MacNair recognised that such anecdotes were of a different order from the statistics she'd collated: more indicative of where fur-ther research should be done than conclusive in and of themselves. But it was surely significant that she was able to find very similar tes-timonies from those who'd killed in a range of different contexts. Her book contains, for instance, a brief section on the killing of animals. For example, laboratory workers whose research entailed cruelty to laboratory animals reported experiencing nausea, sweats and tremors in association with their work. It wasn't difficult for me to extrapo-late to the people Eisnitz had interviewed: rage, intrusive thoughts, alienation—her slaughterhouse workers manifested the lot. Again, it was not statistically significant, but interesting nonetheless.

There was, however, something that had bothered me when I'd first read MacNair's book. In her list of groups that warranted further study, she included abortion practitioners. Soldiers, executioners, police, animal experimenters: I could understand analysing these groups for trauma, but a discussion of abortionists as killers seemed to legitimise the propaganda of the Right about baby murderers. So why include abortion?

Her response entirely pulled the ground out from under me. 'It was', she said, 'the abortion issue which got me seriously studying killing'.

'Excuse me?'

'Well, there's an argument as to whether abortion is killing. So I said, OK, if it's really just a medical procedure, doctors ought to react like it's a medical procedure, but if it's killing, they ought to react like they're killing. Reacting to killing, that would be battle fatigue or, as they call it now, PTSD. Therefore PTSD would be what I needed to research. And so I did.' In other words, her entire project had been driven by a desire to discredit abortion—one of the cornerstones of progressive politics.

MacNair explained her work with a woman called Juli Loesch Wiley, the founder of Prolifers for Survival. Where most of the anti-nuclear activists of the 1980s passionately supported women's right to choose, Loesch Wiley's group equated the ethics of abortion with the ethics of the nuclear arms race, since both, they said, revolved around killing. From Prolifers for Survival, MacNair joined Feminists for Life, and then became a leading member of an organisation called Consistent Life. 'Deliberately linking the issues', she explained, ignoring my increasingly ashen face. 'Nuclear weapons, war, poverty, racism, death penalty, abortion, euthanasia, assisted suicide—all issues connected with violence. In all of them, you have scapegoating, you have the psychological mechanisms of moral disengagement and so on and so forth.'

Where reproductive freedom was central to the feminist movement, the so-called 'consistent life ethic' of Loesch Wiley and her supporters turned the argument on its head. Women, they said, would never be free from the primary burden of child-rearing so long as abortion remained an option, since men could simply offer to pay for a termination and feel that they'd discharged their responsibilities. Abortion, then, didn't constitute a choice, since women were so often pressured into terminating a pregnancy by their partners or families.

But, most fundamentally, their case rested on the nature of the procedure. For members of the 'consistent life' movement, terminating a foetus meant taking a life. Hence, they argued, if you were against killing in wars, you should also oppose abortion, just as if you were a pro-lifer, you should simultaneously campaign against capital punishment, the military and—some insisted—the meat industry.

MacNair was, in essence, making the same kind of comparisons I'd been, but using them to draw conclusions that seemed to me entirely reactionary. So what did this mean for my project? Still trying to assimilate this dizzying realignment of political affiliations, I suggested, rather weakly, that MacNair's would not have been a very popular stance in the peace movement. 'Oh, no,' she agreed, 'absolutely not. There were times when I was intimidated about even bringing it up among Quakers and among peace people, and I was thinking, this is ridiculous. I mean, it's one thing to disagree with me and another thing to disagree with me so strongly that you are just glaring at me for having the nerve to bring it up.'

I thought about the leading anti-abortion ideologues, both in Australia and the USA, and wondered what they'd make of someone who insisted on formulations about the 'American war in Vietnam': 'You wouldn't really fit too well into the pro-life movement'.

'The pro-life movement welcomed us with open arms', she shot back. 'That's the advantage of the single-issue approach. I mean, they were delighted to have a left wing of the pro-life movement. I had no trouble fitting in at all.'

My mouth opened and then shut silently. Consistent Life wrenched the conventional activist landscape into contours that I found almost unrecognisable. 'Where would you consider yourself on the Left–Right spectrum now?'

'I mainly don't consider the Left–Right spectrum helpful to anything very much at all, but if you insist, I'm clearly left-wing. The reasoning I use on abortion is left-wing reasoning.' It seemed almost a challenge, like she was daring me to disagree.

I turned the conversation back to her book. What reaction had her thesis received?

'The thing that interested me most', she said, 'was that there's been no controversy about the basic argument whatsoever, which is remarkable in any scholarly field. After workshops at the American Psychological Association in 2006, I got up and asked the question: well, is killing one of the ideological stressors? The army officer answered, yes it is. And so on to the next question. It's not that they're denying it; it's that they're not interested in it. From their point of view, any individual is going to have a dozen things that led to their trauma, and killing is just one of them.'

The point had occurred to me, too. MacNair's analysis of the Vietnam veterans represented the most impressive empirical study of killing that I'd seen. But the more I thought about it, the more questions arose.

She acknowledged the uncertainties. 'All I had in the survey data was the question "Did you kill or think that you did kill anyone while you were in Vietnam: yes or no?" We're absolutely relying on self-reports. There could be Frank Burns [the character from *MASH*] types who couldn't admit that they didn't kill anybody. There could be people who couldn't admit that they did kill. There was no way of verifying. Also, I didn't have any context. I don't know whether it was self-defence; I don't know whether these were people who killed in battle or outside battle; I don't have any information. We're still at the very beginning of this field. It simply has not been studied enough. What that book did was coalesce the evidence that was available.'

Fair enough. But the conversation revealed, once again, how very difficult the subject is. 'A lot of times trauma doesn't get expressed', she explained, 'because people who have these feelings learn very quickly that others don't want to hear it—which makes the research very tricky. You don't know to what extent people who don't express feelings of trauma are hiding feelings even from themselves, or alternatively, they don't express them, because they don't have them. On the other hand, if you go in and say, well I'm expecting to hear that you have some traumatised feelings, the responses may be overblown because they are being polite to you, telling you what you want to hear.' In particular, there was a difficulty establishing causation: 'In general, people don't get into killing situations unless there's something traumatising going on'.

I'd already been thinking about this after my meetings with Jerry. A maximum security prison was a pretty stressful place, even if you weren't executing people. The same might be said for working on a high-speed production line in a slaughterhouse. As for abortion clinics, the stress there came from a different source. If you worked in a facility performing abortions in the USA, you confronted systematic harassment from the bigots of the pro-life movement. But I didn't say that.

Instead, we talked about Robert Johnson's work on execution teams, how people in Jerry's team focused so much on process, and how worried they were about the routine breaking down. 'That's called hyper-vigilance,' MacNair said, 'and that would be a post-trauma reaction. But here's another problem: a lot of post-trauma reactions like avoidance are, like, duh. The movie *Munich*: did you see it?'

I nodded.

'Well, that showed a prime case of perpetration-induced traumatic stress. In particular, it showed the hyper-vigilance of the Israeli assassins, but nobody in the audience was mystified about why these men were having hyper-vigilance about people killing them in the exact same way they'd been killing others. It's not a mystery, but it's also a post-trauma symptom. So you have to ask to what extent these are symptoms and to what extent they are just reasonable fears in particular circumstances.'

Our inevitable argument started over euthanasia. In the book, she lists it as another area that needs investigation. She made the same point to me. 'It's not about freedom to choose', she said. 'It's about killing. Euthanasia creates a situation where the old and the sick can be pressured into allowing themselves to be killed. Nothing progressive about that.'

A few months earlier, Dr Philip Nitschke, the Australian assisted-suicide campaigner, had launched his election campaign against the then Minister for Immigration and Citizenship, Kevin Andrews, in the seat of Menzies in Victoria. It was one of the most peculiar political events I'd attended: a political rally that began with Nitschke outlining his policies (against the Iraq war, pro-refugee, pro-environment, pro-union) and then segued into a workshop at which the candidate advised his supporters on how most effectively to take their own lives.

Most of the participants were elderly, and they didn't necessarily agree with Nitschke's positions on asylum-seekers or Iraq. But they were adamant that they didn't want to end their days helpless, incontinent and in terrible pain, and they insisted that Nitschke's workshops gave them a feeling of control. 'I've got the Nembutal at home,' one old lady had told me, 'and if the time ever comes, I know what to do'. I'd been to lots of political events, and I knew empowerment when I saw it. Long after the proceedings ended, the frail, white-haired men and women stood around debating passionately the relative merits of drug cocktails and suffocation. In a peculiar way, the discussions about how they might die filled them with energy and life. Or that was how it seemed to me.

MacNair did not agree. She quoted a Dutch doctor who had been involved in euthanasia and then hadn't been able to sleep for a week afterwards: a trauma symptom, she said. Then she spoke of the most famous euthanasia advocate. 'Take Dr Jack Kevorkian—you know, Dr Death. Now Jack Kevorkian has an obsession with death. He's going to tell you that he's not traumatised, but you look at the art he's obsessed with and it's clear: the man has an obsession. Is that a post-trauma reaction? You see, this is the thing: post-trauma does not need to be about people defining themselves as traumatised.' She mentioned secondary or visceral traumatisation, and the impact it had had upon the staff at the Truth and Reconciliation Commission in South Africa.

OK, I could accept that in theory. But her snap diagnosis of euthanasia advocates seemed pretty close to simply psychologising away political or ethical disagreements. Surely that cut both ways. If Kevorkian was obsessed with death, what about the pair of us? She'd written a book on killing; I was working on one. Were we both crazy too?

More than that, there wasn't anything progressive in passing laws to prevent people taking their own lives. You didn't have to subscribe to everything Kevorkian said or did to believe that there were times when life became unendurable, and that your decisions about your own failing body should belong to you and not the state. I'd met Derek Humphry, the British euthanasia campaigner, and seen him quietly weep describing how he'd provided the medicine to kill his first wife, Jean, after cancer had gutted her body. Not only had he been forced to watch the death of someone he loved dearly, but his act of love procuring drugs for her had also made him a criminal and could have sent him to gaol for decades.

For MacNair, euthanasia enabled the young and the healthy to pressure the old and the ailing when they became inconvenient, just as abortion allowed men to control women. To me, this seemed entirely arse-about. Of course, it was all well-trodden ground and our increasingly sharp exchange didn't resolve anything at all. If the discussion never entirely escaped the bounds of civility, it skirted pretty close, and we parted significantly less effusively than we'd met.

Afterwards, making my way back to another depressing motel, I told myself that I should have kept my stupid mouth shut. I almost certainly had less in common with Ron McAndrew, a devout Christian prison officer, than with Rachel MacNair, and I'd managed not to argue with him. The difference was that her cluster of alignments made me think about my own project and its assumptions in a very different light.

Travelling back to Richmond, I felt more confused than ever. Consistent Life did, at least, follow through its arguments to their logical conclusion. It's just that it arrived at a place I didn't want to go. As I'd discovered, you did many of the same things to kill a man as to kill a hog. And the medicalised procedures favoured by the euthanasia movement resembled quite closely the medicalised procedure of lethal injection, so much so that the euthanasia campaigners with whom I'd spoken were able to weigh-in learnedly on the debates about the chemical combinations used in executions. They knew, after all, how fatal drugs worked.

Yet people were not hogs. I'd abandoned vegetarianism precisely because I couldn't see how a movement for animal rights contributed to a struggle for human rights, which surely had to be the priority. So how had I got into this muddle? I wasn't actually a pacifist, and choosing a vegetarian curry in Mela didn't make me an animal rights activist. It was just that, surrounded by all this death, any arguments about life seemed inherently attractive, and I'd been identifying with political positions without really thinking them through.

Abortion had always seemed to me entirely legitimate on the basis that personhood did not arise merely from the accrual of cells. After all, if that was the criterion, a baboon was clearly a more sophisticated, intelligent life form than a human foetus. Unless you were religious and wanted to talk about souls, a lump of tissue became a human being when it could, at least theoretically, interact as a human with the social order. We could argue about the moment when an embryo reached that threshold, but the concept seemed to me sound.

The problem was, after watching all those animals die, I'd become too fixated on the biological process of cow turning into meat, when what really mattered was the social setting.

10

A BUTTON, NOT A SWITCH

At Richmond Airport, I turned my mobile phone back on and discovered that I'd missed a call—which was strange, since almost no one had the number. An abrasive voice on the message bank: 'Jeff, this is Fred Leuchter. I'm sorry I haven't been in touch. I've been very busy. My mother is ill and I've been trying to look after her. She won't eat and I'm very worried about her. But I am happy to be interviewed. Call me back and let me know how long you are in Boston, and we can arrange a time for an interview.'

Leuchter, who had loomed so monstrously large in my imagination, suddenly came through the phone's little speaker as a human being, a man grappling with his own family tragedy. It was profoundly disconcerting, and phoning him back was even stranger. Even Hitler was kind to his dog, I told myself. But still, in Leuchter's rasp, I couldn't hear a sinister Holocaust revisionist; only a desperately worried older man. 'She's in her nineties. She just won't eat any more. I don't think she wants to.'

'I'm sorry to hear that.'

'Well, there's nothing that can be done. Anyway, I am happy to do an interview. One night after work would suit me best. Let's find a place that suits.' And that was that. I would worry about it later. For the time being, there was Jerry.

I booked into a Super 8 motel not far from the airport, a much shabbier place smelling of cigarettes and disinfectant. Jerry had promised to pick me up outside the reception area after five o'clock— we'd drive somewhere and have something to eat, he said. For the rest of the afternoon, I browsed aimlessly on the motel's intermittent Wi-Fi before rousing myself for a walk by the side of the inevitable freeway, using the chain restaurants as milestones: so many paces to the Burger King, on past the Taco Bell and the Ruby Tuesday before turning back after the second McDonald's. The winter was cold and the cars flashed by, and there was no one else walking along the cracked sidewalk strewn with Cheetos packets and road debris, so that even my drab room eventually seemed more pleasant.

By 4.50 p.m., I was waiting outside the foyer, staring out at the car park of the convenience store and watching the overweight white men pull up in their SUVs to buy beer. It was already darkening, and the equally corpulent hotel clerk came outside for a Marlboro Light. Through the smoke, she looked my way with mild curiosity and it occurred to me that this pacing in the cold air probably made me look like a twitchy drug addict anxious for new supplies. 'Just waiting for a friend', I said. 'Fresh out here.' She nodded, not really terribly interested, and then busied herself, cigarette between fingers, writing a text message.

Then 5.30 came and went, and so did 5.45. The clerk stepped out again and looked into the approaching night. 'I don't think your friend is coming, honey.' I'd arrived at the same conclusion, but then a big black car was pulling up in the car park and there was Jerry. He waved me over. 'How you doing, man. Good to see you.' He was sorry; he'd had to work late. But now there was a celebration with his extended family that night. He wanted me to come. 'Y'all eat seafood in Australia?' We did. 'All right then.' But was it all right? How would we talk about executing people in front of his relatives?

Was that a topic for a family dinner? Perhaps sensing my discomfort, he clarified. 'We talk first, then we eat.'

In his powerful car, we headed down the freeway along which I'd been walking earlier until we left behind the outer suburban sprawl and came to downtown Richmond, a streetscape that suddenly seemed disconcertingly seedy. Streetlights didn't work; there were security grilles on all the windows. Jerry pulled up the car. 'Some people I want you to meet.' What were we doing? I barely knew this man; insofar as I did, it was because he'd killed sixty-five people, which in normal circumstances would not be a recommendation. Yet I followed him—what else could I do?—across the street and into the barber shop where, he said, his cousin worked.

There were no other white people there, and the scene—the old fashioned barber's chair, the youths lounging around waiting their turn, the girl getting her hair straightened, the raucous conversations—seemed straight from a Spike Lee movie. Jerry's cousin, as it happened, wasn't in, but Jerry introduced me to everyone else, staff and customers alike, as a visitor from Australia. I shook hands all round as Jerry enumerated my antipodean idiosyncrasies—I'd tried, for instance, to get into the wrong side of his right-hand-drive car—and then the talk turned to kangaroos and the Crocodile Hunter and all the other inevitable subjects. The barbers, their clients, the hangers-on: everyone was genuinely friendly, but it was difficult to relax, and I found myself alternating between a ridiculously stiff politeness and an unnatural casualness—the same as at the abattoir, except even more uptight and gauche and, of course, incandescently white. Again, I wondered, did these people know about Jerry's other life? If so, how did they feel about it? Could an executioner just walk around like this, talking and laughing as if he hadn't seen and done the work of the death chamber?

Back in the car, he explained that we were going to the restaurant first and his family would meet us there later, after we'd had time to talk. Red Lobster was a chain restaurant but with an older clientele: more like a genuine family place rather than simply housing the sullen teenagers who congregated in McDonald's and Taco

Bell. It sold Americanised seafood: deep fried and with sufficient sauce and cheese so as to taste nothing like fish.

We sat in the bar and ordered water—Jerry didn't drink—and I took out my tape recorder. Then I hesitated. Asking someone about the first man he'd killed felt wildly inappropriate in a public place, but the cable football coming from the TV nearby provided a certain privacy, a kind of aural screen.

'Remember, when I joined the team, they didn't have anyone on death row', Jerry explained. 'It wasn't until 1982 that we got our first prisoner. Man called Frank Coppola.' Coppola was an ex-cop, self-confessedly guilty of a violent murder. What's more, he wanted to die, and that made the process easier. 'He said, sarge, I don't want my family to grow up knowing their father is incarcerated on death row. He said that's why he was doing this [volunteering for execution]. I couldn't say, well, go ahead and do it, but I worked with him and the execution wasn't that hard because here was a person who was volunteering to go along with it.'

But Coppola's willingness to die didn't entirely negate the stresses of killing him. It was the first electrocution in Virginia after the informal moratorium, and the procedure attracted enormous attention. 'The place was packed', Jerry said. 'From the front door to the back. Because it was the first in twenty years, it drew a lot of media attention. They were taking pictures and stuff like that. I was worrying about making a mistake; I don't want to overdo it, because I haven't did this before.'

'Did you practise pulling the switch ...' I began, but he interrupted, a little exasperated.

'It's a button you press, not a switch. I don't know why people always say switch—it's a button.' It made sense that an electric chair operated with a button: just about every modern piece of electrical equipment does. So why did the word 'switch' come so inexorably to mind? Perhaps because it was an image from a horror movie: the mad scientist commencing unspeakable experiments, loosing the lightning with an enormous lever. A button seemed more clinical, more modern: that, perhaps, was why Jerry needed to correct me. Yes, he said, they did practise, or at least they tried to, but they couldn't rehearse the actual act itself without a live body on which they could test the level of current.

I nodded. In interviews, Leuchter talked about that point, about how much of the uncertainty in an electrocution depended on the conductivity of the human body. The Coppola execution had featured in one of Deborah Denno's articles, precisely because on that occasion the current hadn't been correct. According to her account, he received two separate applications of electricity, until flames danced around the leg electrode and an oily smoke filled the chamber.

Jerry didn't go into such details but when he spoke of how the first execution had affected him, he implicitly confirmed Denno's account: 'The smell of burnt flesh got into my nostrils. And I could smell it even when I got home, and I wondered whether it was in my clothing, and I took my clothing off and washed it, and I could still smell it. Then when you smell something cooking, when your wife is cooking meat, it brings you back.' We were talking in a restaurant, and though the air carried more garlic than meat, the kitchen smells made his description that much more visceral.

Virginia eventually adopted lethal injection as well as the chair, giving the prisoners a macabre freedom to choose how they wished to die. Like McAndrew, Jerry learnt the new method by observing teams in Texas, a state that operated like a de facto college for executioners.

'Lethal injection.' Jerry enunciated the words as if tasting them, checking they were as bitter as he remembered. 'We had a guy in Texas, and he sung a hymn, and he'd almost repeated that hymn before the chemicals took effect. Electrocution is like flicking a light off and on. But lethal injection … it's a slow process … Then a lot of them were ex-drug-users who didn't have the proper veins, so you might have to do a cut-down or a cut-away, but we didn't have the knowledge to do that.' He shook his head. 'So, if the condemned had asked me, when he was making that choice, I would have told him die by electrocution, because I knew we could do that. But lethal injection was different.'

In everything I'd read so far about killing, process seemed to be crucial. So I wanted to ask him about that. What were the steps that he followed? If I came to him on death row, what would be the procedure in the weeks leading up to my execution?

He nodded, as if to say, yes, that was a good question. His voice lost the mournful timbre that had crept in during his discussion of Texas and became more brisk, more businesslike, a re-creation, perhaps, of the efficient officer he once must have been. 'Fifteen days prior to your execution, you come to me. You leave death row; you come down to the death chamber. When I receive you, what I would do, all your belongings, I would X-ray them. Everything you own, everything you bring in, I would X-ray it.'

Robert Johnson had written about this: the psychological effect upon the inmate of watching their pathetic bundle of prison possessions graded and judged as if they were already dead, their time on earth assessed through the miserable objects they'd accumulated.

'I would give you give you a complete physical,' Jerry continued, 'or the doctor would give you that. Ask you different questions, get your history if you were a drug addict or whatever. You know, if you were a drug addict, we know that we might have problems if you chose death by lethal injection. Those were some of the questions that I might ask. When you make that choice, you say electrocution, then it's no problem: I know that I got to fix up my head piece, my leg piece and so on and so on.' Above the buzz of conversation in the gradually filling restaurant, he was utterly matter of fact, ticking off the tools of his trade like a plumber explaining what he'd need for a particular drain.

'You would stay there for fifteen days during all your appeals and whatever. Your lawyers, your clergy, they would come down. I would have a nurse come to see you on a daily basis; if you want medication, I'll make sure you get your medication. During those fifteen days, I'll have a death watch set up for you. Trained officers who would watch you twenty-four hours a day. Everything is logged: the time you get up, the time you go to sleep. Inmate Sparrow is sleeping; inmate Sparrow got up to use the rest room; inmate Sparrow took a shower; inmate Sparrow used the telephone; you know, inmate Sparrow out to the visitors' area and so on.'

Inmate Sparrow had invited the use of the second person by the way he'd framed his question, but the casual discussion of the process by which he would be executed still seemed rather chilling, a tiny taste of the thoroughgoing impersonality of the protocol. If the circumstances had been different, if I'd really ended up on Virginia's death row some time in the 1990s, Jerry—the pleasant, friendly man sitting across from me in a restaurant bar—would, like everyone else in the prison system, have converted me into a surname to be marched inexorably to death.

'The date of your execution,' he continued, 'it's a twenty-four-hour watch. That means I would post a person right at the top of your cell to watch you, to give you the telephone, anything you want. At that time, you request what you want for your last meal, who you want to send your property to, who your body going to: all those things come out. Then that last date, you get a shower, you eat your last meal, the warden comes and reads your death warrant, and says if the governor don't intervene and give you a clemency, a stay of execution, then at nine o'clock, you will be executed. At that time, you take a shower; the clergy person comes; you can get on the telephone and call; at quarter to nine, that's when stuff happens.

'After you get out of the shower, you go into another cell; you get different clothing, all the stuff that's been examined, so I know that there's nothing wrong with these clothes, there's no weapons [or] anything in it; I know that everything is ready. You are strapped either on the table, on the gurney, or you are strapped on the chair.

'You have the doctor ready with the stethoscope to pronounce you dead. And we look at the body for marks; we have to circle where all the marks are, so you have a mark on your arm where we insert the thing, or for electrocution you might have a burn mark on your leg or on your head. All those things the doctor puts on the death file. Then your body is taken to the morgue to sign off. And that's it.' He looked at me across the table. 'That's it', he repeated, more softly.

In other accounts, it had been explained how the chair melted the joints of an electrocuted man together, leaving the body locked in a sitting position. Some prisons weighed the corpse down with sand bags to straighten it out for burial. But those were not details I wanted to discuss. Besides, I was still thinking about the process through which inmate Sparrow would slowly progress. How did the condemned person react to all of that? Was there a particular time at which they accepted the reality, a point at which they said, yes, I really am going to die?

'I notice that once they see that it's seven o'clock or eight-thirty and they haven't heard anything from the full circuit court, I think it kicks in then, about the time you take them to shower. I just let them stay there, I don't rush them out of the shower—just wash, let me know when you finish. They will wash and wash and wash. Some of them will be in there crying and washing or praying and whatever; some of them will be singing, joking, "I don't want to go to heaven dirty". A lot of them ask me, "Is it going to hurt?" I tell them, "It ain't going to hurt". I pray with them, you know. I extend my hand and we have prayer. Even if the guy didn't want prayer, I placed my hands over his head back while I was cutting his hair for the chair, praying to myself and hoping that it would sink through. Because a lot of guys, there was a pride thing: I'm too bully; I'm a killer; I don't need God. They took that approach, and that was the attitude they carried. But 97 per cent of them found some type of closure with God before they died, before they went away.'

If there were no atheists in foxholes, it made sense that there weren't too many in the condemned cells. But did last-minute conversions from men who'd spent their lives being 'bully' actually bring any comfort? Jerry nodded. 'If the guy really accepted it, if he really believed that he's gonna leave this body and go with God, then it could be something that he could look forward to. Naturally, he's kinda shaky. I would be, 'cos I'm human—that's the human side. But I tell them, you have the advantage over us, because you ready to go to heaven. But I'm gonna stay here in this cell and I don't know when I'm going; I might beat you there. Sort of to relieve the guys, to prepare them, you know.'

It was a point Jerry made several times: the advantage the inmate possessed over those executing him, a unique chance to save his soul. In our first conversation, he'd even reversed the perspective, so that, for a moment, he'd talked as the condemned and cast me as the person putting him to death. 'If I was on death row and you was the executioner, you would say, "Jerry, you have the advantage over me because you know that if the full circuit don't convene and the governor don't give you no stay, then you going to die, so you can ask the Lord right there and then for your forgiveness".' Across the table, he pointed at me. 'But you are thinking, I'm going to go home. I'm going to enjoy my family, after the execution is over, I'm gonna do this and do that. You're planning ahead—but you might go before I go. You don't know.' Then he slipped back into his real role, the executioner once more. 'So I'm telling this guy, "You have a chance to repent". Death is not the worst thing that can happen: if you read the Bible, it tells you that to be absent from the body is to be present with the Lord.'

Here was a clear instance of moral disengagement: the belief that by pressing that button, you weren't blasting someone into nothingness but transporting him out of the bleak chamber into a different and better place would obviously help you carry out a death sentence. On paper, Jerry's words seem like glib self-justifications; it was different listening to him talk. These were, one sensed, not easy things for him to say. At times, he seemed so distraught that you felt the weight that his religious convictions helped him carry.

'If they asked for forgiveness, I think God will forgive them. I had to look at it this way. I'm an executioner—I'm going to kill them—so I've got to ask God for forgiveness. What? God's gonna grant me forgiveness?' He spoke the words with incredulity, as if such a thing were unimaginable. 'God don't need me to do favours for Him! You have to look at it from that standpoint. If God can forgive me, God can forgive them.

'You know, just because you're from Australia and I'm from the United States, that don't mean that you're not my brother. I should have the same love for you that I had for my brothers over here, my brothers in Africa. Whether you are black or white or whatever, we should love one another as God loved us. You are not going to find that love until you clear your heart of all that hatred that you have. I always had to hate the crimes that they committed, but I loved the individuals that I killed, that I executed. And it's hard to say that, you know. It's real hard.'

When I asked him if there was anything in particular he did beforehand to prepare for an execution, he nodded emphatically. 'I had to change. You've got to be transformed to take a life, to become—I hate to say an animal—but a person that you are really not. You are tense. You go up and down. Is the execution going ahead? Will they get a temporary stay? It takes a while to come down afterwards. It might take two days. It might take three days. It might take months. And sometimes you up and down after that anyway, and then when you got another one scheduled, you got to get ready to do that all over again. And then you try to live a normal life.'

Hence his family problems, the troubles he had at home. For years, he hadn't told his wife what he did, leaving her to cope without explanation as his moods swung according to the execution cycle. 'I wasn't a perfect husband. I messed around on her, you know. Had I given her that information prior to me doing this, I don't know if I'd been in a position to take the job. I don't know if she would have approved. But I didn't speak about it to no one.' And, all the while, the executions kept coming.

Were there any of the men in particular that he thought about?

'Sometimes, they say things that will stay with you the rest of your life.' He paused, playing with the recorder, recalling an example. 'We had a guy in a wheelchair', he said, eventually. 'You got to pick him up, his legs dangling, put him in an electric chair.' That would have been, I later calculated, Charles Stamper, a man who had killed three restaurant workers, and had then been paralysed in a gaol fight. Stamper's lawyers, with the desperation characteristic of capital defendants, tried to argue that, as a paraplegic, he didn't represent a threat to society and so shouldn't be killed. The ploy failed, and he was carried to his death in 1993.

Again, the same point: Coral Hull's abattoir goat; the Green Beret and the Vietnamese boy: that instant of recognition, individuality rather than abstraction, brought on by any variation from the practised routine. 'You got guys complaining about their veins. You can't find a vein; you're hurting him; he's going through pain. Things like that. It locks in and stays with you, and anytime you hear about executions, these things pop up.'

If those moments in which the protocol went awry became nodes of trauma for Jerry, the suggestion of deeper, institutional failure troubled him even more. Much like Robert Johnson, Jerry seemed never to have considered the possibility that anyone on death row might be innocent. But in 2000, his faith in the system took a blow. In that year, he went to gaol himself.

He tried to explain the details of his conviction, but it was complex and I couldn't really follow. It seemed he'd been found guilty of money laundering and perjury, after helping an old friend who was a drug dealer. 'I knew this guy for years and years. I knew him as a kid, and he used to clean my cars and different things ... Anyway he was into drugs and I was trying to steer him in the right direction, 'cos if you caught for a king pin drug dealer you're subject to being executed, and you know, I didn't want that.' He laughed—but turned quickly serious.

When he went to court, he couldn't, he said, adequately defend himself, in part because of his work in the death chamber. 'I was scheduled to perform an execution—that day, when I was in court. So when they started asking me questions, I can't get my thoughts back that quickly—there's no way. I did that execution and I had several more scheduled that month, but I couldn't get through those. I knew I didn't do anything, but I wasn't given a fair trial. The judge said he'd never seen a case like it, because I wasn't myself—and I wasn't. I wasn't myself; I was the executioner.'

He was convicted. He resigned his position and he served his sentence, but the experience forced him to reconsider the assumptions he'd made about the men he'd killed. 'Because I know that the experience I had with the court system was unfair and I couldn't imagine what these guys were going through, and it sort of makes you wonder ...' He trailed off and then gathered his thoughts and began again. 'You know, the Commonwealth of Virginia might say, well, we made one mistake and execute one innocent person and that's not too bad, but how do you think I feel as an executioner, knowing that I took an innocent life? They don't have to suffer the consequences: they didn't take a life. They recommended it, but I actually did the killing.'

I wanted to ask more about his time inside—I couldn't imagine other prisoners responding well to a former executioner—but he stood up and waved over my shoulder to a large family group coming into the restaurant. 'Come and meet my people', he said, and I did.

My memories of that evening are like shards of stained glass, brightly coloured but fragmentary. I never really sorted out the relationships between everyone present, but I sat between Jerry and his wife, with Jerry's son across the table from me. The son was a career soldier—a recruiter for the Marine Corps—and our encounter struck me as preposterously ironic. It was one thing to be eating dinner with an executioner on my right-hand side; it seemed almost too much that the man with whom I earnestly discussed the Virginia weather was a US marine.

Yet they were nice, nice people. Jerry's wife went out of her way to include me, a complete stranger, in every conversation, even though she must have known I'd come to question her husband about the people he'd killed, which scarcely seemed any kind of reason to think well of me. Jerry's son dandled on his lap his own child, to whom he was obviously devoted; he, too, politely asked questions about my travels and about Australia.

After we'd ordered from the menu and the food had arrived, in heaped American-size serves, Jerry said grace in his deep, slow voice, giving thanks for the meal and the company and mentioning me, as a guest, by name. He'd just been telling me about praying with inmates before he executed, and taking his hand and bowing my head should, by rights, have felt sinister, a reminder of all that killing. Yet the ritual was unexpectedly poignant. Nearly as primal as dying, eating was a natural focus for ceremony, and it was comforting, so far from home and in such a strange setting, to be draped in the fabric of someone else's observance, even without believing in the Lord to whom Jerry's simple words were addressed. As he thanked his God, I suddenly knew that if I were preparing myself to die in a comfortless death chamber, separated by stone walls from anyone who cared for me, I would almost certainly accept the invitation of my executioner to pray, not out of a sudden faith in an afterlife and a day of judgement, but in recognition of the human communion the gesture represented.

The rest of the evening I don't remember. Not because I was drinking—they were teetotallers, and out of politeness I remained stone sober, though I longed for alcohol—but because the interview had been so emotionally draining. I recall struggling to hold up my end of the conversation and compensating for an inability to speak by consuming heroic quantities of seafood, until Jerry took pity on me and offered to drive me home.

Lying sleepless in the lumpy motel bed, I tried to make sense of what I'd learnt. I liked Jerry—in some respects, I liked him as much as anyone I'd met in the USA. He was kind; there was something warm and reassuring about him. You wouldn't know that he'd killed so many people. At the same time, occasionally he said things that jumped out at you. In the car on the way back to the motel, he'd told me again about how, when he read about executions or saw them portrayed in movies, images from the seventeen years he'd spent putting people to death returned to him—intrusive thoughts, just as MacNair had described.

Again and again, he'd returned to the dilemma faced by an executioner. As team leader, he'd monitored the performance of his co-workers—not just what they did but why they did it—because he felt that anyone who was enjoying putting people to death shouldn't be on the team. If you liked killing, he said, you needed treatment, and if you hated it, you struggled to keep working. Killing, then, was impossible. Yet he'd done it for nearly twenty years.

11

TECHNOLOGY

All the way back to Boston, I tried to plan the interview with Leuchter. I didn't want to get caught up talking about physical processes. Instead I would speak with him about capital punishment as an institution. I'd press him about the psychology of killing and how that shaped the machines he built. Most of all, I'd focus on his own feelings, the coping mechanisms he used.

But there was another problem. I'd argued politics with MacNair, and my disagreement with her was far less significant than with Leuchter. So what to say to him? What about the Holocaust? Did I want to simply ask him to explain himself? Was I going to argue with him? Berate him? What was the right thing to do?

By the time the plane landed, my mind was made up. I would tell him what I thought. I didn't want any misunderstanding. I'd make it clear how odious and evil Holocaust revisionism was: perhaps not at the start, because he might cancel the interview, but definitely before we finished. I would establish my own position, so that I didn't come away feeling any dirtier than necessary.

He'd suggested meeting after he finished work, nominating the Dunkin' Donuts on Broadway, just near a Honda dealership. On the phone, I scribbled down his directions, with the familiar sinking sensation always associated with the phrase 'you can't miss it'. This time, rather than embark on another long trek into the unknown, I caught a cab. The avuncular driver explained that he knew exactly the place, though his confidence became noticeably more brittle when we came to the area and confronted the full extent to which Dunkin' Donut franchises infested Broadway.

'It must be one of these', he said eventually, pulling over to the curb. It occurred to me that such casual assurance would be easy for someone remaining in a warm car rather than stepping out into a freezing evening entirely unsure whether the destination was any-where nearby.

It was, inevitably, the wrong place, the locale nothing like what Fred had described. The staff suggested, with indifferent shrugs, that I walk half a mile up the road, since the Dunkin' Donuts there was, indeed, near a car dealership. Yet, when I arrived, sweating from hurry-ing in my cold-weather clothes, there was nowhere to sit down—the place sold takeaway only. Surely this was not really where he'd nominated to meet? Eventually, I called him. He answered and asked me where I was; he was waiting in an entirely different franchise. Though I offered to go find him, he decided, probably wisely, to come and pick me up.

That was my first glimpse of Fred Leuchter: a big, old-fashioned car pulling up outside the donut shop. Leuchter seemed much, much older than in the Morris film. He'd put on some weight, perhaps, but more than that, he'd lost the preppiness that made his movie presence so striking. He was dressed casually in a vest and blue shirt rather than the suit and tie in which he was usually photographed, and the clothing contributed to a sense that he was somehow less crisp, his hair not so sharply cut, and his shirt not so carefully pressed. But I didn't have time to think about the change in his appearance and what it meant because he hadn't come alone. There was a woman in the passenger seat and, behind her, an enormous, savage-looking dog.

Leuchter came into the shop; I called his name and we shook hands. I apologised for the mix-up, and he suggested, in that raspy voice, that we drive back to the Dunkin' Donuts where he'd originally been waiting. I looked over at the dog in the car. There was nothing I wanted to do less than get into that vehicle with his animal—a German shepherd, no less—but I couldn't think of any plausible excuse to refuse.

When he opened the door, the dog whined and strained to get away from me. 'She's very timid', Fred said, affectionately, as I extended my hand and the dog flinched again. He introduced me to the woman, his partner. She hadn't come to defend Leuchter; she was there because they were on the way home from work, interrupting their normal routine for my sake. Later, during the interview, she read a romance novel while Fred talked to me about electrocutions and autopsies and IV cut-downs. I'd look over her way occasionally, and she'd smile politely and then put her head back down, returning to the world of true love and happily-ever-after.

The second Dunkin' Donuts was, predictably, almost identical to the first, except bigger and with red plastic tables at which we could sit. The radio played commercial hits; the warm air wafted a distinctive corporate cooking odour, almost a parody of authentic baking. One bored teenager steered a mop over the grubby floor; another lounged by the counter. There weren't any other customers, which was fortunate, because the conversation became, almost at once, extraordinarily gruesome.

I knew something of his biography, I said: I'd seen the film and I'd read Stephen Trombley's *The Execution Protocol*, a book that devotes several chapters to Leuchter. But what I really wanted to uncover was not so much his narrative in itself but how he felt about what he'd seen and done. For instance, when he first contemplated commercially manufacturing execution equipment, did he worry about how controversial it would be? Did it cross his mind that there might be consequences for his own wellbeing, his own mental health?

Fred answered in a roundabout fashion. He wanted to stress that his peculiar career was not a matter of choice as such. 'As you'd know, my father worked for the Massachusetts prison system for years, and I was contacted by an official who knew I was an engineer. He asked me if I could look at the Massachusetts electrocution system and see what had to be done, if they were ever going to use it. Which is what happened.

'It's a very strong community, and my name was given to other states. They sought me out because there was nobody who knew anything about it. I didn't know anything about it, either. I had to learn. I had to go back and dig through medical archives and things that were published in the 1800s, the 1890s, dealing with electrocution, how they developed the procedures, what they did. Anyway, there was a lot of information available, which I got. And I developed, I designed, a better system based on what problems they had. I was lucky because there were almost a hundred years of executions, and I could see what was being done wrong and I could address the problem with modern technology, which was what I did.

'The first thing I made that was used was a helmet, for South Carolina. I made it; they paid for it, and they had it. I never thought too much about it until the week before the first execution. It was only then that the shock hit me. There wasn't any going back: I couldn't go down and take it away from them. And once they did it, once they used it, it was something that I made that had taken a life.'

'How did you feel about that?'

'It was kinda ...' He hesitated. 'I had mixed feelings about it. I didn't make these things because I was a proponent of capital punishment and I believed that these people should be executed. I mean, I believed at that point that capital punishment had its place, but I became involved basically because the prison wardens were crying for help. They had equipment that was old, in most cases didn't work, and whatever they did, they were going to torture the inmate.'

I knew this argument—I'd heard him put it in the film, as well as in every interview I'd read—but what came next was more surprising. 'It's a toss-up anyway, for if I build the system and we do everything right, there's probably a 20 per cent chance that there's going to be a problem. The human physiology varies so much. I can do it in most cases, and there are some cases where it just isn't going to work. That's why I'm no longer a proponent of capital punishment. I'm not avidly against it, but the problem I see now is: whether it's a deterrent or it isn't a deterrent, if we can't do it right ... we lower ourselves into the same gutter. If we torture people, and we know we're going to torture people, we're in the same gutter as the murderer that we're executing.'

It seemed a conclusion of some significance: if Fred Leuchter, of all people, no longer believed executions could be conducted humanely, then the dream of painless death that the US judiciary had pursued so assiduously since the 1890s was no more than fantasy.

But he still hadn't said anything about his own feelings. I tried again: 'Let me take you back a step. I'm interested primarily in the psychological basis, and I could imagine that one of the reasons why wardens might be calling out for help is that it might be hard to get very many people willing to involve themselves in such a taboo ...' I wanted to ask whether that had given him any cause for hesitation. Taboos usually exist for a reason, marking, even if obscurely, a point of demarcation and the risk of some kind of danger. Had he worried before crossing that line?

But he was already responding—and the question that he wanted to answer was a much more practical query about the difficulties in finding execution expertise: 'You have to remember, at that stage everybody who had been involved in an execution was retired, and most of them were dead, because most of the people who were responsible for the executions were older people. Because the wardens were in their fifties and sixties, forty years later, what are your chances of finding them alive? The only people who were left who had seen executions were young guards, and they didn't really do anything except strap the individual into the chair. They didn't know anything about how it was done. All the executioners were dead. The officials who may have talked about it to the executioners, they were dead.'

'That's not quite what I meant', I said. 'OK, I understand that there was a practical reason why there was a shortage of people, but did you have any sense of moving into a taboo area, a field that was something ...'

Again, he interrupted: not rudely, but in a way that suggested that this was a tired issue, not worth spending much time on. 'I've been asked hundreds of times, do I sleep at night? Yes. Because I went into it for what I consider the right reasons: I wanted to ameliorate suffering. Even so, the first execution that took place, the first time my helmet was used, I was up most of the night listening to the radio to find out what happened, whether or not there was a problem. It was well designed; it was well built; there wasn't a fault with the rest of the equipment, but if there had been, I was concerned about it. I'm concerned now, actually, because I built the complete system for Tennessee ...'

He broke off, and then asked: 'You know about my background with the alleged gas chambers in Europe?' I nodded, feeling utterly craven as the word 'alleged' scuttled past me and slithered out the door. 'You know about all of the difficulty that I had with the Jewish organisations? OK. Well, you also know that they threatened prison officials; they even threatened to pass legislation prohibiting states from dealing with me. They cajoled the Department of Corrections in the state of Tennessee into having the power supply for the Tennessee electric chair reworked and the voltages and the current levels changed. It was reworked by a fellow named Jay Wiechert— I don't know if you recognise the name?'

I did, but only because of our earlier email correspondence. After Leuchter told me about the forthcoming Tennessee execution, I'd read something about the loathing that Leuchter and Wiechert reserved for each other. 'Jay Wiechert', said Leuchter, with palpable contempt, 'is the man responsible for the Florida electric chair where they have had so many problems. I have a problem with Mr Wiechert. I have a personal problem. I think he likes to torture people. I don't see any other reason. He knows better. He's an electrical engineer. He has the same information available as I had, but he uses voltages and currents that he knows are questionable. It looks like everything went well in the most recent execution, but I'm waiting for the autopsy because there are several things that I can look at that might give me an answer and might not. Sometimes the individual is tortured but you can't tell; you don't see it and it doesn't show up in the autopsy.'

Trombley's book went into Leuchter's use of autopsy results in some detail. Among the factors that Leuchter considered was the amount of liquid remaining in the dead man's bladder. In a successful execution, the inmate voided himself as he died, which was why the electric chairs Leuchter designed handily contained a pan to catch the faeces and urine. If the coroner's knife punctured a full bladder, death had probably not been instant.

Such were the kinds of details that made me glad Dunkin' Donuts was empty, especially since Fred made no attempt to moderate his voice. 'I'm very concerned, because that was my equipment and simply because Wiechert went in and changed the circuit board; the world was going to view it as if I had built the torture device.'

In my view, it seemed extremely unlikely that the success or otherwise with which Tennessee had recently executed someone in a Leuchter-designed electric chair would have much impact on the reputation of a man synonymous with Holocaust revisionism. But that was by the by. I was more interested in the pattern that seemed to be developing through the interview. I'd ask Fred about his feelings; he'd answer with a technical discussion, and his evident reluctance suggested that it was worth pursuing his emotional response.

There was one last card to throw down. Trombley quotes Leuchter as saying that when he began manufacturing equipment professionally, he started with one great insight into the potential market: the problem with the existing arrangements was psychological rather than technological. I read the passage to Leuchter and asked him to explain what it meant. He blinked. He couldn't remember saying that, he answered. He took off his glasses, rubbed them and put them back. 'There's more to the execution than just good equipment', he offered, somewhat tentatively. 'Lethal injection was touted to be the best method a number of years ago, and I designed a system for it based on the chemicals that were defined by law. I don't know if you are familiar with this controversy about the chemicals?'

I nodded. Yes, I knew about that. In fact, I told him, I wanted eventually to ask him about that as well. That was a mistake, because we immediately veered away from the emotions and towards the chemicals. 'I believe it's a lot of hogwash. I did the research on the chemicals, and I knew more about them than anyone. I was the one who extrapolated the dosages from the rabbits and the pigs when they first tested Pentothal and pancuronium bromide, and what I extrapolated worked. I don't believe that people are paralysed and feeling pain—I mean, that might happen one in a million cases because of a physiological difference, but that would be all. But let's assume that we have the best piece of equipment in the world and it works all the time and I can guarantee that it's going to be humane and painless. We strap a man down on a gurney forty minutes before his execution and we put an IV line in his arm with saline going in. He lays there for almost an hour in some cases. I don't call that humane.'

Neither did I. Over the previous weeks, the image of an inmate strapped on a gurney, waiting to be killed, had been one to which I'd often returned. I'd been thinking about Jerry's description of the Texas inmate who'd completed an entire hymn before the chemicals took effect. The moment of agony produced by an electric chair paled in comparison to a drawn-out process by which someone was prepared for a lethal injection.

I'd thought we were on the same page with the cruelty of that procedure, but then Leuchter continued. 'He's in a room', he said, referring to the inmate—or, to use Leuchter's preferred term, the 'executee'. 'It's a room that's got painted grey concrete walls. He's in a gurney that's either a hospital gurney or something that they made in the metal shop or some place, and it's not comfortable. I mean, he should be laying in one of those dentist's chairs that they have: contoured and plush, the same type of thing they use for donating blood. He should have closed-circuit TV; he should have music; he should be in an environment in which the walls are panelled or painted or something. That's humane. It's not humane to throw him in a dungeon and make him lay there for almost an hour before we kill him.'

My mouth opened; I shut it again. Was he really suggesting that the inhumanity of lethal injection might be in any way alleviated by better decor and a more comfortable gurney? Then it occurred to me that he was focused so intently on the technicalities of design that he couldn't see any context at all. Roughly built machine-shop gurneys bothered him because they represented a failure to think through all the engineering challenges posed by the death penalty—almost an aesthetic reaction, as much as a moral one. It upset him that the job wasn't being done properly.

So perhaps that was the answer. Perhaps I needed to rephrase my question into an enquiry about design. 'When you were constructing these machines, did you give any thought to the psychological impact on the people who have to use them? If so, how did you deal with that in the devices you constructed?'

He beamed. 'The most pressing problem was that of the warden. And in some of the states—let's say in Missouri—it was really a problem because the warden in charge had to do the execution. He was required by law. So the equipment I gave them had two buttons, with a small computer chip that could go either way. He and the deputy warden pushed a button, and they never knew which one of them did it. And that alleviated the warden's feelings somewhat, because at least he could say, I don't have to know that I did it.'

Did he think that made a difference?

'Yes. Yes.' He nodded emphatically. 'I think that makes a great deal of difference. I mean, you don't know how much this wears on him. The warden at Texas who has done the most executions is retired now. His name was Jack Pursley.' I'd heard of Pursley. With Texas the execution capital of the USA, Pursley had inevitably been involved in a number of grisly botches. 'He kept asking for a machine and they wouldn't buy him one. They kept patting him on the head and saying, you're doing a good job, Jack, keep it up. Well,

Jack did the first lethal injection, utilising dosages that I had computed for the State of New Jersey. And he had a lot of trouble. He had lines rupture; he had veins rupture. And there are all kinds of inhumane things that go on with the lethal injection process that we haven't even mentioned yet. But the bottom line is that in ten years he aged thirty. That was simply because he had to do this. He didn't want to do it. But it was his job and he did it. But that doesn't mean he liked it.'

There was something distinctively boyish in Leuchter's own enthusiasm for the technical: he was like the child who painstakingly builds models of fighter planes and tanks, without ever thinking about what his toys actually represent. Yet it occurred to me that Leuchter, like Jack Pursley, had also aged greatly, though in his case the process seemed to have started not from the period in which he participated in executions but, rather, from the time in which he didn't—that is, from the time he'd been sacked. There was an obvious reason for it, too. But, I promised myself, we would get to that in due course. In the meantime, I wanted to know if there was any way around the distress that Pursley felt. Would a machine have made a difference, or was it just a manifestation of the basic odiousness of taking a human life?

Leuchter didn't hesitate. 'I think having a machine that at least looks humane makes a difference. Because the warden doesn't know he tortured someone, he assumes that he didn't. If we go for lethal injection for a minute, remember most of the people that are in the criminal justice system by the time they get to the end of the pipeline where they're being executed, that's the worst place you could be. Those are the worst felons you got. Most of them are former drug-users. They've got vascular systems that almost are non-existent. So how do we find a vein? Well, a doctor has a problem. But they don't have any doctors because the AMA won't let them participate. So somebody has to do an IV cut-down. We have to go into the carotid artery, or we have to go to an artery in the groin. Now I'm not qualified to do an IV cut-down, but I'm a hell of a lot more qualified than some guard that's gone to the ninth grade. He takes out a pen knife and he does the IV cut-down. But they don't tell you that.'

Not wanting to descend once more into the particular abyss of veins and IV cut-downs and clumsily wielded pen knives, I did my best to steer us in a different direction. Did he know of other executioners who had been affected like Pursley, either ageing prematurely or manifesting different symptoms?

There was, he replied, a distinction between those states where the wardens themselves were obliged to carry out the execution and the jurisdictions in which they could employ specialist executioners. He mentioned Don Cabana as an example of the first category and its results. 'He bears up better than I'd expect,' he said, 'but I think something's going on with him'. As for the second group, Fred was surprisingly severe with them: 'I know several people who work for the system, mainly in the South. We got some oddball people down South. I don't think it's affected any of them. But these people were affected at birth. They have a different mental outlook from you and I. They think it's macho.'

The image of hayseeds yee-hawing it up in the death chamber must have caused me to react, because Leuchter became slightly defensive, as if I'd held him personally responsible for their lack of professionalism. 'I can't control who they pick to do it. To be quite frank, even if I could, I might get one of those people to do it, too, because I figure it would do the least psychological damage. If I can get someone who it doesn't bother, let them do it. Maybe that's a good choice.'

We were on the scent now. 'So you think there's an inevitable human reaction to performing executions? I mean, in a normal person, someone who is not maladjusted.'

He nodded quickly. 'Yes, yes. If you have to do it all the time; if that's your function. I have had some of the states ask me if I'd be willing to do the execution, and I've said no. I don't do that. I'm not an executioner. I'm dealing with the humanity of the situation and I'm going to hold your hand through this thing to make sure you don't torture the guy, but I'm not a state functionary and don't make me into one.'

That distinction seemed very important to Leuchter. He was a humanitarian; other people were executioners. But what exactly did it mean? His lethal-injection machine allowed a certain ambiguity about whose button triggered the needle, but only in the most literal, technical sense. Obviously, an execution is a collective event. How could you distinguish between the guard who escorted the inmate into the chair and the official who pressed the button? The execution required both of them. They were both responsible for what occurred.

I put that to Fred, and he talked, rather obscurely, about the training he'd provided to some death-row teams, and about how he'd schooled them beyond the letter of the protocols to understand something of the medical processes taking place in the execution. How was this relevant? He wanted to stress, I decided, the contribution he'd made to ensuring a quick death, the claim central to his putative humanitarianism. Yet his provision, in his training sessions, of a theoretical grounding for executioners hardly weakened the argument about his own responsibility for what took place in the chamber.

I tried another approach: 'What distinctions do you draw? Would you find it difficult to attend an execution? Or is that a line that you maintain: "I don't want to be there when it happens"?'

'I don't want to be at an execution.' He seemed appalled at the suggestion. 'I've never seen one. I turned down numerous invitations. I could have—I couldn't now—but at one time I could have called up any warden and said I'd like to come up and see the execution and they would have said, "Yeah, come on up, Fred". There would have been absolutely no problem at all.'

Why didn't he?

'There's no need of it. This is something that you do that has to be done. It's not something that you do for the fun of it. If you're a warden and you say, hey Fred, do you want to come watch? No thank you! If you say, I need your help to set it up, that's a different story.'

'So is there a psychological difference? Are you saying that it would make a difference if you saw the execution with your own eyes?'

He surprised me again. 'I think if you see someone die, it affects you. When somebody dies, we all die a little bit, and if you are close to the death, you die more. In combat, if they kill people—if they see people die—they die a little bit inside. They're never the same.'

In some respects, this wasn't a particularly profound point—in normal circumstances, an easy cliché. But you didn't expect to hear an execution technologist explain that those who witnessed deaths— the people for whom he manufactured his products—were never the same afterward. Wasn't this, in some ways at least, an argument against capital punishment per se? Wasn't employing a punishment that necessarily damaged the staff who administered it as unconscionable as, say, asking guards to work with asbestos or some other material that inflicted long-term injuries?

'Society has dirty jobs that have to be done', he said, flatly. 'No, my argument with capital punishment is that we can't do it right. On that basis, I oppose capital punishment. If a state is having a problem and they ask me for help, I'd still help them, because I don't want them to torture a man to death, but I feel that we can't do it right. You know, if anybody can do it right, I can. And I can't do it right. And I will defy anybody to do it right, all of the time. I can build a piece of equipment that's flawless. I can write a protocol, and you can carry out a protocol that's flawless, and 60, 75 per cent of the time, maybe 80 per cent of the time, it will work perfectly: there will be no pain, no suffering. But there's gonna be a time … The machine does its thing as it's supposed to, but there was something else in the system that we weren't aware of that leads to a torture session.'

Again, we'd diverged a long way from what I really wanted to know, but it seemed worth following the argument to its conclusion. 'And you're saying these failures happen regularly?'

He nodded. 'I think it happens all the time.'

He began discussing a particular technical dilemma implicit in electrocutions: a problem related to Ohm's law and the characteristics of saturation in an electrical circuit. The details lost me entirely, but the difficulty seemed to lie in the inverse relationship between the voltage in the circuit and the temperature of the inmate's flesh: as the chair super-heated the condemned prisoner, the executioner struggled to maintain the correct voltage without increasing the current. 'If we over-current the individual, we're going to cook him,' Leuchter said, 'and meat's going to come off the body'. His own design incorporated a device that overcame that particular difficulty, through some technical process that he tried to explain at length: the Leuchter chair, it seemed, delivered a first jolt to knock the inmate out, then let the body cool before a second jolt stopped the heart's natural pacemaker. Or something like that.

My inability to follow Leuchter's complex explanation stemmed not only from my ignorance of electrical engineering but also from an appalled realisation that, right at that moment, the store's radio station had begun broadcasting a 50 Cent song, so that, as Fred talked about Ohm's Law and cooking human flesh, Justin Timberlake was wailing, 'I'm tired of using technology, I need you right in front of me'. It was all too weird and gruesome, and I decided to move on.

I'd already asked Leuchter about the Trombley book, and he'd told me that he didn't like it: 'Trombley was more interested in blowing the inmates' horn than dealing with the situation as it was', he'd said. Now I wanted a reaction to *Mr Death*.

He sighed. 'Errol Morris contacted me a number of years before the film came out and he asked me about doing the film. He wanted to tell a story much like Kennedy's *Profiles in Courage*—this is how he explained it. He said that he believed in the Holocaust and he didn't agree with what I said. He believed something happened and he didn't want to get into that: I got a right to my opinion; he's got a right to his opinion. He wanted to explore it from that standpoint, where I did nothing wrong but I received all this venom and animosity and problems thereafter. And he did that.

'He came back a number of years later and said, "I want to finish the film". And I talked to him and said, "Look, Errol, I think you are going to get your tit caught in the wringer on this thing. You don't know what's going to happen." He said, "I'm Jewish. I understand that." I said, "No, you don't understand. I was firebombed; my life was threatened; I had Mossad agents chasing me: all kinds of things happened. You're asking for trouble." He said, "I believe in freedom of speech. I believe you had the right to say what you said, and I want to tell that story." And he said he was gonna do it strictly neutral. Which is what he did. In all his documentaries, they're always one-person documentaries; you stand or fall by yourself.

'So he released the film. He had a pre-showing at Harvard; he had a pre-showing at Toronto. The Jewish organisations went wild because people were coming out of the theatre saying, "Maybe this guy's right". So … they put a lot of pressure on him; they threatened him, and they had him increase the length of the film. It became the first film he'd made with more than one person in it. And the second half of the film, he tried to make me look silly. He had this big cup of coffee that he used. I hadn't smoked for fifteen years. I told him I don't smoke; I don't see why you want to keep putting these cigarettes around me. But he said, "It's part of the flavour".

'The second half ruined the film. I had a lot of people say to me the first part was a great film; they learnt a lot from it. But the second half, there was nothing there; they were just trying to make you look ridiculous.'

I hadn't known that Morris had reshot the ending, nor that he'd faked the scenes of Leuchter smoking, though when I checked later, the first claim, at least, seemed to be true. But the notion that a mainstream film-maker would model a documentary about a Holocaust-denier on John F Kennedy's book *Profiles in Courage* was so palpably absurd that even if Morris had really made that promise, Leuchter had only himself to blame for believing him.

In any case, this was my cue to probe the crux of Leuchter's story. 'The suggestion in the film', I said, laying words down like stepping stones across a dangerous river, 'was that you were an eccentric individual. That eccentricity was reflected in your views on the Holocaust, and it came from your work in the execution industry. What would you say to that?'

'But it changed. If you just take the first half of the film … all that extra material was re-photographed. He really was put through the wringer. And in the process, he probably lost himself an Academy Award.' To me—and to most of the reviewers I'd read— the second half of the documentary was far more powerful than the first. The idea that the film would have won an Academy Award if it had only shown Leuchter in a better light was entirely delusional. But that wasn't the point I was trying to pursue.

I tried again. 'But what would you say to the suggestion that there was some relationship between working in an industry that necessitated a certain desensitisation and your position on the Holocaust?'

He wouldn't budge. 'Morris knows better, and that's not what happened. Besides, it's not what appears in the first half; it's only what appears in the second part.'

'So you'd reject that: the implication in that film and perhaps also the Trombley book that there was some connection between the desensitisation of the execution industry and then …'

He cut me off, beginning to get impatient. 'I've never been desensitised because I've not participated in the executions. If anything, I'm very sensitive to the issues, and I'm very outspoken about the fact that we can't do a competent execution.'

Well, what did I expect? He was scarcely going to say, yes, I hold these repellent views because I've been driven crazy as a bedbug by the work that I do. Still, it was interesting that, for Leuchter, desensitisation could only relate to direct involvement in the death chamber. You could not ask for a clearer instance of moral compartmentalisation than a man who, at one time or another, had advised most capital states in the USA on their death-sentence protocols but still insisted that he didn't participate in executions. I asked him if he was still involved with the field today.

'No. I have been called after all this stuff started by wardens who were having trouble. I supplied them with sponges [for electric chairs]; I've supplied them with things that I've paid for out of pocket to prevent a torture session, but I received no recognition for it. And as far as they're concerned, it never happened. But ... it doesn't happen any more because the people that I dealt with are gone and the new wardens don't know me. If you were one of the new wardens, you probably wouldn't call me up because you don't know me well enough to say, we've got to do this on the QT.'

What did he do for a living now?

'I was a driver for a homeless women's shelter; I'm now a driver at a drug rehab shelter. I'm no longer an engineer; I can't get any work. The last person who hired me was threatened. I'm unemployable: if you hired me to do something, the Jewish organisations would threaten you. I can't work for the prison system any more. And it's a shame, because somebody should be doing something for the people who are being tortured.'

I would never have imagined Fred Leuchter—execution technologist and Holocaust-denier—working in the community sector, in drug rehabilitation, of all things. As he'd laboriously explained, heroin addicts, with their flattened veins, were the particular bête noire of executioners. Now here he was carting former drug-abusers around. Perhaps this was a redemption. Leuchter was no longer working with death. He was restoring people to life, and now that he didn't spend his time obsessing over electric chairs, he'd come to a different perspective—even, perhaps, realising why his Auschwitz stunt had been so wrong.

I hoped so, because, despite everything I knew about him, there were times—or, more exactly, contexts—in which Leuchter seemed very personable. If he'd been an expert on washing machines or antique motorcycles, his goofy technical enthusiasms would have been almost endearing, like any other passionate eccentricity. The notion of him turning his back on his fascist friends and their death chambers and reinventing himself in a healing profession possessed a certain romantic appeal. At least it did for me; for Leuchter, not so much. 'Do you have any sense of relief about being out of the execution business?' I asked.

He shook his head. 'No, my gut wrenches every time I hear about an execution that goes badly because I know that shouldn't have happened.'

Taken aback at his vehemence, I asked again: 'No relief at all in not grappling with these issues any more?'

'No', he said, flatly. And that was pretty much that. If it were up to him, he'd still be working in his old business. He hadn't turned to the community by choice but by necessity, and that necessity still irked him.

I was now at the moment I'd been imagining ever since I'd first emailed Leuchter. I'd promised myself I would confront him, challenging his complicity with those who would revive fascism and its death camps: the enemies of life. At the very least, I would make clear where I personally stood.

Yet, now that the time had arrived, I struggled. I couldn't shift mode, couldn't force myself into combativity. Leuchter's support for neo-Nazism was vile and unforgivable, I'd planned to say, in a flat, unambiguous statement which would establish my position and, most probably, end the interview. Yet when I spoke, the words twisted around in my mouth, emerging as an anaemic question rather than the bold message I'd intended. 'Ernst Zündel', I said, 'has a clear neo-Nazi agenda. Didn't it occur to you that he was using you for that purpose?'

It hadn't, Leuchter said. He was a functionary of the court, not of Zündel. Yes, he'd been paid by the defence, but he'd been recommended by the federal court system because he'd previously been an expert witness in the US system. Before he went to Poland, he did wonder about whether he should go, but two things decided him: 'First, Zündel's got the right to the best legal defence he could muster. They were talking about giving him twenty-two years in prison. Second, there's a freedom of speech issue: whether I agree with what Zündel says, he has a right to say it. I do think that every-one—and I'm sure you agree, too—that everyone has the right to think what they want and say what they want.'

His 'I'm sure you agree' unbalanced me further. I didn't agree. Of course I didn't. I didn't think Zündel's proselytising for a new Holocaust bore any relation to freedom, whether of speech or any other kind. Zündel's activities were the antithesis of freedom, and I would have been quite happy to see him and his evil co-thinkers spending twenty-two years in gaol. But I wasn't sure I wanted to make that argument to Leuchter. I wasn't going to convince him. So what exactly would it achieve, other than making me feel better? I hesitated, and the moment passed. There would be no confronta-tion; there would be no sudden denunciation. I'd finished my ques-tions, I'd turned off the tape and now I would leave.

Together, we stepped outside. The rain that had been falling gently earlier had become a solid sheet. Leuchter noticed my invol-untary shudder at the evening bleakness. 'Do you know where you are going? Do you need a lift? We can drop you somewhere—it's no trouble.' I desperately wanted to get back to Cambridge. I was leav-ing for Australia in the morning, and I wanted to sit down and think about something other than killing people. Besides, I was already beginning to shiver. But, at the same time, I didn't want to accrue a greater moral debt to Leuchter than I already had. I refused and they offered again and I refused again, and eventually they drove away.

Waiting for a cab, stamping my feet against the chill, I tried to make sense of it all. After our dialogue, I didn't think Leuchter was a Nazi, though neither did I believe him to be as politically naive as he made out. After his testimony for Zündel, for instance, he'd been represented by Kirk Lyons, a white-supremacist lawyer who openly admired the Ku Klux Klan. You did not innocently hire someone like that.

Still, my impression was that compartmentalisation more than ideology was the explanation for Leuchter. Many of the articles on him made the obvious reference to Adolf Eichmann, the Holocaust functionary whose career Hannah Arendt famously analysed. Yet because the Nazis had become unambiguous symbols of evil, such comparisons often muddled Arendt's central point, which was about structure as much as ideology. Leuchter had, after all, devoted himself to perfecting a process that broke down human connections from beginning to end, not simply by the indeterminacy of the buttons on a lethal-injection machine, or through the rehearsals by which Jerry's team turned execution into discrete and simple tasks, but by the scores of separate actions that combine to send the prisoner to the chamber, with no one—not the prosecutor, the judge, the jury, the appellate courts or the governor—ever taking responsibility for the process in its entirety. The division of labour whereby each guard in the death team worked a certain limb represented the entire capital-case bureaucracy in microcosm, a system in which scores of people who never met performed their allotted part in putting a man to death. That anonymous collectivity was why any breakdown in the rehearsed process caused such distress to prison officers, since the collapse of routine forced them to confront their own responsibility, their own autonomy, whereas if they marched through the killing like robots, they could think of the inmate as robotic, too.

Talking with Leuchter just reinforced the weird impossibility of executions. He no longer thought that a humane procedure could be guaranteed. As he said, if anyone could kill humanely, he could—and he now accepted that the variation in human physiology made that impossible. But surely variation meant that humans were not abstractions. Because they were living, they were unique—and not just because of the state of their veins. Leuchter might have been primarily referring to technical problems that prevented an electric chair from killing cleanly, but his words also explained why traumatic moments would occur when the guard caught the eye of the victim. It was impossible to negate entirely the individual humanity of each inmate.

But there was more to it than that. The prison management understood that botched executions upset their staff, that the instants when the abstraction broke down were particularly gruelling. That was why execution methods had evolved from the days of Governor Hill. But what if death row did everything right? What if Leuchter designed the perfect execution, a procedure in which the capital sentence was fulfilled so quickly and easily that neither the inmate nor the executioners experienced any distress whatsoever?

Jerry had put the executioner's paradox simply. If you don't like the work, he'd said, it will damage you and you should get out. If you do like it, you're already damaged. But there was a third option. While executioners were bothered by killings that went awry, they were also troubled in a more fundamental way by the process running smoothly. Both the studies I'd seen recorded prison staff distressed by their lack of distress. 'The hardest thing for me', one man confessed to Osofsky, 'is that the first one really affected me and the next two to three didn't. It affected me that it didn't affect me.'

'I just cannot feel anything', an officer said to Johnson. 'And that was what bothered me. I thought that I would feel something, but I didn't feel anything … [Y]ou're supposed to feel something … It's laying over my whole life.'

If an absence of sentiment worried guards as much or more than its presence, then the humane execution contained its own negation, not because the technology wouldn't always work but because sometimes it would, since a procedure that allowed one to kill without any emotion at all induced, by definition, something almost like psychosis. Leuchter himself was an illustration. It was not that he was mad or in any way unstable; it was that he'd devoted himself to the logic of killing humanely. His machines were predicated on making work as easy for executioners as possible, rendering the extinguishment of human life a question of mere engineering efficiency. Yet humans weren't machines, and acting as though they were fostered an outlook in which even Auschwitz mattered only as a technical challenge—essentially what Arendt argued about Eichmann.

That was why Leuchter seemed so odd. Others might be enthusiastic proponents of the noose or the chair, but they retained a certain queasiness about the actual act, a sense that, as Singletary had told McAndrew, 'That's some real dirty work there!' Leuchter didn't think like that. If the autopsy results showed that sufficient urine had been voided from the bladder, then there was no reason for second thoughts about the machine he'd designed. He'd ensured efficiency in the chamber and thus performed a service to society. It was an ethic calculated with a slide rule, and it meant he didn't feel that shiver, that instinctual revulsion, that the Nazi death camps induced in normal people.

In another context, a different setting, Leuchter might have been a decent man, an amiable eccentric. The problem wasn't that he was amoral per se; it was more that he possessed a morality divorced from any bigger picture, and he would not or could not trespass beyond the limits he set himself.

I was thinking about that when a cab finally came past, and I waved sufficiently frantically to induce it to stop. 'Where to, man?' The driver was black—Haitian, he said—and as we sped back to Cambridge, he told me about the indignities he'd endured sorting out his citizenship papers.

In the motels I'd stayed in, the American schizophrenia about immigrants had been perpetually startling. Each room offered the same cable channels and the same nativist blowhards railing against 'illegals' and queue-jumpers, and calling for stouter fences and more border guards. Yet the motels, like much of the country, depended on the labour of immigrants, from the maid who cleaned your room to the old man who emptied the bins—an invisible army of Spanish speakers without whom the hospitality industry couldn't function.

I said something along those lines. The driver nodded. 'These Americans wouldn't know what it was like to work like we work.' It felt good to talk about something unrelated to executions. We discussed the rallies for refugee rights in Australia and in the USA, and the weight of the last hours shifted itself slowly from my chest. We were a street away from my stop when the conversation reached its climax. 'We do all the work', the driver complained, 'and you know who benefits?'

'Who?' I was thinking of families like the Hiltons: the menial, backbreaking work of hundreds of thousands of hotel maids and cleaners funding the empty lifestyle of Paris and Nicky. But the driver had something else in mind.

'The Jews.'

'Pardon?'

'The Jews. They run this country.' The oldest hatred sat itself down beside me, grinning its death's-head grin.

The driver wasn't a fascist, nor was he necessarily a hardcore bigot. Most likely, he was just another harried immigrant, finding it easier to scapegoat someone else than to make connections across the divisions of the world. But there were questions on which you couldn't be neutral, and times at which journalistic objectivity masked a betrayal. And when you stared into the abyss, sometimes the abyss stared back at you.

12

SAD CELEBRATIONS

The sound shook me the most. Concentrating on the instructions—the firm two-handed grip, the slight forward lean, the little notch that should line up with the little bump and then with the printed ring of the target—I pressed, too gingerly, too tentatively, on the trigger. It yielded more than I expected, and without any apparent effect, so that I was half-ready to conclude that I'd committed some kind of inexplicable rookie error, when the gun exploded, not with the incidental bang you hear on a TV show, where the crack of a weapon merely complements the action taking place, but with a detonation so violent and so overwhelming that, even through the padded ear-muffs, it became instantly and unavoidably the only focus of my attention.

The first few weeks after returning to Australia, I was something of a mess. The bad dreams had begun in the USA, but now, back home, I simply didn't sleep. At three each morning, I was awake, nerves taut and mind racing, lying there until there was enough light to cease pretending and get up for the first pot of coffee. Days passed in a fog of fatigue, in which simple tasks loomed like mountain ranges, and any decisions were clouded by an amorphous dread, a perpetual sense of imminent catastrophe.

I'd been thinking about pistol shooting ever since the trip with Demetri, but like so much else, the idea had been pushed out of the way by my growing obsession with the death penalty. After talking to an executioner, I no longer really believed that handling a gun would provide any insights into killing. But what the hell—it couldn't hurt and it might be cathartic.

Holding a gun in the booth felt instantly familiar and weirdly foreign. Images of soldiers and cops and their handguns saturated the culture, and because I'd seen these weapons handled and aimed and fired a million times in film and on TV, the touch of the .22 automatic seemed right and proper. Still, the pistol surprised me with its heft: weightier and more substantial than the shadowy weapons I'd imagined since childhood. I'd assumed the guns would become at once part of my body, like the cocked fingers you aimed playing cops and robbers, but the grip the trainer wanted me to take was never quite comfortable, and he pushed my clumsy hands into a position awkward enough that its maintenance required, for a while at least, an element of conscious thought and ongoing effort. Yet the more I concentrated on holding the pistol, the more I lost track of the sight through which I was supposed to be aiming and which displayed an alarming tendency to wobble up and down, more or less uncontrollably.

Then came the noise, which astonished me, not just the first time I fired but throughout the session. We wore earmuffs; later, watching one of the others shoot, I surreptitiously lifted the padding from an ear and was rewarded with a ringing deafness lasting for several minutes. We were inside, in a concrete range that, despite the rubber sound-proofing, probably both concentrated and amplified the blast, but still, these weapons were, as the trainer explained, pretty small beer in the gun world. A few minutes with pistols crashing and you couldn't help wondering how anyone could have survived the mass artillery barrages of the Great War, bombardments during which a million or more high-explosive shells might land, each explosion infinitely more violent than the discharge of my little .22 automatic. The noise 'did not move', wrote one soldier, 'it hung over us. It seemed as though the air were full of a vast and agonised passion, bursting now with groans and sighs, shuddering beneath terrible blows.'

Nor had I expected the recoil, which, though I'd been warned, still kicked the gun back far more than I'd thought possible. Thereafter I harboured the entirely illogical fear that the muzzle might, snakelike, twist back in my direction before I pulled the trigger, sending the slug crashing back into my face. We'd been set a target close enough that we couldn't really miss, but even though my bullets mostly landed within the inner circle of the cardboard sheet, I never truly felt fully in control of the process, almost as though I were astride some half-trained horse that galloped in the direction I wanted but only for reasons of its own, entirely unrelated to my hesitant tugs at its reins.

The .32 Ruger revolver—the gun traditionally carried by Australian police—was even worse. Bigger and bulkier, the force of its recoil was such that I tensed my whole body in anticipation each time I touched the trigger. When all the bullets were gone, I realised I'd been concentrating so intently on the mechanics of firing that any broader questions about what I was actually doing—that is, propelling, at over 300 metres per second, a piece of lead designed to penetrate the human body so as to cause catastrophic injury or death—simply didn't cross my mind.

The only time during the session that any hint of violence arose was when the instructor suggested that my friend Kath should summon up some more aggression. Perhaps because she lacked a certain masculine competitiveness, she had been firing a Glock automatic rather nervously, spraying her bullets across the target. Thus admonished, she sent three or four slugs in rapid succession into the bullseye. But this was less about attacking the target and more about attacking the gun, an assertion of control over a weapon previously handled too tentatively.

Gerard, the third in our party, was a natural, the instructor said, and his target came back with holes neatly drilled through a narrow band in the centre, without the wild outliers with which we decorated ours. On the drive home, he explained. He constructed furniture as a hobby; he was accustomed to working with heavy machinery. The noise didn't bother him, he said, and he felt comfortable wearing safety goggles and earmuffs, and wielding tools that required careful handling. That was, in fact, what the gun reminded him of: a noisy and dangerous piece of equipment, a circular saw or something similar.

The point had never occurred to me, even though the shooting range nestled in between warehouses and panel beaters, and its steel and concrete shooting area recalled the small manufactory it had probably once been. It was an industrial setting, and the guns themselves, with their smoke and their noise and their recoil, belonged with the rattling and crashing machines of the factory—a place where sparks showered and steam hissed and, every so often, someone lost a hand.

Maybe that was why, as a stress-buster, it was less than successful. There wasn't much relaxation in shooting. The idea of it was fun, when you were still thinking of yourself as Dirty Harry, but after you'd become accustomed to the noise and the recoil, the whole thing became too much like work, and expending your allotted bullets almost a chore.

Certainly, the session made no difference to the obsessions I'd brought back from the USA. As soon as I got back from the range, I returned, as I'd been doing almost compulsively since meeting Leuchter, to more accounts of punishment in the pre-modern era: the French breaking wheel, in which prisoners' limbs were progressively smashed with a hammer; the stake, at which the British burned traitors or heretics; the elaborate process of hanging, drawing and quartering. These cruel ceremonies promised, I thought, though I couldn't yet articulate how, a way of understanding the strange affectlessness of the modern death chamber.

Take Robert-François Damiens, the would-be assassin of Louis XV of France, famously put to death in 1757: publicly tortured with molten pincers; burned with sulphur, boiling oil and molten wax; harnessed to horses, which attempted to pull him apart; and finally cut into pieces with knives. Next to that kind of barbarity, the claims of humanitarianism for Governor Hill's innovations became suddenly more credible.

Damiens's ordeal had been much studied, but not from the angle that interested me. I wanted to understand the contrast between Samson, the French executioner, and someone like Jerry. They worked in the same trade, but their roles seemed almost inversions of each other: Jerry's job was to send the condemned from life to death as painlessly as he could, while Samson sought the most spectacular agony possible. A botch in a modern execution meant that the inmate suffered, but Samson failed because his draught horses couldn't entirely pull Damiens apart. The modern death chamber did its work as the culmination of a long bureaucratic chain. The execution team worked anonymously and with no control over the procedure: unless something went wrong, each member of the team simply performed a discrete task that he had rehearsed many times before, a task that could not be done in any other way. For Samson, it was different. He was a public figure, the focal point in a well-attended public ceremony. Authority for the execution was direct rather than bureaucratic, and though the participants had particular functions to fulfil, these were not the interchangeable tasks of an assembly line but positions that took their meaning from the specific person who filled them, just as characters in a play depend upon the specific actors playing the roles. Most fundamentally, since the elaborate tortures depended on his unique skills, Samson exercised control in a way that someone like Jerry simply did not.

The deskilling of executioners was, in fact, even more profound than the deskilling of meatworkers. What had Bruce said, when comparing the master butchers to the labourers in a modern abattoir? They took pride in their work, he'd explained, since the end product was all theirs. Might Samson have said the same thing, once Damiens was no more? What emotions ruled a man like that as he performed his abominable deeds? Perhaps imagining that he felt pride in a job well done was going too far, but it was hard to believe he felt nothing at all. Anyway, there was no comparison between what happened in Paris in the eighteenth century and what happened in Virginia in the twenty-first. And yet ...

I'd meant to talk with Jerry about racism. Everyone knew about the racial dynamic of US capital punishment: about how death row was full of black men, about how blacks who killed whites were far more likely to receive a capital sentence than whites who killed blacks. But when I asked Jerry, he'd chuckled. The first man he'd killed, he said, had been white. 'Black or white, it don't make a difference.'

I'd dropped the subject then, but after the conversation with Leuchter, I was more curious than ever. Leuchter had shown no sign of prejudice to me, but he was still, of course, an internationally famous poster boy for murderous anti-Semites. And trying to think that through, I came across the case of Henry Smith.

In 1893, Smith had been accused of molesting and killing the daughter of a police chief in Texas. After his apprehension, he'd been seized by a mob and placed upon a carnival float—in mockery, the *New York Times* reporter explained, of a king upon his throne. Paraded through the streets before an immense crowd, Smith was eventually dragged to a 10-foot-high scaffold in the middle of town, to which he was secured with ropes. The father of the dead girl, alongside the uncle and sundry other relatives, rolled red-hot irons down Smith's stomach, back and arms, while the citizens of the town cheered his every scream and moan. He was tortured publicly for an hour or so, before his eyes were burned out, brands were thrust down his throat, and he was set on fire. This was three years after Kemmler, and yet where the newspapers had enthused over Hill's electrical humanitarianism, the press covered Smith's ordeal with something like approval. The difference? Kemmler was white and Smith was black.

Between 1890 and 1940, over three hundred black men died in public torture lynchings, alongside thousands more killed in less prolonged lynchings. These events, much closer to the ritualised cruelties inflicted on Damiens than to modern executions, took place in the same period that Governor's Hill's ideal of the humane, scientific death sentence was becoming hegemonic. That was no coincidence. The killing of Smith was deliberately atavistic. By cheering his agonies, the Texas crowds affirmed the values that they saw as under threat in a changing world: most obviously, an explicitly racial system of justice. Seeking overt revenge, deliberately causing spectacular pain, they burned the values of an idealised past onto Smith's body, in self-conscious opposition to the modern court system and its commitment to bloodless, humane and impersonal justice. Such unspeakable Grand Guignol performances took place predominantly in the South, in the states that carry out the overwhelming majority of capital sentences today. Texas, the scene of Smith's ordeal, remained, as I'd repeatedly discovered, the place to which novice executioners journeyed to learn their trade.

Did that mean, as was sometimes argued, that the death penalty was nothing more than a legal lynching? Certainly, the demagoguery that assured the continuation of capital punishment in the USA tapped into the same social forces manifested in a lynching. McAndrew had described executions as theatre for the governor. Sending a criminal to their death inevitably produced drama, so when politicians signed execution warrants, they were ostentatiously signalling an allegiance to traditional values, particularly on race. Just as they had in the past, executions provided miniature passion plays, through which populists could demonstrate their commonsense opposition to the bloodless liberalism of Washington: *Why should we house and feed killers on the taxpayer's dollar? Ordinary punishments are too good for these monsters. They need to be taught a lesson. Make them suffer just as the victim did.* Behind this rhetoric, behind the tabloid fascination with the final moments of inmates, and the pro-death vigils outside the prison gates, you could detect the same impulses that led a crowd to watch Smith shriek and moan.

But modern executions were not lynchings. If anything, they were anti-lynchings, for they radically reversed content and form.

Popular enthusiasm for the death penalty might be implicitly directed against people of colour, but even in the Deep South the actual rules governing capital sentences were scrupulously non-racialised. While politicians and shock jocks might talk of stringing killers from the nearest tree, the procedures for executions remained fussily bureaucratic. Lynchings took place according to customs rather than rules, but death sentences involved an almost autistic concern for the letter of the law. Despite what Leuchter said about 'capital torture', Jack Pursley had never subjected condemned men to anything like what Smith had experienced. In fact, like every other contemporary executioner, he'd done everything he could to make the procedure both pain-free and antiseptic. The sentiments informing Texas's defiant enthusiasm for capital punishment might not have changed, but the actual executions were entirely different, far more Governor Hill than Samson of Paris.

Robert Johnson had given me a perfect illustration of this weird inversion and its consequences when, a few days after our conversation, he'd emailed me a poem he'd written after witnessing a last supper on death row:

A fried steak, diced into little squares,
arrives at the death house,
neatly reassembled, like a puzzle,
laid to rest in the center berth
of a standard white Styrofoam box,
bordered on one side by soggy, sagging fries,
on the other by wilted greens, curled and brown,
long past their salad days, like the man himself,
who ordered this meal as the sad celebration,
culmination, of a dreary, wasted life
that is even now slipping away,
as he ages before our eyes right there in his cell,
called the 'last night cell' in some prisons,
'the death cell' in this one.

The final meal was an age-old gallows custom, another manifestation of the carnivalesque tradition invoked by that Texas crowd when they hoisted Henry Smith into a float and crowned him their king. In pre-modern executions, the condemned man's final feast was part of the ritual whereby all the participants in the killing made meaning out of what was taking place—in some traditions, the executioner would even break bread with his victim.

But Johnson's poem documents how, in a modern prison, the last supper no longer represents, as it once might have, a Bacchanalian leave-taking from the pleasures of the flesh but comes instead pre-packaged and plastic, served up as if from a fast-food restaurant. The prisoner chooses his menu, but his choices don't underscore his individuality so much as emphasise his disposability: the inmate will also, Johnson says, be 'boxed without frills in a plywood coffin/the mortuary's answer to the Styrofoam box'.

What interested me most were the lines on how this McDonaldised killing directly diminished the prison staff. In a later verse, Johnson writes:

We look at each other tentatively, almost furtively,
Lawyers, chaplains, even officers speaking in low tones,
Words directed toward the ground,
As if we are greasy, dirty, our mouths dry,
Tongues swollen, sticking to our teeth...

A pre-modern execution—or, indeed, a lynching—used violence to bring the participants together, with the pain inflicted on the transgressor bonding the rest of the community. The crowd watching Jack Napoleon Tunermenerwail and Robert Smallboy hang in Melbourne in 1842 shouted and laughed; so, too, did those at Smith's death. The killings were ventings: they purged the community of wrongdoers and the racially impure, and in their deaths the onlookers became one. In its modern incarnation, though, the ancient ceremony of the final meal passed in uncomfortable, foot-shuffling silence, and the lawyers, the chaplains and the guards came away feeling more rather than less isolated. They were awkward, unable to speak except in whispers, and they felt greasy and dirty and uncertain.

I could see why, in a contemporary execution, any divergence from routine caused so much distress. In a bureaucratic procedure, no one was responsible and everyone, including the killer and the victim, became object rather than subject. Even the slightest variation threw that schema out of whack, confronting the executioner simultaneously with humanity and with responsibility. When the business went smoothly, the problem was different but related. A successful execution was a relationship between things—and things didn't have relationships. That was why the last meal was so utterly empty.

Suddenly, I felt greasy and dirty myself, and I laid down Johnson's poem on the table with an overwhelming sense of shame, as if I'd been caught prying into something private. All of this was supposed to be an analogy for war. But how? The head from Gallipoli had seemed, at first, such a straightforward thing. There was a mystery, sure, but a simple mystery, a puzzle to be resolved by just the kind of historical detective work that made archival investigations so addictive. But that story came to an abrupt end—or, rather, the expected narrow path opened up into a broad one, and it was no longer clear which way to go. I felt lost and uncertain and very, very tired, sick of wandering the intricate cruelties of capital punishment as a tourist of other people's pain. The pornographic power of suffering—the way that these accounts both disturbed and fascinated—had been proven by nowthatsfuckedup.com. I'd thought I was above all that: not a voyeur but a researcher. Now I wondered whether that distinction held.

It wasn't simply that I didn't seem to be making progress. It was also that, these days, the papers and the TV news left you more convinced that the wars could sputter on indefinitely, like the dull ache of a bone fracture. The new Rudd government no longer showed enthusiasm for Iraq, but nor did it campaign against it with any conviction. Iraq had become another Gaza, a running sore that would never heal but, with the US death toll falling, didn't bleed sufficiently to make the front pages very often. And Afghanistan had, without anyone noticing, somehow transformed into another Iraq.

I still didn't really know what I'd learnt about the death penalty or, for that matter, animal killing. But I realised, only a month or so after returning to Australia, that it wasn't important. I no longer wanted analogies. I wanted to talk to soldiers themselves, to hear their thoughts on what they'd done. I put away the texts on executions and started making the arrangements.

13

KNOWN AS KILLERS

'The first time I fired my rifle at a human being was 23 December 2004. I got trapped in a house, me and my squad. You know about that?' I knew about that. The savage combat through which Jeremiah Workman had earned his Navy Cross had been chronicled in detail in the *Washington Post*: three hours battling on the second floor of a Fallujah building, in an engagement that began with an insurgent ambush and ended with an M1A1 tank destroying the entire house and everyone in it. During the encounter, Workman personally killed more than twenty insurgents with grenades and small-arm fire. I also knew something of the second battle of Fallujah and the carnage that had ensued there, with house-to-house fighting reminiscent of Stalingrad. It sounded utterly horrific.

Before that, Workman explained, he'd led a squad in a mortar platoon. Their rounds killed plenty of insurgents, he said, but not up close. The Fallujah ambush was different. 'Well, a lot of people ask: do I have what it takes to pull the trigger and kill another human being? But when you're watching your buddies being shot … it was easy for me. Once I started on that trigger, I didn't want to stop. I never felt weird during that firefight until I put my rifle down to throw a grenade and then I felt naked because I wasn't firing. Never once did it cross my mind that this was a father, this was a brother, that I was killing.'

It had taken months to get back to Virginia—scraping more money together, finding a way to delegate my responsibilities at *Overland* to my longsuffering co-workers—but even just making the decision to go left me feeling appreciably better. At least I was doing something, and the organisational intricacies kept my mind away from the grim places it had been loitering.

As well as the veterans themselves, I wanted to see Dave Grossman, not simply because his theories remained the most systemic account of killing I'd found, but also because their implicit optimism, their assertion of a human distaste for violence, seemed more and more valuable. Grossman operated an organisation with the unfortunate name of the Killology Research Institute. While the secretary there was unfailingly polite, her answer never varied: Lieutenant Colonel Grossman wasn't giving interviews. He was concentrating on his training commitments and his research; he didn't have time to spare. Despite pleas about his importance to my work, she remained adamant. The lieutenant colonel was flattered by the interest, but unfortunately it was not possible.

The institute website displayed Grossman's booking calendar, with all of his speaking engagements in army bases and police colleges listed for months to come. The Killology Research Institute seemed, in fact, to be booming, and that, I realised, was the solution. Grossman was due to deliver a day-long seminar entitled 'On Killing' at the Northern Virginia Criminal Justice Training Academy, a kind of university for cops. The organisers, rather to my surprise, had no objection to me attending. It wasn't exactly what I'd had in mind, but it would do: I'd hear Grossman lecturing about killing to a room full of Virginian police.

When it came to the plane trip, I'd learnt my lesson. Leaving the more overt killing literature behind, I took as my reading Siegfried Sassoon's two classic novels of the Great War, *Memoirs of a Fox*

Hunting Man and *Memoirs of an Infantry Officer*, both sufficiently canonical, I thought, not to repel any fellow travellers. In any case, despite his reputation as a war writer, Sassoon's prose lingered not on violence but on rural England, in an elegy for the childhood destroyed by the mechanised carnage of war. In *Memoirs of a Fox Hunting Man*, the narrator is solemnly told to do everything in his power to eliminate the barbed wire springing up around the village—the most dangerous enemy of the hunting man. It's meant literally, of course, but all of Sassoon can be found in that central opposition of the new century of wire and tanks and poison gas contrasted with the old century of village cricket and chestnut geldings and blacksmiths with cloth caps.

Washington Dulles International Airport was most definitely no place for a fox-hunting man. It had been winter during the last trip, but now summer had come, and everywhere the concrete shimmered with heat and fumes. That week, oil prices in the USA had reached an all-time high, and every cab driver muttered that things could not go on like this.

I understood what they meant. The oil profligacy struck you everywhere you went, like the arctic blast from your hotel room, where the airconditioner had been running all day to keep an empty bedroom cool. On cable TV, the pundits worked themselves into their habitual vein-popping fury, but their only proposals were for offshore drilling, and that seemed more like a pre-emptive strike on the environment than an appreciable change to the economics of the industry. And outside, on the five-lane freeway near my window, the muscled-up SUVs charged past in their thousands, each super-powered vehicle blithely transporting its single occupant.

Though Jeremiah Workman was still in the armed forces, he wasn't in uniform. But he looked unmistakeably the soldier. It was not just the buzz cut and the tattooed weightlifter's biceps emerging from his casual shirt. It wasn't even the square jaw, the kind of stone-hammered profile you found on recruitment posters, that gave him away. It was his intensity, the fixed, Alpha-male gaze he maintained as he spoke.

Workman grew up in a little town in Ohio, where both his parents worked in factories. He'd been a football player in high school. His father had been in the army; his grandfather, too. He'd wanted to join the state troopers, and he'd become a marine to fill in time between leaving school and reaching the mandatory age of twenty-one.

On killing, he was characteristically blunt: 'Yes, you do get trained to kill. Especially in the Marine Corps—I mean, we're known as killers. They talk about that from day one. In boot camp, the drill sergeants would say to the weak recruits, the ones who weren't keeping up with the pack: the American taxpayers sent you to us to protect the nation. You're supposed to go out and kill bad guys—and this is how you are. What they're basically doing is tearing you down, taking the individual out of each person and building us up as a team. It instils confidence and discipline, and so when you leave, you do think that you're a trained killer. Bayonet, rifle, hand-to-hand combat: whatever.'

The obvious way to reach Iraq veterans was through their organisations. These, however, were deeply divided. Traditionally, returned soldiers skewed rightwards, but the deep unpopularity of the Iraq invasion had changed that, and alongside very conservative organisations such as Workman's Veterans for Freedom (VFF), there were now quite radical groups: most notably, Iraq Veterans against the War (IVAW).

Interestingly, the Left/Right distinction in the veterans' groups pertained not just to the ethics of the war but also to the fighting of it. So, when IVAW held their Winter Soldier event—modelled on the famous Vietnam-era conference—many of the speakers directly addressed the question of violence: talking about what they'd done but also talking about what their deeds had done to them. The sessions were all available on YouTube, where you could watch, for instance, Jon Michael Turner, a former marine, describe receiving the personal congratulations of his company commander for his first kill, and how he'd tattooed 'fuck you' in Arabic on what he called his choking arm. Turner began his speech by throwing away his medals with the words 'I don't work for you no more'; he ended with the declaration: 'I am sorry for the things that I did. I am no longer the monster that I once was.'

VFF also hosted an event at which its members told their stories. The speakers on the National Heroes' Tour, one of whom was Jeremiah Workman, characterised Operation Iraqi Freedom as necessary, justified and successful, but the speakers also, either explicitly or implicitly, described military service—and sometimes combat itself— as character-forming rather than corrosive.

Back in Australia, I'd been in contact with one of VFF's founders, David Bellavia. Like Workman, Bellavia was a Fallujah veteran, and he, too, had a heroic reputation, single-handedly storming a building full of insurgents and then, when he ran out of ammunition, killing the last Iraqi with his pocketknife. After that, he'd become a high-profile media commentator on military matters, repeating VFF's hawkish talking points with the authority of a decorated soldier: the war was necessary; it was going well; troop morale was high; the liberal media did not tell the truth. Our emails had been very cordial—until I arrived in the USA, and then he stopped responding.

Workman was undoubtedly conservative, too, yet he didn't seem overtly political—at least, not in the sense of wanting to debate geo-strategy or, say, the relationship between the Iraq war and the USA's Middle Eastern presence more generally. His was an over-whelmingly physical presence, a straightforward Americanism: an acceptance of the flag and the president and the war he'd been ordered to fight. He wasn't, he said, a Bible-thumper, and he didn't go to church each Sunday, but, yes, he believed in Jesus—of course he did. The people he'd fought were 'bad guys'; the world was a better place without them.

I asked him what it had been like the first time he'd killed an insurgent. Had he felt like he'd crossed any kind of barrier?

He growled a deep, rumbling affirmation, like a cartoon bear. 'Yeah. After that day, I went back and thought to myself, damn: I shot a lot of rounds and went through a lot of magazines and threw a lot of grenades, and there are people who harm one person back in the United States and they go to prison for the rest of their lives. But here, clearing this whole house out ...' He shook his head, in wonderment. 'Never once did I think, wow, I'm a bad person, gloom and doom, anything like that. But it was like, holy shit, I just shot another human being!'

If not doom or gloom, what were his emotions?

'Once you kill that first person, it's like deer-hunting. You know how some guys, when they fish and hunt, they catch a big fish, kill a big deer, and they mount them on their wall?' I nodded, although, in reality, I didn't actually know any people who put animal heads on their walls, which was probably one of the differences between us. I couldn't imagine Workman needing any special expedition to analyse kangaroo-shooting. 'That's like how it was in Fallujah. It turned into almost a sport. There was no feeling of, holy cow, we just killed a guy; it was more high fives, there's another one gone. That was the only... I hate to say that we rejoiced and we were happy, but that's kinda ... it's a game. We lost three marines in the house that day, and I had a lot of emotions about them. But there was definitely no pouting or boohooing about killing. Even to this day, I wish the hell that we could have killed more of them—rid the world of these people.'

I asked whether he knew anyone else who'd felt any resistance to killing.

'Do you mean like they had a hard time doing it or something?' Yes.

'Nuh-uh.' Then he corrected himself. 'I only knew one guy—and I can't even remember his name—but when we were in Iraq, he would tell people that Iraqi children were coming to his bedside at night in his sleep telling him that he was a killer and he was killing innocent people and things like that.' He laughed. 'But we thought he was just saying that to get out of there. I've never met anybody who said, man, sometimes I sit around thinking about that sniper who was trying to kill me.'

Partly, he suggested, that was because of the nature of the particular war being fought in Iraq. 'Sometimes I've stopped and thought: would I still have the same thirst to kill these people if they were uniformed, and followed the Geneva conventions? In Iraq, you obeyed the rules of engagement, but if you had the chance to kill somebody, you killed them. Whereas if it was a respectable fighting force, like in the Second World War, you'd be more apt to take somebody prisoner rather than pulling the trigger on them. But with those guys over there, if you know anything about their religion and what they're trying to do in this world, there's a very simple solution—kill them.'

Had it been suggested to him, beforehand, that there might be anything traumatic about killing?

He gave one of his growling laughs. 'No, not at all. The drill instructors, the people who teach you bayonet techniques and close combat: it's go get 'em, get 'em, get 'em. Once you get one, you move on to the next one. The instructors never sit down with you and say, look, you've done all the attacking and you killed ten bad guys, and now what?' Still, he wasn't overly concerned about that absence. Recruit training was not, he said, about psychology. It was about training marines, giving them the tools they needed to get on with their job.

We talked then about combat. 'It's hard to describe. My heart would start beating so fast, and my adrenalin would start pumping, flooding my body so much that it had a reverse effect on me, it drained me, to the point of being nauseous, every little thing …' He fell silent for an instant and then resumed. 'It wasn't something I expected. Up to that point, the closest thing to combat that I'd ever seen was hand-to-hand combat in boot camp with other recruits, and my adrenalin pumped then—just like when I was in high school, playing football. But this … it takes your body over, to the point of making you sick to your stomach.

'It is addictive. I tell people now that I love living life on the edge. Once you've been to that point, it takes a lot to get your body there again, and I think you're constantly looking to do it. For me, when I came back, I bought a motorcycle, just to get out on the high-way and to go 150 miles per hour and get my adrenalin going.'

'Do you get used to it in any way?'

'Nah, you don't … I didn't get used to it. I don't think you ever get used to people trying to kill you.'

Then he said something that unexpectedly brought the Gallipoli head back into frame. I'd asked a question about exposure to violence and whether it brought with it a desensitisation. He growled in the affirmative again. 'Yeah. Here's an example. When I came home, I had a bunch of pictures and stuff on my computer. Insurgents, you know, with bad wounds. I'm talking legs, arms—bloody, gory stuff. I pop my computer open and sit down with my wife and start showing these to her, and I'm like, laughing, as I'm showing her the pictures, and she's sitting there in sheer horror. And I'm like, what's wrong?' He laughed, and I laughed, too, because although this young man was so big and demonstrably deadly, there was still, it seemed, a naivety in him, and the picture of him unthinkingly showing his wife a laptop horror show and genuinely not anticipating her reaction seemed instantly plausible and not a little comic. But, of course, in another sense, it wasn't funny at all. The dead men on his laptop had been people, too, as human as the Gallipoli head. They weren't just props in someone else's anecdote.

I was back where I'd started. Workman hadn't taken an actual body part, but then modern electronics made that unnecessary, since the camera gave you an instant, permanent representation of your enemy's crumpled form. Surely it was the same. Here was the chance, then, to ask him why he'd taken the photo, to find out what that kind of souveniring meant.

The problem was that he didn't know. He shrugged his big shoulders. 'To me, those kinds of things were just, like, normal.'

We were sitting outside at a wire mesh table. Three young girls drank Cokes nearby, giggling as they compared text messages. The traffic surged past, and men in suits walked by with iPhones on their ears. The house-to-house combat of Fallujah seemed frankly incredible, a tale from the Dark Ages. He thought so, too. 'The amount of dead bodies that I saw ...' he mused, and then he looked over at the table opposite and lowered his voice. 'It's weird. We're sitting here, normal, but you get on a plane, you get off and you're in a combat zone. It's seems like right around the corner that these things are going on.'

When he came back, he'd been diagnosed with post-traumatic stress disorder. 'Solely because of the marines that I lost', he added, in case there might be any misunderstanding. 'Nothing to do with the people that I had to kill. It was in December when I lost my guys, and I didn't leave Iraq until April. Didn't have any symptoms; I didn't think anything was wrong. I came back; I started drinking real heavy. We talked before about being on the razor's edge; well, I just started doing things to give me the same excitement ... Then my father-in-law flew up to California to visit, and I went to pick him up in the airport, and I popped the trunk on my car to put his luggage in and it was just full of empty liquor bottles, and I, like, took the luggage and slammed it in there and tried to shut the trunk, and it won't shut. I was, like, jumping on the luggage, and he looked at me: you think you might have a problem?'

Had he been prepared for anything like that before he came back?

'Before you leave the country and again, when you get back, you do a lot of suicide training, talking with the chaplain and things like that. They can't sit everybody down and say, look, you've been a killing machine for seven months, but now we're going back to the States, so don't kill nobody. It's not like that. They would never be able to go through all the battalion, for a start—you've got a thousand marines there. So as far as making the transition from, wow, a week ago people were shooting at me, you kinda just figure it out on your own.'

But the biggest issue he was facing was anger. 'I avoid conflict at all costs now, so I'm not forced into that situation, because when I feel threatened … it's normal for me to neutralise the threat. Even just a simple scuffle in a bar or a disagreement at a restaurant. Because I don't want to end up in a conflict situation, because I know what I'm capable of, and once you do it once, you know … I know that I have an issue with that. Am I different now? Oh, yeah. Definitely. Definitely different now from when I went over there. I'm hyper-vigilant; I just get angry easy, you know. It's hard to deal with it here, because over there, the threat arises and you neutralise it and that's it. Your mind … you can breathe again: the guy who was trying to hurt you is no longer on this planet.' Another chuckle. 'Here, you have to find ways to live with people and to deal with it. If you've got somebody you can't stand working with, guess what? He's here; you work with him; you gotta deal with it. That's been tough for me.'

It sounded, I suggested, like life over there was simpler. 'Yeah. Oh, yeah. Just about anyone you talk to—marines—that have been over there, they want to go back. It's very dangerous, but life is so simple. You wake up; you're given a set of instructions—patrol this road, locate roadside bombs—and if you find anybody out there who appears to be planting the things, neutralise them. It's a simple way to live. It's instant gratification. It's not like the guy's going to death row and he's going to have fifteen years' worth of appeals and wasting taxpayers' money and everything; it's instant. The guy's gone. And you know that you just personally did your part to rid the world of evil. So it is kinda like … you just feel like you're doing something, doing your part.

'In that one house, with that many insurgents killed, I had visual proof, instant gratification: damn, we just put a hurt on those guys. And I tell people all the time, nothing I do from this point on in my life is ever going to compare. Ever. I do a lot of panel discussions and things, and I tell people, I could win the lottery today, have two hundred million dollars, have fast cars, mansions, you name it, and still, it's not going to compare to that feeling of leading marines, other human beings, into combat and doing what we did there.

'It's almost like I'm going through the motions now for the rest of my life. It's a hundred per cent true. If I went out today and became a doctor, a chemist, and found the cure for cancer, I mean, nothing … I can't see anything that will ever compare to that feeling of leading marines in combat and ridding the world of evil. I was young: I was twenty-one years old. The thought of them having that much trust and confidence in me: I mean, what other job here in the United States are you trusted with life-and-death decisions on a daily basis, where the decisions you make could end up getting people in body bags? What else could compare to that?'

As we shook hands and parted, I still had the afternoon free to spend in Arlington before flying out the next day to meet with some-one from IVAW. The obvious place to visit was the Arlington Cemetery, but I'd heard how big it was and didn't think there'd be time. So instead I wandered the city streets, more or less randomly.

Arlington was prosperous, without the panhandlers or the home-less that you encountered elsewhere. The shops were full, the pedes-trians well dressed, the roads crowded with new cars. There was a big military presence because of nearby bases, but still, the war seemed no closer than in Melbourne.

There'd been no self-pity in anything Workman had told me. If anything, he'd wanted to stress the value of what he'd been through. Still, his sense that his life now would be simply a coda to those few hours in Fallujah, and that only alcohol or deliberate risk replicated the luminosity of combat, seemed almost unbearably poignant. The man was only twenty-four, after all.

Of course, I'd just read something very similar. 'For me,' Sassoon had said, 'the idea of death made everything seem vivid and valuable. The War could be like that to a man, until it drove him to drink and suffocated his finer apprehensions.' So how common was that?

14

THE ANATOMY OF A KILL

'The weight of knowing that you've killed another person: it's heavy. I've seen guys lose religion over it, and I've seen guys gain religion over it. Especially if you are certain—if you are *certain*—that you killed someone. I know the guys that I hit with my sniper rifle. I've shot guys with my M4; I've shot guys with an M60; I've shot guys with a 50 calibre machine gun that I *know*. People I watched die, I watched them get hit by my round and go down.'

From the air, Colorado Springs looked gorgeous, with rumpled mountains extending to the horizon. From the ground, it was the same as everywhere else: another budget room on a flat highway surrounded by nothing. I knew intellectually that there was another America, an America of scenic walks and quirky neighbourhoods and restaurants that weren't fast-food chains, an America where different cities showed distinctive personalities, with cafés and galleries and alleyways away from the arterial roads and the airports. There was such a place, but not for me, not on a trip like this, with a schedule even tighter than last time, and with each interview rolling inexorably into the next one. My America consisted of powdered coffee creamer and early morning taxi rides on the way to ask complete strangers about who they'd killed and how they felt about it.

Here, it was Garrett Reppenhagen. He worked for a group called Veterans for America; he was also a leading member of Iraq Veterans against the War (IVAW). Veterans for America was an advocacy organisation, helping returned soldiers with their rights and benefits. IVAW, founded in 2004 and with members in forty-eight states, was more directly political. It advocated an immediate withdrawal from Iraq as well as the payment of reparations for the damage caused by the occupation.

The leftish program accompanied a far more grassroots structure than that of Veterans for Freedom (VFF). When I'd contacted VFF, I'd gone through a secretary in an office somewhere, but chasing down members of IVAW involved a far more ad hoc process of hunting up email addresses and mobile numbers. It eventually gave me far more contacts, but it also contributed to this ridiculous schedule, since the veterans were scattered around the country. I was due in Grossman's seminar in a couple of days, so I'd be heading back to Arlington from Colorado Springs almost as soon as I arrived.

Reppenhagen nominated a pizza and pasta place on North Tejon Street late one Saturday afternoon. I knew the city was ringed by military bases—Fort Carson, Peterson Air Force Base, Schriever Air Force Base, United States Air Force Academy—and I'd expected to find another Jeremiah Workman, all square jaw and buzz cut. But Reppenhagen wasn't like that at all. He had tattoos, too, but with his stubbly beard and Loved Ones T-shirt, he seemed less like a soldier than the bass player from some hardcore band. Ordering a beer with his pizza, he looked and talked like anyone you'd meet in an inner-city pub in Melbourne. Here, though, we weren't speaking about gigs or girls or the state of the scene. We were discussing his career as a sniper in Baquaba, Iraq.

'My dad was a Vietnam veteran: served for twenty years and died the year he retired from Agent Orange–related cancer. So I never wanted to join the army. But I dropped out of high school, started working job to job, and so, by about my mid-twenties, I was like, I gotta do something to get into college or else I may as well just trade my life out. I knew I had to sacrifice, and I figured the biggest sacrifice would be to do something I told myself I would never do: join the army. So I did.' He grinned, rueful. 'It was a month before September 11.'

Reppenhagen had read Grossman's *On Killing* and knew where my questions were coming from. But he said at once that he'd never encountered any resistance to killing. 'You're so afraid of the enemy that you just toughen up and shoot to kill. Most of the guys I was with, no matter how incapable they seemed, when they were in a firefight, they were putting rounds down range. They were trying to kill.'

The only reluctance he'd felt had been political, a reflection of his views on the war rather than any innate or biological resistance. On the way to deploy, he'd gone drinking in Germany with members of the punk band the Bouncing Souls. They'd encouraged him to send emails of his wartime experiences, which had then been posted on the band website. The feedback his correspondence from Iraq received—especially when he and some other soldiers established their own site—encouraged him to think more about what he was doing, and his changing ideas eventually brought him into conflict with his officers. 'I started being sympathetic to the anti-war movement. I was thinking: this is retarded. These guys are trying to kill us because we raided their house the other night. They don't hate Americans; they just hate us being here right now.'

That attitude made killing harder. But he still did it. 'I realised that the people we were fighting were just the resistance against the occupation of their country. So I felt really bad when I killed them. But I never hesitated. When they were firing at me, I fired at them. I was on the red team; they were on the blue team. I wasn't going to go home dead, and the friends that I'd been serving with for the last three years were not going home dead, and that meant that this guy who I didn't know was, unfortunately, going to die. That was the way I put it to myself. When I was a sniper on sniper missions, it was much harder. I had to really convince myself that a person—who mostly didn't even know I was there—was trying to hurt my friends, so if I didn't kill him he was going to kill my friends or me. But it was a lot more difficult.'

I knew something about the snipers of the Great War and the peculiar stresses they'd come under. When the famous Australian marksman Billy Sing had first been appointed, an officer asked him whether he was sure he wanted the job, in a variant of the conversation McAndrew had before transferring to Florida, and for precisely the same reason. Sniping seemed a little like an execution: you were killing a man in cold blood, a man you could see talking and laughing, up close in your telegraphic sites. Sing's comrades nicknamed him 'the Murderer', a designation that hinted at the ambiguity of his profession.

In sniper training, Reppenhagen had gone through a course entitled 'The Anatomy of a Kill'. 'It was about what bullets do to people. How they tumble through the body, what kind of damage they do, the difference between soft organs and hard organs, what happens when the bullet hits what, how to deploy the round earlier so it pulls earlier and does more damage.'

Yet when I'd first asked about whether the army talked about killing, he'd said no and then yes, and then he'd laughed. 'We were trained how to do it—but we were never trained what to do afterwards.' The attitude to mental trauma was, he said, still very backward. In his thirteen weeks of training with the cavalry scouts, a particular recruit couldn't cope psychologically—and so he became the favoured target of the drill sergeants. 'They took his shoe laces away; they took his belt away, and they put a big orange vest on him with the letters LOS. That meant nobody could ever let him leave their line of sight. He had to be watched, twenty-four hours a day, because he was thought to be a suicide risk. It wasn't to make him feel better; it wasn't to get him the help that he needed or to make sure that he would come around and rejoin the unit. It was to make going down that road of mental illness so awful that no one else would want to follow. Instead of having courses where they say: "Yeah, you'll be in combat and you might see some horrible shit; your buddy might die next to you; you might take a civilian life, and this is what you're going to feel and this is how you're going to deal with it", their message was: "Don't let mental illness happen to you, because if you do, we're gonna make an example of you and you're not going to like it." It was, like, suck it up, drink a beer, do whatever you have to do—and don't show anyone that you have a problem. And everyone said, roger, we got it. We got the message.'

The trophy-taking, the death porn: what did he think was behind that?

'People want to prove that they were there, that they did the thing, you know. But I didn't see that much of it. Nothing at all with the sniper team. With the scouts, a few of the guys got little things, and I guess there were a couple who took photos of corpses, though nothing where they posed with them or any sick shit like that. We had to take photos of bodies for military intelligence, and some of the guys would download copies before they turned in the cameras. Since then, though, I've tried to find some of those pictures for journalists, and almost all of my friends—the scouts that are out now—destroyed them, got rid of them, erased them, burned them. It was something that they weren't too proud about after coming home.'

But then, in response to Workman's laptop photos, he told another story. Snipers were trained to shoot for the triangle of death. 'The triangle of death', he explained, 'is the area right around the nose and mouth. If you aim there, you are supposed to sever the spinal cord, and then the body can't operate, so that even if they want to pull the trigger, they can't. In a perfect shot, that's where you're supposed to hit.' Theoretically, sniping was supposed to be a matter of clinical, dispassionate killing. 'Even when we were in Iraq, killing Iraqis, it was target one, target two. Target one's on the left; target two's on the right. OK, scan target one. Target one's down. Scan target two. Fire. Target two's down. That's it. They're just targets; you try to convince yourself of that.' Imagining a man purely as a target was not easy when you had to aim specifically at him and fire and then watch him fall over, screaming and arching his back in agony, which was what happened with some of the men Reppenhagen killed.

But much of the time, one-on-one sniping—what he called 'doing it by the book'—gave way to massive, brute firepower. 'When we got in theatre, we tried to, you know, take one shot, hope to kill the guy. But sometimes you hit him and he doesn't die. Sometimes you miss him. So we started setting up 240 Bravos and M16s or M4s. The sniper takes his shot and, as soon as he fires, everybody else'—he made the rata-tat-tat sound of a machine gun—'opens up and takes the guy out. We stopped getting all fancy about it and just tore them up.'

Hence the photo: 'I had one 500-metre shot where I was actually shooting for the guy's chest area but hit him right in the chin—a perfect shot. I'd sometimes show the photo, and say this is exactly where you're supposed to hit if you're a sniper. I'd tell them about the triangle of death and I'd get what the Vet for Freedom guy said, that "OK, let's move on" look.'

Combat had changed Reppenhagen, too, though not, he said, at his core. 'Nobody comes out of that experience and says, yeah, I'm exactly the same dude. I think the fundamentals are the same, but it's changed part of me, definitely.'

What were his feelings in combat?

'So much goes through your mind. I mean, I remember I was afraid to let everybody else down. So I just kept going; I didn't want to be that guy who just couldn't do it, who dropped his end so that somebody else got hurt. There's frustration and anger, from being shot at, knowing someone is trying to kill you. And there's fear. Tons of fear. I've been in firefights where the guy in front is laughing hysterically and the guy behind me is crying, bawling his eyes out. I think soldiers have a dark sense of humour to process these extreme situations; everybody laughs about everything, even when awful things have happened. I've never felt more alive than after a firefight.'

I wondered if he felt the addictiveness Workman had mentioned. 'Oh, definitely. There's a lot of my friends that are just completely addicted to it, and want to go back. All they understand is that the feeling they had there, they don't get it when they're sitting in a

restaurant ordering beers or standing in line in a Starbucks or working at a 7-Eleven. They say: I've changed; the only thing I understand
is over there. I hate it, but I'm still going back. And I can understand
a little bit of what they mean.'

I quoted him Workman's comparison of combat with peacetime.
He frowned. 'I can agree with his words but probably not the sentiment behind them. He's probably talking about single-handedly
saving America, keeping his friends and family safe from the evil
terrorists. But then, if that's what he means, you can see why he thinks
like that. I mean, we've taken human lives. That is a significant
burden to carry. And it would be almost better if soldiers could convince themselves about the nobility of the cause, because perhaps then
they wouldn't kill themselves in the same numbers that they do now.'

The numbers were indeed astonishing. According to one count,
eighteen US veterans killed themselves every day. In California alone,
more than 650 veterans committed suicide in 2006, with returned
soldiers comprising over 20 per cent of the suicides in the state that
year. 'That's why, when I go to Walter Reed veterans' hospital to talk
to soldiers, some of them—most of them—hold onto a belief that
they've sacrificed for a good cause. Because that's what they have to
do to convince themselves that they weren't fucking shammed, that
they didn't lose a leg or lose their sanity, lose their innocence on
some fucking bullshit lie.'

He took another slug of beer and then continued. 'But, you
know, there's the other side of the coin, with those people who do
start questioning what it was about. They have to take on responsibility, take responsibility for having killed for a lie, which is why
quite a lot become political activists. We're mobilised by the demons
that we feel. That pressure that comes from having done something
so horrible—people feel like they need some sort of atonement. I
know a lot of my veteran friends are trying to … well, they feel like
criminals. They come back and everybody treats them like heroes,
but they feel like they're criminals, that they're getting away with a
crime, and that there's been no judgement and no absolution for

what they've done. If you had committed murder, you'd get put away in prison, and then when you got out, you could say, alright, I did my time; I paid a price for what I did, and now I can move on. But it's not like that for these guys. That's why, for many, joining the movement is so important: they won't quit; they don't sleep; all they do is organise. I know a lot of veterans who aren't even political who go just full-blown with veterans' issues to try to help veterans, and they're driven by that same thing: I've got to do something good; I've got to give back.

'At night, I often go through a lot of what-if scenarios. Sometimes, I'm thinking that I should go back to Iraq, because I could do it better, you know, because I understand it. We've got a couple of nineteen-year-old kids in the active duty section of IVAW ready to deploy for the first time this Christmas. Shit, back in September 11, they were fucking babies! I feel like saying: this isn't your war; it's not a burden on you; at least let people my age or older fight it, people who have already been there once or twice.

'You know, they say that guys supposedly think about sex, like, a certain number of seconds in a minute. For me, the rest of the time, I'm thinking about the war. Do I want to go back? No, I'd never choose to go back. But is there a portion, little desires here and there? Yeah, sure. I think there is. I think there is. While I was there, I experienced the ultimate highs as well as the ultimate lows.'

15

WOLVES AND SHEEP

'd called my avatar Buttercup: in a game so relentlessly macho, you took your laughs where you found them. Buttercup stood beside a trestle loaded with digitalised guns and digitalised ammunition while Major Amerine yelled at him. 'This is a live fire exercise, soldier. Listen up to my commands. You're going to execute MOUT— Military Operations in Urban Terrain. Please set up an M4 carbine or an M9 pistol.' We were undergoing, in virtual form, the realism training by which the army had suppressed the resistance to killing identified by SLA Marshall. 'At this time, pick up your weapons and ammo and range walk to the front door of the shoot house.'

I was back in Arlington. Dave Grossman's seminar wasn't until the next morning, and I'd vaguely contemplated going out to see something of the city. But there was something I needed to do first.

In his books, Grossman accuses the media in general, and computer games in particular, of fostering lethal violence, using exactly the same mechanisms as the army uses to train its soldiers. The conditioning that induces recruits to fire relies on realism, a constant rehearsal of the movements required for combat until they become reflexes strong enough to override the natural reluctance to kill. Teenagers who spend hours aiming and firing in a first-person

199

shooter game are, the argument goes, doing the same thing: the screen flashes a target, they pull the trigger and the target falls. Interactive video games are thus, he says, identical to the pop-up trainers used by modern armies, except that the adolescents who practise with them aren't subject to the discipline that controls the lethality of soldiers.

The ubiquity of video games therefore helps explain the contemporary phenomenon of school massacres. In the early twentieth century, a mixed-up teenager toting a pistol would have been far less capable of killing than Marshall's soldiers. But the computer game generation is different since they rehearse slaughter each evening on the Xbox.

More generally, the rise in violent crime since the Second World War can, Grossman suggests, be attributed to a media that revels in realistic bloodshed. Teenagers today model themselves on socio-pathic antiheroes and suppress their instinctive revulsion at suffering, and the results show in the crime statistics.

It was a popular liberal argument, a natural reaction to the mainstreaming of cruelty in films such as *Hostel*, *Wolf Creek* and *Saw*. In the 1990s, when *Reservoir Dogs* first screened, when Mr Blonde sliced a man's ear from his head, the giggles in the session I'd been at had not seemed a healthy cultural development—and compared with today's films, Tarantino's efforts were tame. That the unselfconscious enjoyment of simulated pain had real world consequences appeared an entirely reasonable supposition.

Yet identifying those consequences was not easy, and Grossman's straightforward relationship between representation and reality seemed unduly simplistic. To pluck one problem at random: which way did the causality work? Those torture films coincided with Abu Ghraib and Gitmo. Were Jack Bauer and *24* responsible for waterboarding, or was it more likely that the cultural and political shifts that brought George W Bush to power also changed the tastes of audiences? You could scarcely blame teenagers for a fascination with celluloid cruelty when the world's most powerful men reverenced the real thing.

The specific case against video games seemed, perhaps, more convincing, especially since, in the years since *On Killing*'s first publication, powerful computer simulations had been integrated into US military training, with soldiers on their way to Baghdad discharging modified assault rifles against blue-screen digitalisations of the Middle East. The people running such simulations spoke admiringly about how even off-the-shelf games prepared troops to kill. Lieutenant Colonel Scott Sutton, director of the technology division at Quantico Marine Base, explained to the *Washington Post* that soldiers of the video generation felt 'less inhibited, down in their primal level, pointing their weapons at somebody', something that 'provides a better foundation for us to work with'. Retired marine colonel Gary W Anderson, former chief of staff of the Marine Corps Warfighting Lab, agreed. He compared gamers to the Spartans: from childhood, they'd been constantly rehearsing combat.

That was why, before leaving Australia, I'd downloaded onto my laptop a program called *America's Army*, a huge and complex game playable both by individuals and by teams in which the minutiae of military life—weapons, uniforms, insignia—had been rendered in obsessive detail. It was a first-person shooter, exactly the experience Grossman describes as a 'murder simulator'. Furthermore, because the gameplay began with your character signing up for military training, it not only simulated combat but, in recursive postmodern fashion, allowed you to simulate the experience of combat simulation, even with your physical body located in a tiny room in the Extended Stay Hotel in an industrial park near Arlington.

So, the evening before Grossman's seminar, Private Buttercup grabbed, rather robotically, his M4 and clicked its magazine into place. The shoot house was open to the roof, with a supervising officer looking down from above. The signs on the closest door read, 'Caution: High Noise Area Wear Ear Plugs' and 'Caution: Eye Protection Required'.

'Soldier! Ready your weapon', called an officer somewhere above. 'Enter the shoot house and engage enemy targets!' Buttercup did his best. He kicked the door open to reveal a couch, some packing crates and other objects strewn around randomly in a simulacrum of a lounge. The floodlights shone down from the platform above to accentuate the staginess, while an old electric timer counted down seconds like a basketball scoreboard. And then, to the right, a wooden figure with a mask slid out. A terrorist! An ecstasy of fumbling and Buttercup raised the M4—but not quickly enough, because the target twirled out of position and the lights flashed to signal time was up.

And it was onto the next room. As Buttercup progressed, he managed to launch some shots at the plywood jihadis who popped up on sticks, shuffled out on tracks and otherwise obligingly presented themselves. Those he hit dropped down satisfyingly; unfortunately, so did a representation of what seemed to be an unarmed civilian. He pressed on, bashing through the doors one after another, spraying as much as aiming—and, then, the gun was clicking on an empty clip. That was bad. 'Soldier,' shouted the trainer, 'you have expended all of your allotted ammunition for this exercise'. He barely disguised his contempt. 'You failed to meet the minimum training standards and must restart this training. You are a NO-GO!'

Most of Buttercup's missions ended as No-Gos, a depressing electronic counterpart to my misadventures with Demetri. Gaming on a laptop was hard enough, but I was outside the target demographic and lacked the intuitive sense of how the play worked, so Buttercup often found himself marooned in a pixelated limbo with the action paused and the other characters staring at him expectantly, while his controller stabbed randomly at buttons, trying to comprehend what was meant to happen next.

Even when Buttercup graduated from the MOUT and ventured briefly and disastrously into combat, *America's Army* never seemed likely to condition anything more deadly than RSI. Yes, he unloaded his magazine into sundry swarthy no-goodniks, but the gameplay was far more stylised than realistic, at least in comparison with the training that Grossman described. Buttercup was controlled with touchpad and keyboard, and thus, if his bumblings conditioned any reflexes, it was only to click desperately whenever a target appeared. Wouldn't that make you less rather than more deadly with an actual gun?

Even with a specialised gaming console, I couldn't see how a plastic controller replicated in any meaningful sense a real M4. Going out with Demetri had been an overwhelmingly physical experience: the sound of the rifle, the space of the paddock, the smell of cordite. Sure, the automatic weapons in *America's Army* crashed, and the empty rounds tinkled when they were ejected onto the ground, but the tiny sound from my laptop speakers resembled gunfire only to the extent that a seashell mimicked the roar of an ocean, and I was always acutely conscious of my real location on an uncomfortable hotel armchair.

No, no matter how superficially attractive it seemed, the indictment against video games didn't convince. Even with first-person shooters, the enemies weren't human much of the time: back in the day, when playing *Doom* seemed an attractive alternative to my undergraduate degree, I'd shot at monsters, not men. If conditioning depended upon realism, how could mowing down space aliens (or demons, or whatever they were—the *Doom* story-line had always been a little cloudy) facilitate a school massacre? Besides, only a minority of violent games presented the player with a first-person point of view. *Grand Theft Auto* might have been as murderous and as self-consciously amoral as its critics suggested, but it couldn't possibly condition kids in the way Grossman described, since the *GTA* player looked down on the action from a bird's-eye perspective impossible in real life.

My head was aching and my shooting fingers sore, and I'd reached the stage where the onscreen action made no sense whatsoever. The next day, I would be taking a real course in real killing, and it was starting to get late. With the push of a button, I sent Buttercup and Major Amerine back into the digital void, and then I stared numbly at the hotel TV until I fell asleep.

The information sheet from the Northern Virginia Criminal Justice Training Academy warned, with military precision, that the session would begin at 0700 hours sharp. I woke suitably early, to a morning that, even before the sun came up, already threatened more sticky heat. On the way, I reviewed my instructions. I was to be prompt, the sheet said; I was to dress appropriately; I was not to bring guns into class but to store them in the lockers provided.

All of that, I duly obeyed, overcompensating so much on the promptness that the taxi deposited me, in ill-fitting suit pants and entirely *sans* weapons, on the college's over-greened lawns, about fifteen minutes before anyone else. Inside the foyer, I passed the time looking over at the framed graduation photos of generations of police, feeling decidedly out of place. This was Copland, and my classmates, slowly arriving, were mostly cops: chunky white guys with cropped hair and open-necked shirts and the military swagger of the characters from *America's Army*. Amerines, I decided: a whole army of them, with me the lone Buttercup.

Near the registration table, a stylish red-headed woman sipped at some coffee. At 0700 hours, that was something I needed. Where had she found it? She gestured towards a cafeteria down the hallway. When I came back, a little more human, she asked me what agency I was with. I wasn't with any agency; I was from Australia. 'An academic', I said, apologetically, not wanting to explain the complex relationship between *Overland* and Victoria University. 'Sort of.'

'Oh. I'm with the FBI.' We nodded companionably, and for an instant, I thought we might compare professional notes: she, say, talking serial killers, me, poets. But the lecture was starting, and we all shuffled into the theatre, past the display table loaded up with Grossman's books.

The last time I'd been among so many police, I'd been under arrest. Still, that was a long time ago and in a different country, and here, in the context of police school, everyone was very friendly. A big officer took the seat next to me, offered a knuckle-cracking handshake and then, when he heard my accent, asked where I was from. I explained, and we chatted amiably until he hailed some men in the row in front and they all began discussing cop-like things.

These guys weren't FBI agents: they didn't talk about international man-hunts or special operations or glamorous stake-outs but instead bitched happily about new procedures for logging shifts.

When Grossman took to the stage, he was smaller and thinner than I'd imagined, not a gym-built soldier like Jeremiah Workman, but wiry and intense in blue shirt and jeans. He introduced himself, gave his background and then explained that he came from Arkansas. Which gave him, he said, the right to tell Arkansas jokes. 'A feller from Arkansas …' he began, and the room relaxed into the anecdote. 'This feller from Arkansas and this feller from Virginia, they went on holidays together. The feller from Virginia sees a note down by the beach: ocean cruise five dollars, go to room 222. All right! So he goes to room 222, knocks on the door, says, "Hey I'm here for the five-dollar ocean cruise". Bam! Someone smacks him over the head, takes his wallet, and he wakes up strapped to a log floating out on the ocean.' He paused, anticipating the slight titter as it rose from the audience. 'Feller looks over and realises that strapped to a log right next to him is his friend from Arkansas, name of Bubba. 'He thinks, I can't let ol' Bubba know it's got me down. So he says, "Do you suppose they gonna serve us any food on this five-dollar cruise?" Bubba says, "Well, they didn't last year".' He delivered the line in a good ol' boy accent, and the theatre erupted.

From then, he owned the crowd. Grossman was a consummate professional: a man who evidently spoke often and did it well. He held the cordless mic just so to maximise audibility and minimise popping; he paced up and down without any notes, and he let the laughter subside before continuing. 'The moral of the story is simple. We had a hard time last year. Let's not do it again.'

The voice changed: no longer the avuncular master of ceremonies but deadly serious, like the veteran cop delivering the eulogy for a colleague dead in the line of duty. 'People, we've been having us a hard time. Littleton, Paducah, Springfield, Jonesboro, Edinboro, Santee, Hillsborough, Virginia Tech, World Trade Center, Columbine, Oklahoma City, little Amish school in Pennsylvania …

but we all agree: we don't want to go on that ocean cruise no more. Can we take the lessons learnt in blood and lives in Jonesboro, Columbine, Virginia Tech, World Trade Center, Oklahoma City? Can we take the lessons learnt in blood and lives and apply them?'

Most of the names he recited were now synonymous with schoolyard killings, and it was schoolyard killings that he discussed throughout his opening session. 'Juvenile mass murders in schools have never happened in history. But in the last ten years, there have been hundreds and hundreds of murders, and attempted juvenile mass murders in schools.' He described some in detail, dwelling on the impotence and terror of the teachers as they watched a deranged shooter walking the halls killing the students one by one. Such scenes were taking place more and more frequently, he said, and we, as law enforcement officers, had to be ready. 'Throughout today, I will show you that our enemy is denial. We will hunt down every bit of denial. We must prepare for the unthinkable as if it were inevitable. We live in a world where kids are coming to kill the kids.'

The focus, for the first twenty minutes or so, seemed merely odd. Why use massacres to frame a seminar on killing? Surely ordinary officers—these regular cops next to me—would be more likely to be exposed to lethal force during drug busts or domestic quarrels or other prosaic, everyday scenarios. An unmedicated schizophrenic, an armed drunk: wouldn't something like that be a more appropriate example?

Instead, Grossman was stalking up and down the aisles, explaining that the killings we'd seen so far were straws in the wind, the merest taste of what was to come. The movies, television, the Internet and—especially—video games were training kids to kill, and the kids would put that training to use. There was, he said, a game called *Postal*, in which players scored by shooting cops and then urinating in their mouths as they lay dying. Children spent thousands of hours playing such things—'interactive, total-immersion criminal simulators'—and law-enforcement agencies needed to prepare for the consequences, especially since the Columbine generation, tutored since infancy to be lethal, were entering the workforce. 'The kid playing

Postal-piss-in-the-mouth-of-the-dying-cop today, he'll be your school killer tomorrow, your college killer next year and the workplace killer in years to come. We will reap what we sow for a generation to come. Folks, we're sitting on a powder keg right now. If we get a major recession, and twenty million of the Columbine generation go six months without a job, they will make you feel their pain!'

Then he brought an overhead up onto the screen: a shot of two brain scans, with the swirls of green and orange on the one clearly different from those on the other. This was the hard evidence of how gaming companies rewired kids' neurons into murderous patterns. He pointed at the first: 'This is your brain'. He moved to the second: 'And this is your brain on video games'.

It was a dramatic display—or it would have been, had I not read an account of that study, which, like all the other literature linking media violence and reality, was actually very tentative. Yes, emotional arousal seemed to increase after game-playing, but exactly what that arousal meant and how long it lasted was not clear-cut, and one might equally have pointed to entirely different research suggesting that boys who didn't play violent games were more likely to get into trouble than those who occasionally did. The whole field was like that: for every paper making one claim, there was another rebuttal, with no real consensus about the media's responsibility for violence—and especially not about the straightforward causality Grossman posited.

Besides, if violent games were so problematic, why not rail against the US Army? *America's Army*, the game I'd been playing, was designed and funded by the defence forces, specifically to influence impressionable youngsters. Peppering the little vignettes through which Buttercup had fumbled were messages about military values, and Major Amerine, who explained the shoot house, was the digital incarnation of an actual soldier, about whose swashbuckling Afghanistan career we were invited to learn by visiting the 'Real Heroes' gallery. The moral was simple: if you like the game, check out the real thing.

And they did. Perhaps 30 per cent of visitors to the *America's Army* homepage (from which the game could be freely downloaded) also clicked on the real-life recruitment page, while about the same percentage of soldiers joining the military academy had acknowledged playing the game. The product had, in other words, been stupendously effective—the most successful recruiting campaign, some said, since the Uncle Sam 'I Want You' ads of the Second World War. That was why the army funded gaming tournaments and poured development money into other military-themed projects, most of which were far more widely available and popular than *Postal*. Grossman was ex-military; many of the police in the room had an army background. Shouldn't they be looking closer to home rather than blaming the game companies?

As for the general thesis about a red tide of violence engulfing the USA, that, too, seemed problematic. Data from around the developed world for the last decade actually showed a steady fall in violent crime. Grossman explicitly disputed the homicide rates, arguing that, since contemporary medicine kept alive victims who would previously have died, it was impossible to make an accurate comparison with the past. But even if you allowed for that, where was the evidence of attempted murder or assault spiralling out of control? This almost existential crisis of violence: what exactly was that based on?

I was so busy scribbling little rejoinders in my notebook that the segue from school massacres caused by video games to school massacres caused by al Qaeda initially passed me by. 'Six years ago they came and murdered three thousand of our citizens. What are they going to do next? We don't know. Nobody knows the future. If we knew what they were going to do, we'd be waiting for them and they wouldn't succeed! We don't know what they're going to do. But the one thing they do with every nation they mess with is they come and kill your kids.'

I put down my pen. Now this I had not expected at all. 'Folks, they do this to their own Islamic people. Every single nation they mess with, one of the first things they do is come kill the kids, because they know there's nothing that will destroy your way of life and cripple your economy better than that.' Not only had al Qaeda masterminded the Beslan massacre in Russia, but bin Laden had also promised that more such attacks were coming for the West. And if terrorist school massacres in the USA seemed unlikely, well, that was precisely why we should prepare for them.

'These are terrorists!' His voice cracked with emotion. 'They don't piss in your water. They don't sprinkle doo doo from your skies. You imagine the most mind-numbing, gut-wrenching, horrifying thing that can happen, and that's at the top of their list. They can destroy our way of life; they can cripple our economy; they can modify the behaviour of every family. How? By pissing in your water? No, by coming to your kid's school tomorrow.'

And not just to one of them. 'Nobody knows the future. But al Qaeda likes four. Four planes hijacked on 9/11, four bombers in London on 7/7, four bombers on the second wave. So let's say they come to four schools in heartland America tomorrow …' A queasiness grew in the pit of my stomach. Where Grossman's media theory seemed overheated, his argument about terrorism was becoming positively hallucinogenic with each rhetorical escalation. 'It's not your job to stop the plane sprinkling anthrax over the city. It's not your job to stop nukes or anthrax or smallpox coming across the border. It is, by God, your job to put a chunk of steel in your fist and kill the sons of bitches who are coming to kill your kids. That is your job!'

Grossman was talking, for the most part, to ordinary, everyday cops. The men (and the few women) hanging onto his words were the officers who patrolled the streets outside, the people who dispensed traffic tickets and returned stolen cars, and they were here, hearing this white-knuckle hysteria about nuclear terrorists, and learning that all that stood between the children of Virginia and Osama bin Laden's evil schemes was their personal willingness to kill.

'I bring you a message from a young Green Beret', Grossman told them. 'It's a month after 9/11. This young Green Beret comes up to me and says, we're going to Afghanistan and we're gonna kick their ass. While we're going there, you tell all those cops you teach, "Don't let 'em come kill my kids". Folks, they believe in what they're doing. They've kept the bastards off your back for six and a half years. They only ask one thing: watch my six, cover my back, do your damn job. "Don't let 'em come kill my kids."'

The War on Terror was not, he said—more conversational now—against all of Islam. It was only against a tiny minority of extremists, but the difficulty was that mainstream Muslims weren't acting against that minority. They were sitting the conflict out, just like the perfidious Turkish government, stubbornly refusing to fight either in Iraq or Afghanistan. We should, therefore, remember the Sepoy Rebellion. Did we know what that was? No? Well, what happened with the Sepoy Rebellion was that, on one particular day, all the Indians of the subcontinent arose against British rule. All of them combined and they gave it their best shot. That was the worst case scenario for America. On a certain date, all the Islamic people in the USA would give it their best shot. 'If the word comes down and just one in a thousand answers the call to jihad, the rest will sit there and do nothing. That means we're looking at thousands of Washington snipers and thousands of Virginia Techs, all on the same day.'

Where precisely this incendiary word would originate and how it would be delivered to the millions of American Muslims, Sunni and Shiite alike, was not clear. Still, Grossman said he'd spoken to cops who were particularly concerned that 'the Islamic folks' were buying up all the gas stations. 'All you got to do is drop all the gas into the sewer system and drop a match and the entire city will explode, you understand, and burn the city to the ground, yeah. You don't need bombs when you own a gas station.' After this Sepoy-style rebellion, the USA would, in his opinion, have no choice but to intern the entire Muslim population—and making that happen was, he said, a goal of al Qaeda.

Mind you, we shouldn't jump to conclusions. 'Nobody knows the future. That's just trying to give you a worst scenario. But if you start seeing a bunch of indicators all pointing to one thing, don't be in denial.'

Again and again in the margins of my notebook I scrawled, 'Did he really just say that?' But, yes, he did. He explicitly and repeatedly told cops and FBI agents and whoever else was in the audience that local Muslims couldn't be trusted, that they were either indifferent to terrorism or active supporters of it, and he made those declarations in the context of preparing armed law-enforcement officers to kill.

Grossman had always made his military background clear. But that, in a way, had only made his theory more attractive. 'I tell you the reason I take an interest in Grossman', Rachel MacNair had said. 'I need to be able to say that it's not just that I have this evidence because I'm a pacifist—there's even a lieutenant colonel in the army who thinks the same thing. Grossman can do things; he can say things that I can't.' She was right. There was something tremendously powerful about a career military officer arguing that killing was gut-wrenchingly awful. That was why his assertion of an innate human pacifism had been a source of comfort. And now here he was pushing the crassest Islamophobia in a lecture theatre full of people who spent their days armed.

Quite clearly, I'd misunderstood everything. His analysis of the media—the thesis I'd been testing on my laptop—was neither *bienpensant* liberal hostility to Hollywood nor an unfortunate but secondary extension of his argument into the realm of social policy, but a central part of his program. If you thought that game violence was bringing a tsunami of crime, what did you do? You could campaign for ratings systems and bans on particular content, and you could encourage parents to turn off the television—and Grossman advocated all those things. Yet media violence wasn't going anywhere soon. In the here and now, someone needed to protect the schools, to fight back against the angry kids with their Tech 9s and their Uzis. And, if ordinary folk found wielding deadly violence difficult or impossible, those who could successfully kill became a precious asset in the defence of civilisation.

That was something he emphasised over and over again. Most people, he told us, were sheep: productive and placid and incapable of violence. A small percentage were wolves, sociopaths adept at violence and thus able to prey off the sheep. We in the audience belonged

to a third category. Police, soldiers and others with the lawful authority to carry guns were sheepdogs: able to wield violence but fundamentally protective of the flock. The sheepdogs who fought off the
wolves were, he explained, those who 'walked the warrior's path'.

But the warrior's path was not an easy one. 'The sheep aren't
too sure they like the sheepdog. You go out to the meadow, you ask
the sheep, "Hey, just between me and you, what do you think about
the sheepdog?" You know what they say? "He's a baa-aad man!
He's always carrying a gun; he's going to hurt someone!" Now the
sheep are pretty leery of the sheepdog until when? When do they
change their mind? When the wolf shows up and the whole flock
tries to hide behind the one lonely sheepdog!'

Naturally, he was talking about September 11. 'Notice how for
a little while after 9/11 the American public appreciated the warriors? Three thousand dead, the enemy is at the gate: "We want you;
we need you; we thank you; we will nev-baa forget!" How long did
that last? A lot of people went like this: "No one's come to kill me
for over a year—baa. No one's come to kill me for six years—baa!
What are you still doing out there? Go away and leave us alone!
They are sheep: they sink back into denial. They're sheep: they've
got two speeds—graze and stampede.'

But the warriors didn't forget. They prepared each morning as
if it were September 11, so when the day came again, they would be
ready. Such was the sheepdog: the man or the woman who moved
towards the sound of guns when everyone else was moving away.
When it came to September 11, ordinary people—the sheep—said to
each other, 'I'm glad I wasn't in one of those planes'. The sheepdogs,
on the other hand, said, 'I wish I could have been there. I might have
been able to save some lives.'

It was a rhetoric of permanent war. Joanna Bourke had tried to
warn me about this, when she'd given a seminar in Melbourne,
months earlier. She, too, had been nothing like I'd expected: much
funnier and more personable than you'd expect from the author of

one book entitled *Killing*, a second called *Fear* and a third, *Rape*. I'd asked her why she'd never mentioned Grossman's book in hers.

'Look, I strongly respect David Grossman. Very strongly respect him. But to my great shame, I only read *On Killing* when my book was done. So I actually didn't know about it. Very shameful, I know.' But then she said that their approaches were so different that when she did engage with his theories, she didn't actually find them helpful. 'I'm opposed to the evolutionary psychology aspect of Grossman's book. I think it's a pernicious doctrine. It's used in military history and it's absolutely everywhere in arguments about rape, and I'm absolutely opposed to it.

'Obviously, we are biological creatures. But what is interesting about us as biological animals is precisely that war and rape are social things that are created by human minds and that they change really dramatically even within very short periods. In the end, well, what does an evolutionary model actually tell us? The answer is absolutely nothing. I only deal with a very short period—between 1914 and the 1970s—but within that time there's dramatic changes in attitudes to war. Which suggests that war and the way we relate to it is not this biosocial constant. Even within short periods, it changes dramatically, and I think that's a really hopeful thing. If we can show that things change quickly, then they can change in other ways: different ways, better ways.'

This was the classic problem with biological explanations of human behaviour: innate differences between human beings would inevitably become evidence that social hierarchies could not change. The feminist movement confronted it again and again: whatever qualities you defined as 'naturally' female quickly became assimilated into arguments for male superiority.

I'd known this—of course I had—but I hadn't thought it through properly. But if you accepted that killing was sometimes necessary— and most of us did—then a biological resistance to combat was not an argument against war. Instead, it was an argument that successful killers were unique and special, possessors of a necessary ability denied to the common herd.

'The model I want you to take away from here is that of the knights of old', Grossman explained. 'Today, for the first time in centuries, there are warriors who wake up every morning. They don armour; they hang a weapon from their hip; they hang a shield on their left side, and on that shield was on whose authority they went and fought, administered justice and did good deeds in the land. If that is not a knight, you tell me what is. If that is not a paladin, you tell me what is.' Again, emotion hoarsened his voice. 'The new knights, the new paladins, are the champion of the weak and the oppressed, and they must be the master of their realm, and as the firefighter knows fire, you must know violence. Violence is your tool. Violence is your enemy. Violence is the realm you live in. You are men and women of violence. You will master it or it will destroy you. You are the warriors who man the ramparts in a dark and desperate hour. You are the thin line of heroes who hold together the tattered fabric of our civilisation in a dark and desperate hour.'

Shortly after that, he called a short recess and put down his microphone. The big cop next to me yawned and then stretched out his arms. 'He's good, isn't he?' he said, gesturing to the stage. 'Makes me want to go out and kill someone right now.' He was joking, of course, but there was something of that in the air. After the word pictures that had been painted—those visions of us all as paladins fighting epic battles against evil—the sudden consciousness of a prosaic Virginia lecture room, now slightly stuffy from our body heat, came as an undeniable wrench.

I'd planned to ask for an interview, but Grossman was down by his merchandise table, signing and selling books. Besides, I felt too depressed. I'd spent so much time thinking about Grossman's work and I couldn't believe I'd misunderstood it so badly. I'd come expecting the humane, wise voice I'd heard in *On Killing*, the voice that made the taking of life seem truly terrible, and instead I'd found Dick Cheney. Once again, I needed to rethink.

16

INTO CLEANNESS LEAPING

During the Great War, it was said that even when the dead couldn't be seen, the very earth of No Man's Land was itself corpselike. Arlington National Cemetery was like that, too, though its resemblance was not to an untended body so much as the cadaver on which the morticians had already been at work. On the great field where the USA buried its veterans, the grass was so green, so lush, that it seemed painted and powdered, as if it too was prepared for a final viewing in an open casket. But the care lavished on the cemetery only accentuated its sadness. Nothing you could do with the dead—tributes, flowers, eulogies—changed the basic truth of a funeral: someone was gone and would never come back. That was Arlington, except on an unimaginable scale: 300 000 dead over 200 acres, the human tally from all the US wars since the revolution.

I walked in from the east, past the Iwo Jima Memorial, where a scrum of giant stone marines perpetually pushed their enormous flagpole skyward, and onto the grounds themselves, moving beside the hundreds upon hundreds of white crosses in their agricultural rows, until I arrived at the Tomb of the Unknowns. There, on the marble steps, the guard was changing, and a small crowd had gathered to watch. Twenty-one paces, the ceremonial soldiers stepped to each other, and then the same number away, clicking their heels and shouldering their rifles in an intricate, almost mathematical pattern.

Drill was about control, ensuring that men placed orders over instincts even in the face of death, for as Frederick the Great explained, if soldiers were allowed to think for themselves, not one would remain on the field. That was what gave the performance by the tomb its power: the sense that, come what may, these men would step and salute and present muskets to each other, even as the cannons fired and the bullets kicked. Their inexorability implied danger, some peril against which their mechanical exactitude became necessary, and it was the perception of flesh willed against fire that made their precision different and more fascinating than that of dancers or cheerleaders.

I'd been thinking a lot about that, about the enchantment of violence. For weeks before I left Australia, I'd been corresponding with Jon Kulaga, a forty-seven-year-old spice-buyer who, on weekends, donned the uniform of a Seaforth Highlander Lewis gunner in the trenches of Pennsylvania. In the USA, so many ordinary people dressed in the colours of long-disbanded armies and skirmished with blank cartridges and blunted swords that military re-enactment had become the fastest growing hobby in the country. The Great War Association (GWA), in which Kulaga was an official, owned a full-scale Great War battlefield, with shell holes and barbed wire and the lunar landscape of No Man's Land rendered exactly as in the old sepia photographs. At the GWA's most recent event, two Great War–era aircraft had buzzed overhead as twenty-first-century Americans fired combat rifles, threw grenades and launched trench mortars at each other, though as yet they couldn't, Kulaga admitted, replicate heavy artillery.

Why did they do this? The most interesting insights came from a young Melbourne man called Andrew Nolte. When I'd visited him at his house (or rather, his parents' house—he was only twenty-one) in Greensborough, he'd answered the door dressed as a Great War soldier and then ushered me into a lounge with a full battle kit spread on the carpet.

Melbourne re-enactors couldn't manage mayhem as impressive as that regularly inflicted upon Pennsylvania, partly because there weren't enough of them and partly because of the Australian gun laws. Kulaga went into his ersatz battles with a fully operational Lewis gun, capable of firing 550 rounds in a minute, but in Victoria, Lewis guns were seriously illegal, so illegal in fact that you couldn't even tote a pretend one—the legislation outlawed replica machine guns as strictly as the real thing.

Nolte and his friends mostly did static displays: ceremonials for Anzac Day or at country shows, where they displayed their stuff on trestle tables and drilled and raised flags and so on. That was, he said, the only way you could get a gig.

Still, for Nolte, the real pleasures of the hobby lay in collection as much as performance: 'When you collect, you acquire a whole lot of expensive gear but no way of showing it off, no way to use it. Re-enacting means you can actually wear your gear. You do some work out in a trench, and eat the bully beef and biscuit and smoke the tobacco and drink the water and the rum from the same containers, and it gives you a feeling of what it was like.' He smiled, almost embarrassed. 'In a vague way, at least.'

When we switched off the recorder and turned to the objects on his floor, I understood something of what he meant. He'd replicated the basic kit of an average soldier: a drinking flask, a packet of thin cigarettes, an ammunition belt and so on. They were objects for use, rather than pieces of craftsmanship, and they demanded to be handled. The belt wanted to be buckled, the pack worn, the combat rifle hoisted to the shoulder. Yet you could not touch any part of the collection without registering its authenticity, its historical weight, as if the past still clung to it like loam to a tree root.

Nolte showed me a light-horseman's shoulder bag and explained how to carry it. Then he pointed out the bloodstain. 'They used to salvage whatever usable equipment they could find after a battle', he said. We both looked at the mark and fell silent, calculating where the wound must have been and the likelihood (slim) of its owner's survival.

Kneeling amid Nolte's collection, I understood, for the first time, the appeal of re-enactment, a hobby that, until then, had seemed faintly risible. He'd acquired a metal trunk for the storage of medical equipment, and he'd tracked down, item by item, its original contents, from the bulky pads used to staunch bleeding to the forceps with which bullets were removed. I looked down at the assembled display of Great War medical technology and, for an instant, historical distance evaporated. The war became not an ancient abstraction but an event palpable and solid, where real people writhed with agony at a makeshift dressing station and the staff treated the damage from machine guns with this primitive array of bone saws and placebos.

But why war, and only war? Nolte said that to re-create soldiers' tinned supplies authentically, he'd searched the National Archives copyright section for the original labels. OK, I understood the pleasures of historical detective work. Yet why did it require legitimisation from war? There were canned foods in the 1920s, too. What made them less fascinating than the almost identical tins served to soldiers a few years earlier? Nolte's confidence faltered momentarily. 'I don't really know. I suppose you could re-enact something else. I'd never thought of it before.'

With the American practitioners, the question became even more acute, simply because they were so much more extreme. There were men so devoted to re-enacting the American Civil War that they starved themselves to achieve the emaciation of the malnourished rebels. They waxed their beards with bacon fat; they practised 'the bloat', lying on the ground with stomachs protruding so as to resemble Confederate corpses decomposing in the Southern sun; they welcomed the hacking cough obtained by sleeping rough on a freezing battle site as an accurate representation of the phlegm rolling around the permanently infected throats of the 1860s.

History happened during peacetime, too, and the Great Depression changed the world as much as the Great War. Why didn't thousands of Americans dress up as hoboes, jumping mock freight trains and lining up at fake soup kitchens? What made an industrial dispute or a flood or the discovery of penicillin innately less suitable for re-enactment than war? Why were Roman centurions a popular choice of character for re-enactors and not, say, Roman orators or farmers?

There was something different, in a way I didn't quite understand, in the contemplation of times when people deliberately sought to kill each other. Even with the few examples of non-military re-enactment, violence always seemed to creep in: no Renaissance Faire was complete without its mock executions and its sword fights. Re-enactors weren't mumbling gun-nuts or bug-eyed fantasists, secretly yearning to turn a Lewis gun on their neighbours. But, still, the hobby did seem to hint at a peculiar glamour attaching to violence, one strong enough to persist over time.

The guards eventually completed their transition, and the spectators turned off their camcorders. I walked back the way I'd come, looking out across all those headstones, the gardens of stone. There was an empty bench where I could sit and watch a squirrel playing across the graves, its feathery tail floating serenely behind it. I tried to make sense of what I'd learnt.

Despite the differences between Bourke and Grossman, there were definite affinities in their theories. Both described the initial abhorrence that new recruits felt in relation to killing; both chronicled the physical and psychological training techniques the army had developed to break down that resistance to killing. The main difference was in emphasis. He concentrated on the wartime non-firers, she on those who did shoot, treating the men unable to cope with killing as anomalous.

The central point, then, was the existence or otherwise of an inherent inhibition when it came to killing. Yet the more you thought about that, the more the question seemed undecidable, almost by definition. You couldn't investigate a resistance to killing by studying today's soldiers, since they'd all undergone the training that Grossman said overcame it. The only sources, then, were historical ones, the interpretation of which was always problematic.

Take SLA Marshall and his statistics about US troops in the Second World War. As soon as I mentioned Marshall to Bourke, she'd cut me off. 'I have to stop you there. This myth that's in Grossman's book about how 75 per cent of soldiers did not fire their weapons: it's based on the Marshall book and that book's a lie. When Marshall did his interviews, that question was never asked. He didn't ask anyone, "Did you fire your weapon?" He just invented his statistics.'

That was true—or at least arguable. Later researchers had, in fact, established that Marshall—a tremendously influential military writer but a rather erratic individual—didn't actually conduct all the interviews he'd claimed, and of the soldiers with whom he did speak, none recalled him asking about whether they'd fired or not. Not surprisingly, many military historians had dismissed his famous research as overtly fraudulent.

Grossman, however, had mounted a fierce rearguard defence. Marshall's methodology might have been suspect, he said, but his findings were essentially correct and could be confirmed from other sources, such as the weapons discarded after Gettysburg. And that was true, too. The other day, browsing through an account of the Russian front in the Second World War, I'd stumbled on an account very similar to Marshall's, with a certain Captain Kozlov complaining that the vast majority of his men hadn't fired a single shot during the entire war and that the burden of combat had been carried by heavy machine guns, battalion mortars and the courage of certain individuals.

Yet, despite such corroborations, I could see Bourke's point. Rough generalisations about who did what in particular battles were one thing, but the Marshall statistic had been quoted time and time again as a nugget of fact amid all the uncertainty. Stripped of Marshall's statistical rigour, the thesis of a hardwired inability to kill became significantly less persuasive.

Like many of his readers, I suspected, I'd been attracted to Grossman's argument because it had seemed an implicit critique of war itself, especially when contrasted with Bourke's thesis on the ease with which people killed. Bourke's book opened the door, it seemed to me, to an old fashioned Toryism, a Hobbesian account of ordinary people as naturally homicidal, with their propensity towards violence bursting out whenever traditional authority weakened. A revisionist school of historians now argued precisely that about the Great War: its length and ferocity, they said, could be attributed to the delight of ordinary soldiers in killing each other. By contrast, the Grossman thesis suggested that insofar as Tommy Atkins actually fired at Fritz with hostile intent, it was a denial of all his natural instincts.

That was why the ferocious militarism of his seminar had come as such a shock. But I thought now I could grasp the internal logic. During the first session break, I'd purchased *On Combat*, a subsequent book that Grossman had co-written with Loren Christensen. It was much more practical than *On Killing*—essentially a hands-on guide for preparing for deadly force encounters. The book outlines in detail all the ways by which a resistance to killing might be overcome: breathing techniques to help the body cope with combat stress; rehearsals to make aiming and firing secondary nature; various ways of gearing up to, and gearing down from, the sensory overload of a gun battle.

On the flyleaf, *On Combat* reproduces the poem 'Into Battle':

And life is colour and warmth and light,
And a striving evermore for these;
And he is dead who will not fight;
And who dies fighting has increase.

The words come from Julian Grenfell, the British soldier-poet whose letters feature so strikingly in Bourke's *Intimate History of Killing*. It was Grenfell, an archetypical 'happy warrior' of the Great War, who declared trench warfare 'wonderful fun' and compared it favourably with pigsticking.

Grossman might equally have chosen Rupert Brooke, Grenfell's better-known contemporary, and his famous lines:

Now, God be thanked Who has matched us with His hour,
And caught our youth, and wakened us from sleeping,

With hand made sure, clear eye, and sharpened power,
To turn, as swimmers into cleanness leaping,
Glad from a world grown old and cold and weary,
Leave the sick hearts that honour could not move,
And half-men, and their dirty songs and dreary,
And all the little emptiness of love!

Where Grenfell thought those who would not fight were 'dead', Brooke said they were 'sick hearts' and 'half-men'. Both would surely have accepted Grossman's description of non-combatants as 'sheep', for the sense was exactly the same: where ordinary people recoiled from violence, warriors yearned for the righteous battle in which they could exercise their sure hands, clear eyes and ability to kill. The sheepdog on a plane on 11 September did not want to be somewhere else but instead thanked God for matching him with the hour.

But for Grenfell and Brooke, enthusiasm for war was also a critique of peace. The original happy warriors welcomed the Great War more or less explicitly as an antidote to the diseases of industrial society: isolation, aimlessness, ennui and so on. August 1914 arrived as the whole world teetered uncomfortably on the brink of modernity. The prosperity of the new European cities came with a bustle that, for many, offered only spiritual emptiness. The social ties of a simpler age had dissolved; the new society consisted of atomised individuals, buffeted this way and that by forces they could neither see nor hear nor understand.

The year 2008 wasn't 1914, but the dirtiness and dreariness against which Grenfell and Brooke contrasted the colour and warmth and light of a battle seemed entirely recognisable. The generation of the Great War yearned to escape the pettiness, the smug prosperity of suburban life. Wasn't there more than a hint of that in Jeremiah Workman? Nothing he'd ever do in peacetime would compare to combat, and while Fallujah was deadly, life in a war zone was simple and meaningful and real; day-to-day Washington could simply never compete.

'No one became a cop for the money', Grossman had said. 'So if you ain't here for the money, why are you here? Because you are sheepdogs, because you are paladins, because you are warriors. You've heard the sound of the trumpet. You know there is evil in the land, and you couldn't live with yourself if you were flipping burgers or selling stocks or shovelling shit when the bastards came to kill the kids.' You became a warrior to save the kids, to defeat the Kaiser. But you also knew that flipping burgers or selling stocks or any of the other priorities of the peacetime world amounted to shovelling shit, a demeaning and purposeless activity, an occupation fit only for sheep.

The Edwardian militarists developed a whole language to convey war's restoration of a pre-modern age and its pre-modern values, with battle imagined in feudal, even Arthurian, terms. A horse was always a 'steed'; the enemy was the 'foe'; danger was 'peril'; brave soldiers who won were invariably 'valiant conquering warriors' and so on. That was the genesis of Grossman's paladins and 'knights of old': the cod-medieval vocabulary of twentieth-century militarism.

From the vantage of a century, it's easy to dismiss the happy warriors—indeed, the Edwardians as a whole—as hopelessly ill informed, naifs who imagined the trenches into a rugger match: a little rough, perhaps, but essentially a contest of character, after which winner and loser would shake each other's manly hand. Grenfell and Brooke and all the less famous young men who went off to kill and to die could seem like spoiled schoolboys, rhapsodising about glory with no real understanding of what a .303 bullet actually did to a human skull.

Except that they did understand. As the letters about kangaroo-shooting suggested, their generation possessed far more experience with the shedding of blood than ours did, and Grenfell, in particular, was very frank about combat's appeal. War was violent, and that was why he liked it. 'I have never, never felt so well, or so happy, or enjoyed anything so much …', he explained. 'The fighting excitement vitalizes everything, every sight and word and action.' He was writing from the trenches. He knew of what he spoke.

Even before the Great War, the philosopher William James had identified this sentiment. Young men dreamt of battle, he said, because of the gore, not despite it. The possibility of sudden death was central to romance, and conventional pacifism could never dim the sound of the trumpet, since well-meaning warnings about the 'horrors of war' made violence more alluring, not less. 'The horrors make the fascination', James explained:

> War is the strong life; it is life in extremis ... [War's] 'horrors' are a cheap price to pay for rescue from the only alternative supposed, of a world of clerks and teachers, of co-education and zo-ophily, of 'consumer's leagues' and 'associated charities', of industrialism unlimited, and feminism unabashed. No scorn, no hardness, no valour any more! Fie upon such a cattleyard of a planet!

James talked of cattle and Grossman of sheep, but the idea was the same. Yes, the warrior walked a narrow and rocky path full of tribulation, but the extremity of his trials provided honour and duty and purpose, in a way that the common herd could never comprehend. The ease of peacetime was also an emptiness, and battle gave meaning to those who fought, so that war seemed somehow more human than peace. The sheep dealt with each other through the impersonal nexus of the market, whereas when two warriors clashed, it was a meeting between men, even if at the end of a bayonet.

In Germany in 1914, the soldier-poet Franz Schauwecker enthused about what was to come. 'The petty, aimless, lounging life of peacetime is done with. Life has suddenly been brought back to its simplest terms. Every movement is scrupulously precise, every touch is determined, every action is consciously directed towards its goal ... everything has its clear, palpable meaning.'

That, I decided, was also the lure of military re-enactment. The dim enchantment that possessed Nolte's collection came from objects that had lost their everydayness in violence, things that had passed through a time of direction and meaning, and still retained shreds of it. In another context, you wouldn't glance twice at that chipped enamel mug, but when you knew its wartime history, you experienced an entire sensory world. You imagined a small tot of spirits in the early dawn; you felt a sympathetic stab of the pre-battle terror that the rum helped to suppress.

The militarism of Grossman's presentation wasn't a contradiction of his thesis about the resistance to killing so much as an extension of it. The Edwardian enthusiasts for war didn't, it was true, talk about any psychological obstacles to violence. But an argument about a biological inhibition simply updated and strengthened the old rhetoric. If violence was harrowing, if killing was difficult, if the trauma was too extreme for most people to handle, all that simply made the deed more profound, accentuating the distinction between the sheepdogs, who could kill, and the sheep, who couldn't. That was why his formulation so persuasively revived the language of 1914 in a form for the twenty-first century.

The squirrel abandoned its game and skittered off behind another headstone, and I stood up, too. It was growing late and my plane left early in the morning, and the walk back to the hotel was a long one. It was time to go.

Bidding the graves farewell, I thought of Simonides's epigram from the tombs at Thermopylae: 'Stranger, go tell the Spartans we died here obedient to their commands'. That was how warriors died, and every Edwardian schoolboy had learnt those words. But there was also AD Hope's Vietnam-era treatment of the same passage. Hope's version ran:

> Go tell those old men, safe in bed,
> We took their orders and are dead.

Grenfell had been killed, and Brookes had died and so had Owen, and Sassoon had been wounded, and Arlington, this tremendous city of the fallen, housed thousands upon thousands of others who had taken orders and were now dead.

The warrior rhetoric didn't provide a vocabulary to discuss the purpose of a war. Warriors sought righteous battles, it was true, but in some respects, the value of war lay in the fighting as much as the outcome. You could prove your valour and display your honour in a doomed cause just as well as in a successful one—the campaign for the Dardanelles was an example. But it only took the slightest shift to fundamentally change the frame. From Gallipoli, a certain Lieutenant Richards wrote some simple words that implicitly challenged every monument, every statue. 'The fact that they died well', he said, 'is no answer to the question as to why they should die at all'. All the way back, down the long paths that led out from the necropolis, I thought about that.

17

REMOVE THE THOUGHT

I am making this statement, as an act of wilful defiance of military authority because I believe that the war is being deliberately prolonged by those who have the power to end it. I am a soldier, convinced that I am acting on behalf of soldiers. I believe that the war upon which I entered as a war of defence and liberation has now become a war of aggression and conquest.

With *Memoirs of an Infantry Officer* a constant companion, my wars kept blending together. The passage comes from Sassoon's 'Soldier's Declaration' of 1917, but the sentiment seemed remarkably similar to Camilo Mejía's statements after his 2004 court martial for refusing to return to Iraq.

Miami was even hotter and even more sticky, and I was exhausted again: another early morning flight, and then a struggle across town to find Mejía, the president of Iraq Veterans against the War. When I arrived, red-faced and sweating, he ushered me into a lounge room where the table was covered with anti-war posters and left-wing newspapers. 'Do you want something to drink?' He stepped into his little kitchen and reappeared with a bottle of Australian merlot.

If Reppenhagen had seemed too punk rock for war, Mejía was too ordinary: small, almost gentle and slow-speaking, with a faint Latin accent. But that wasn't the only reason his military career seemed so surprising. His parents had been high-profile Sandinista revolutionaries—his father was the famous Nicaraguan singer Carlos Mejía Godoy—and Mejía's own politics were closer to a South American leftism than to the anaemic liberalism from which most of the anti-war movement took its vocabulary. So why had he joined in the first place?

'I've thought about that a lot, and I wish I could give you one answer. The best I can say is that I'd been travelling so long, and the military seemed a place to get a sense of belonging. When you talk to recruiters, they tell you, yeah, camaraderie, you'll have your buddies; you're gonna be like brothers; you'll do everything together. It's gonna be fun.'

Born in Nicaragua, he'd come to the USA as a baby and then moved, with his mother, to Costa Rica before shifting once again. Amid all that, the army promised stability. And there was also the more prosaic issue of finances. His parents had been relatively privileged, but when he settled in the USA, he experienced a new insecurity about his next pay cheque—and a military career offered financial independence. Besides, this was during the Clinton years, with the economy booming, at a time when war seemed an incredibly distant prospect.

All through his basic training, he'd remained emotionally distant from the reality he was being taught. 'I'd moved around so much that I learnt to adapt well, to emotionally separate myself from situations, because I always knew that nothing would last long. Which was messed up as a kid, but it had positives, too. In basic training, I was equipped emotionally and psychologically to detach myself from everything. Not just the bayonet training and the rifle training but the humiliation, the harshness of it. I remember going into the bathroom, the latrine, during fire-watch late at night and seeing grown men crying, sitting in the toilet, in the shower, hiding from the rest, and crying because it was so tough for them. For me, it wasn't hard at all. I went through it all and I never questioned how using these weapons would feel against a real human being.'

He'd signed up for three years in 1994, but the standard three-year contract included a commitment for another five years, either in the regular army or through one weekend a month in the National Guard. It was a detail the recruiters often glossed over, and its implications for Mejía were immense.

In February 2003, Mejía became a father to a new baby girl. He was enrolled in psychology at the University of Miami and volunteering as a counsellor for a non-profit organisation. He'd created, in other words, the infrastructure for the civilian life into which he'd step when his weekend obligations for the National Guard came to an end in a few months' time. And then he learnt his unit had been activated and he was being sent to Iraq.

Politically, he opposed the war even before he arrived. But his experiences made that general opposition far more extreme. He witnessed the abuse of prisoners; he saw the relentless rise in civilian casualties, and he took part in patrols that seemed to have no purpose but to draw enemy fire. Most of all, he became convinced that the Iraqi people did not want him there. So when he was sent back to the USA on leave, he made the decision not to return. This was no small matter. In theory, an active-duty soldier charged with desertion during wartime could be sentenced to death.

For the anti-war movement, Mejía's decision, like Sassoon's in 1917, had an immense significance. Since 2003, the administration had claimed that the troops all supported the Iraq invasion; here, suddenly, was proof to the contrary. After Mejía had done his time in the Fort Sill military prison, he'd emerged as an important leader of the GI resistance movement.

But, even while he'd been still serving in Iraq, he'd been reluctant to put his men in danger when he could see no good reason for doing so. He'd also gone out of his way to avoid pointless Iraqi deaths. 'You can set up a traffic-control point or a blocking position in the middle of nowhere where it's dark, where there are no lights, just by putting across a strand of concertina wire. When somebody gets to it, you open fire. You're basically setting up a trap, pretty much ensuring that you will fire a weapon at someone, even though that road may be on the way to the hospital. As a squad leader, I'd put chem lights on the concertina wire, "stay away" signs in both English and Arabic, orange traffic cones, flashlights and things like that. I would make it a thousand per cent clear that there was a blocking position here, that if you come this way, you might get shot. And we avoided killing people that way.'

Here was another difficulty in theorising a resistance to killing. Mejía did as much as he could to avoid taking lives, but there was nothing instinctive about his reluctance to kill. It was a conscious political decision, based upon his identification with the Iraqi people—others made quite different choices.

Reppenhagen had said that one of his biggest regrets from Iraq involved an incident in which he'd been ordered to fire on the bodyguards of a deputy governor: men who were actually fighting on the US side but had been wrongly identified as insurgents. 'We got orders to fire and nobody fired. We all kinda hesitated for a moment. The major got really pissed and yelled at us again, fire. Finally one person started and then we all started. We hit a civilian car coming towards us, lit that car up, finished it off, just wasted all these people.

'Afterwards, everybody tried to make excuses—you know, collateral damage; wrong place, wrong time; they had weapons, and if they were insurgents, we'd all be dead—but really ... well, I don't know. Most of these guys [the Americans] were in a security detachment that had been there for half a year without any combat, and they were really eager to get their trigger time. Even the major wanted to get his combat patch. He wanted to see a fight; he was hyped up. Everyone was finally getting their game faces on. That rite of passage: God forbid that those kids might come home from a year in Iraq without a single firefight! They were so ready to cowboy it up and shoot somebody that they didn't take the time to identify the target.' Such men wanted to kill and Mejía didn't, and the distinction came down to ideology rather than biology.

When you looked back more closely at previous wars, the explanation of why particular soldiers could or could not kill became extraordinarily complicated. During the Great War, the American pacifist Jane Addams interviewed soldiers recuperating in hospital. A young man told her that he'd been at the front for more than three months and he'd never once shot his gun in a way that could hit another soldier. His brother, an officer, also fired high, as did scores of other soldiers they knew. At first, it seemed a perfect confirmation of that inbuilt resistance to killing: large numbers of soldiers either firing high or not firing at all, just as Marshall described.

The problem was, however, that they weren't acting involuntarily. Like Mejía, they were choosing not to kill—and that was quite different. 'Why should you kill men who live in other countries,' one of them asked, 'men whom in times of peace you would like and respect?' That sentiment, during the Great War at least, was far more common than is sometimes acknowledged. It manifested itself most dramatically during the Christmas truces that broke out all along the Western Front in 1914 and, despite the best efforts of officers on both sides, again to a lesser extent in 1915.

Even more interestingly, throughout the length of the war, soldiers often developed informal understandings with the enemy to minimise killing. While these arrangements did not necessarily rise to the fully fledged truces of Christmas 1914, they still had a direct impact on the relations between the belligerents. This 'live and let live' system, as it was known, was epitomised by the noncommissioned officer of a particular garrison who explained to the men relieving him: 'Mr Bosche ain't a bad feller. You leave 'im alone; 'e'll leave you alone.'

This was nothing to do with an evolutionary resistance to killing. The unit was operating on the basis that if they didn't initiate combat, neither would the Germans. The soldiers fired their weapons only to propitiate their officers, and when they did, they aimed high or fired randomly. The men actively resented anyone who behaved aggressively towards the enemy, on the quite reasonable basis that such action would invite a German response. In some sectors, combat became entirely ritualised, with, at a certain time each day, the guns firing at an empty area of the enemy trench. The other side would respond in kind, allowing all the soldiers to report a satisfactory expenditure of ammunition without anyone being hurt. Each side understood that a violation of the arrangement would make life harder for everyone; accordingly, they both did their best to keep it.

The system depended on the men recognising their opponents as rational agents, with whom they could make common cause. In the trenches of France, this was not necessarily so difficult: the British and the Germans had a long history of interaction and knew something of each other's culture.

In Iraq, it was different. 'The moment we got there,' Mejía said, 'we realised that they were calling them "*hajis*"'. Among US troops, he explained, *haji* had become a derogatory term for Arabs, 'and they used it to dehumanise everything. *Haji* applied to everything, not just the people. It was *haji* food, *haji* women, *haji* kids, *haji* music—everything was *haji*, worthless.' The racism of US soldiers, he said, while never a formal part of training, was tacitly condoned by commanders. 'They don't prepare you for a different culture, and they don't want you to understand it, because understanding Iraqi culture means you humanise Iraqis. It means you can communicate with Iraqis: "Hey, how are you doing? What's that you're eating? Where did it come from? Oh, your wife made it for you—OK." It's not in their interests that you have those conversations; it's not in their interests that you view the people as people.'

Racial prejudice worked on two levels. First, it undermined any conscious attempts of soldiers to minimise killing, since you were much less likely to establish a 'live and let live' agreement with an enemy you saw as barbarous or irrational. Second, because racism turned humans into abstractions, it made pulling the trigger much easier. The Pacific battles of the Second World War were far more lethal than either those of the Great War or, indeed, combat against the Nazis, since the Japanese and the Americans viewed each other in explicitly racialised ways. The consensus among many US marines was that while the Germans were human beings who had been misled, the Japanese were closer to animals. That was why 44 per cent of US soldiers said that they'd 'really like to kill a Japanese soldier', compared with only 6 per cent who harboured the same thoughts about Germans.

Such was the context for most of the trophy heads about which I'd read. With the military authorities urging soldiers to 'get some more monkey meat' before they went into battle, it was not surprising that some saw Japanese bodies as merely animal carcasses. The sentiment was so prevalent that one soldier thought it appropriate to send as a gift to President Roosevelt a letter-opener made out of Japanese bones (he refused it), and the *Baltimore Sun* reported, matter-of-factly, that a local mother had asked the authorities to allow her son to post home an ear he'd cut from a Japanese soldier in the Pacific.

Joanna Bourke had suggested that the act of killing varied immensely according to the cultural context. I'd quoted her Orwell's famous remarks from the Spanish Civil War, in which, in rebuttal of those progressives who saw the fighting there as fundamentally different from previous conflicts, he'd declared that, regardless of the cause, bullets hurt, corpses stink and men facing gunfire wet their pants with fear. Did she really think that killing would be different in somewhere like Spain compared with, say, the Great War?

'Absolutely. Yes. That's one reason why I restricted myself to simply three situations—basically British, Americans and a few Australians, rather than French or Germans or Russians—because it was one way of narrowing the issues. The Spanish Civil War is a really good example. You talked about bullets hurting. Well, the experience of dying is probably less different—though it does still vary from culture to culture—but certainly for killing, the social context makes a huge difference. The languages people have to make sense of their experiences are drawn from specific histories, and these vary immensely. When you have a strong religious element, a Christian culture, for instance, the language of redemption and sacrifice becomes much more important, which affects the way people talk about—even experience—trauma. These are social experiences and you have to understand them in context.'

Coincidentally, Mejía was in the middle of reading *Homage to Catalonia*, and he too saw more differences than similarities in the war Orwell describes. 'It's nothing like what we went through. He says—and it's one of the parts of his book that I like the most—that the chaos in the International Brigades was not due to the lack of conventional structure and the lack of hierarchy, but was because they were pulling them together with very few resources and under extraordinary conditions, and if you were to try to form a conventional military like that, it would crumble. What kept those people going was that they believed in what they were doing. And that was one of the most difficult things about serving in Iraq is that we didn't have a reason to be there.

'Besides, we were facing a ghost enemy. When US troops get attacked, they retaliate with massive force and against everything that moves. There's no front line; there's no rear. That makes a difference, if you are killing civilians and killing people who are unarmed. The dynamics of the war have a lot to do with how you feel about it.'

How, then, had he been trained to kill?

Workman had claimed that basic training process took the individual out of each recruit, and that was pretty much how Mejía understood it, too. But for him the implications were much less positive. 'When you join up, the first thing that goes is your hair. Suddenly everyone is the same. Then your clothes: everyone wears the same uniform, no nametags or anything. Then the way you walk, because you're marching, all the same. When you go to the mess hall, you take whatever food they give you. The sense of humour becomes one sense of humour; the language becomes one language, filled with profanity. Where you sleep, where you eat, what you do after you eat, what you do when you wake up: everything becomes part of the program. Your individuality, your humanity, your sense of self is destroyed. You become part of the unit. If you do something that you're not meant to do, they'll say, "Oh, so, you want to be an individual". And then they smoke you.'

He caught my incomprehension. 'Smoking means they physically punish you. Or, what's even worse, they punish—smoke—your whole unit. One time this guy got candy when he wasn't supposed to, and so they dropped everybody and they made us do push-ups, and they made this guy call cadence: one, two, three, four; one, two, three, four! People hated him! Because he fucked up—he went and bought candy—and now everybody's doing push-ups for him, because he was an individual, because he didn't want to be part of the program, because he dared to think for himself or do something for himself. So they destroy all of that; they destroy that sense of self; they destroy that sense of the individual, and I think that has a lot to do with not questioning, detaching yourself from the idea that you will be killing a human being. It's what everyone else is doing, and you do it, too. It's part of the program.'

I asked him how important realism training was, and rather to my surprise, he completely rejected the idea that his training was realistic: 'No, it wasn't. Not at all.' I didn't understand. He'd discussed a regime identical to the one Grossman described: firing ranges with human-shaped silhouettes that popped up for a few seconds and fell down again, a process that turned four crucial aspects of using the weapon—correct posture, regulated breathing, aiming at the centre mass and squeezing the trigger—into second nature. Wasn't that realistic?

He shook his head. 'If you see an accident where an eighteen-wheeler truck smashes into a little car, it has an effect. That's reality! You're an active participant and you think about it; you see the people involved as people, and you understand that what happened to them could happen to you. That's why in the military, realistic training would have the wrong effect. You don't want soldiers to think: fuck, we've just opened fire with this 50 calibre machine gun on a car full of civilians. If you think about that, it will kill you. So they don't make it real; they make it *automatic*. Remove the thought; remove the analysis; make it mechanical.'

He illustrated with a story about how, when he and his men had established a traffic-control point, one of the cars coming towards them didn't stop. Fearing a suicide attack, the closest soldiers opened fire on the engine block. The vehicle kept moving until it rolled to a stop near where Mejía and another soldier stood. 'Without even thinking, my rifle was trained on the car, and I was squeezing the trigger and firing. How do you do that without thinking? I didn't think that this was a human being; I didn't think that he had kids; I didn't think that he might have been a teacher or whatever. The whole thinking process—the emotional process—was completely removed. That's how they train you. They train you to not think, because they know if you do think, if you do experience what's happening, it's going to affect you so much that you're not going to be effective.'

Mejía was a squad leader, so it wasn't necessarily his job to pull the trigger in combat. But on a few occasions, it had been forced upon him. 'The first time I actually saw what bullets do to a person', he said, choosing words slowly and with care, 'was the first time I fired at a person who died. I remember him coming out from the crowd and he had a grenade, and then he threw it and we fired on him, and I have no recollection of squeezing the trigger. Later on, I checked my magazine and it had bullets missing. So I know that I fired eleven bullets at him, but the moment when he was hit and he fell and he died— I don't even remember it. I remember him coming out and swinging his arms to throw, and then I remember him being dragged by the shoulders through a pool of blood.'

Like Reppenhagen, Mejía understood his anti-war activism as, in part, a form of atonement. 'One of my great fears when I came back was not knowing whether I would be able to be an effective dad. We had done so many horrible things there. So as an educator and a father, how could you teach morality and good behaviour and love when you'd been involved in behaviour that was so horrible? I knew that I had changed a lot in the time I went to the war, and I just wasn't sure I could do it; I wasn't sure that I could be a dad again.'

How had he changed?

'Before the war, I was about to graduate from college, and I was an excellent student and had everything ready: I was going to a very, very nice school; I had a little kid; I was living a good life. And after the war, when I came home and began speaking out, I just could not go back to that. I could not go back to getting my degree and getting a nice comfy job and making good money and not caring about what happens elsewhere. I think that's because of the pain—having done all the things that we did. How do you live with yourself unless you try to undo some of that?'

We drank the rest of the wine. Many US peace activists, he said, were placing all their hopes on Obama's presidential bid, something about which Mejía was entirely sceptical. Obama would keep the wars going, Mejía said, but he'd just do so in ways that were smarter.

On the other hand, he expected the anti-war sentiment to continue to grow. And in his attempts to organise soldiers, he'd felt that he'd recaptured the most positive aspects of military life: 'The mission has changed, but the culture remains, the sense of humour, the same experiences. This is a place where I'm still comfortable, because the people I talk to have been through the same experiences. That sense of belonging: by speaking out against the war, organising and the rest of it, in a way I still have that.'

18

A DINK FOR JO-JO

'The cowboy thing, the frontier masculinity thing, masculinity defined as conquest: I hear y'all got a bit of that going on back in Australia, too.'

Raleigh, North Carolina, was as spectacular as anywhere I'd been, all oak trees and gentle hills, but we were once again in a Starbucks coffee shop—'you know, one of those crappy corporate places'—because Stan Goff, whom I'd been reading for years online, had nominated it as easier for a stranger to find. I'd recognised him as soon as he'd walked in. He looked a lot like Grossman—the same rangy physique, the same aura of confidence—and nothing like the shop's other customers, mostly over-caloried and under-exercised teens.

Goff had come straight from a building site, where he worked in demolition, but for decades he'd been a soldier, mostly in Special Operations: Vietnam, Guatemala, El Salvador, Grenada, Panama, Venezuela, Honduras, Korea, Colombia, Peru and Somalia. His last mission had been in Haiti, where he'd strongly identified with the impoverished supporters of Jean-Bertrand Aristide and had resisted orders to serve the ruling clique, a group tied to the Duvalier death squads. Driven out of the army, Goff had become a peace activist, with his military experience adding a certain authority to his articles for leftish publications. An evolution from Special Operations to socialism was rare enough, but more recently, Goff had become interested in radical feminism, as his latest book, *Sex and War*, attested.

When I explained about the head from Gallipoli, he nodded, unsurprised. 'Proof of conquest. Hunting trophies—masculinity defined as conquest. If you remember, when Zarqawi was killed in Iraq, and CentCom did the briefing, they had a giant photo of Zarqawi's dead face up behind them. That was a hunting trophy, too, on display to show everyone: we're real men; we've done it; we've bagged Zarqawi.'

Goff had enlisted, like so many young men, after watching *The Green Berets*, a John Wayne movie. He'd understood Vietnam as a struggle to stop evil taking over the world. 'It sounds stupid and simplistic, but we were children, and we really did believe in the world communist conspiracy—just like people a few years ago still believed that Saddam Hussein did 9/11.'

But the all-American ideals of the movies soon gave way to the reality of Vietnam. Within weeks of arrival, he'd attached a human skull to his backpack and was admiring the severed ears that his comrades had taken. How did that process work? How far was the journey from the white-bread heroism of John Wayne to that kind of almost bestial violence?

Goff laughed. 'If there was a distance, it didn't seem to take us long to overcome it. When I was there, I thoroughly believed that if I allowed the idea that Vietnamese were human to penetrate my consciousness, it would lower my chances of survival. And the sentiment was nearly universal in infantry units. People who had not generalised their hatred of Vietnamese, people who were not leaning forward to kill Vietnamese—they were the exception rather than the rule.'

That was why he was so scathing about warriordom, the visions of paladins and knights and the rest of it. For him, the official code of the army idealised a version of masculinity that was almost socio-pathic: 'They've got this list of army values and it's a cardboard caricature, something from the movies, something that only the most obtuse of the officer corps might actually believe: a nationalist manhood that's tough and moral and so on. They want to promote a frontier masculinity and control it—only take it so far so that it's acceptable to everyone back home.

'The problem is that once you expose these kids to what real war is about, some of them are going to get by the best they can, some of them are going to pull back from it and oppose it, and some of them are gonna say, yeah, I'm there ... See, the officer corps wants to ride this military masculinity like a horse with a bit in its mouth. But sometimes the horse will spit it out. You know about Haditha?' This was a massacre of Iraqis by marines. 'That kind of thing was so common in Vietnam—people have no idea. It was like: so and so's a cherry; he hasn't had his first kill; let's send him out in the village to shoot a *papa san*. Common, common, common! The first person I saw killed in Vietnam was just a *mama san* out there hoeing a garden patch. Jo-Jo got killed by a booby trap last month, so we're going to go out there and get a dink for Jo-Jo. They just went out there and hosed down an old woman and made up a story about how she threw a hand grenade. And then they came back and heated up some C rations and smoked a joint.'

He took a sip of his Starbucks coffee. 'You can't put the bit back in their mouth. When they get to the point when they'll go out and shoot another human being just for shits and giggles, you're not going to bring them back. We got a lot of kids coming home right now who, for a whole period of time, are gonna have to play act about giving a shit about anything.'

In *Sex and War*, Goff describes the act of killing as playing out less like Sylvester Stallone than Ted Bundy. Killing, he says, is banal, mechanical, almost under-stimulating. Asked what he meant, he hesitated and then laughed. 'I'll tell you an interesting story. It's kind of a confession—I'm not particularly proud of this.' Given we'd already discussed skulls and ears, that was quite a warning. I certainly didn't expect to hear about Arnold Schwarzenegger.

'I ran out of work some years ago and ended up getting picked up as a military technical advisor for this male revenge fantasy, a Schwarzenegger film called *Collateral Damage*. I did things like choreograph battle scenes, made sure people's uniforms were OK, taught extras how to clean AK-47s, hung around with the director while he asked lame questions—that sort of thing.

'Anyway, whenever they had scenes when people were shot, or there were explosions, I told them, that's not real. Explosions don't have big fireballs like that. They said, it's Hollywood: we have to have the fireballs. I was explaining to them that when people are shot—if it's a kill shot—they fall in the direction that gravity pulls them, but they wouldn't allow that either. It has to be a Sam Peckinpah scene: people have to fly through the air whenever they are hit.

'At another point, I helped the second director do a scene where, after a battle, they stripped the corpses and put them in a pile, which is what soldiers would do. But they said, no, we can't show that. Why couldn't they show that? Because it was banal; it was mechanical; it was very matter of fact and undramatic, and it did exactly what seeing people killed in real life does: it reminds you of the simplicity of your own mortality. It reminds you that, in an instant, you're converted into something that's basically a sack of shit, you know?'

He took another slug of his coffee and put the cup down. 'And that's what people find out in combat. Young men killing people in combat get pumped up thinking this is gonna be some big experience. But the thunder doesn't crash; the sky doesn't open up: nothing happens. It's really ... it's not a dramatic experience.'

'Why wasn't it dramatic though? You've just taken a life. What could be more dramatic than that?'

Combat itself, he said, was sudden and terrifying, so much so that new soldiers were often paralysed with terror. That was the point of military training: to overcome that tendency to freeze; to drill the recruits a thousand times so that, despite the fear and the adrenalin, they continued to react, so that they knew instinctively to breathe, relax, aim, align the sites, squeeze. But killing itself was simple: 'There's nothing complicated about it. Things don't happen; the sky doesn't fall. And so because nothing happens, you're in a dimension where nothing matters, where you don't have to take a moral position on anything. That's what we said in Vietnam: it don't mean nothing.'

War—modern war—wasn't about knights or chivalry. For a start, most people, he said, don't actually go anywhere near combat, since the military was so big and complicated that the vast majority of its personnel necessarily served in some sort of supporting role. Even for those in combat units, combat wasn't about heroism, and competent commanders actively dissuaded glory-seekers and romantics. Successful operations involved cautious planning rather than recklessness, and most victories were therefore enormously one-sided, a brutal and systematic process of gunning down people caught unprepared and in the open. In any case, most of the deaths in combat were civilians, and they weren't killed by individuals but by artillery and bombs and the like. Even when soldiers fired small arms rather than relying on the technical weapons that did most of the damage, they very rarely saw the enemy or knew whether they personally had killed anyone.

'The infantry is factory work', he said, as if the point were almost too obvious to require confirmation. 'It's completely Taylorised. There's a soldier's manual, and it tells you how to do every single task in your job. There's a task condition and training standard, and you memorise those things by rote. Technology just makes it more and more mechanised, since often the main thing you do is maintenance on the vehicle. It's extremely routine. You got a certain place to put everything, and you're basically operating a great big machine, and there is no room in either the technology or the doctrine for initiative or creativity. Even the tactics are rote. They do battle drills over and over again. You know, someone calls out red; you do a red. They yell blue; you do a blue.'

That, he said, was why so many soldiers wanted to join elite units. 'In Special Operations units, they put you in situations that are completely unpredictable and you have to make decisions. You have semi-autonomy. In a Taylorised, factory-style military, Special Operations constitutes an artisan class. The military leadership is constantly trying to impose Taylorised efficiency on those units, and so between the conventional military and the unconventional military, there's constant tension. Special Forces soldiers do not want to wear their uniforms correctly; they do not want to trim their moustaches; they don't want to march; they don't want to call anyone by their rank. They push back, and even though they can't necessarily articulate it, the space to make decisions, to exercise creativity is sufficiently important that they're willing to buck authority to defend it.'

I nodded. When John the kangaroo-shooter had suggested the army could use a squad of roo-shooters because they were independent and capable of taking their own initiative, it was the glamorous Special Operations image he had in mind. Yet Special Operations resembled the army as a whole as little as Demetri's ute did a cattle abattoir.

Which was, historically, what had so confounded the happy warriors of the Great War. They'd yearned for killing as a grand experience, a transcendent act to deliver them from the banality of peace; instead, they'd discovered wartime violence as Goff described it. The contradiction was simple but inescapable: the Great War heightened modernity rather than ending it, inserting men into the very conditions they'd sought to escape. Rather than jousting in a tourney, they found themselves working in an industry of human butchery. Passive perseverance and dreary labour; digging holes and keeping watch; monotonous, rote tasks punctuated by paralysing, jagged instants of danger: that was the Great War.

That was why it eventually produced so many ironic inversions of the warrior metaphors. If, as William James had suggested, many young men in 1914 saw the peacetime world as a cattle yard, then they quickly came to apply the same description to industrial war. Sassoon, for instance, describes troops on their way to France as 'bovine', since, like cattle, they were not going out to do things but to have things done to them.

A snippet of dialogue from Henry Barbusse's *Under Fire* captures the same point. One soldier remarks that, back home, the people 'drool all over the idea' of great charges and glorious advances, suggesting a battle must be a fine thing to see. His comrade responds: 'A fine thing! Oh shit! It's just as though an ox said: "It must be a fine thing, at the abattoirs in La Villette, to see all those hosts of oxen being driven forward".'

Most famously, in 'Anthem for Doomed Youth', Owen asks, 'What passing bells for those who die as cattle?' His point isn't about war's horror. He is suggesting that men died like the cattle I'd seen slaughtered in Melbourne's west, that they were killed systematically, automatically and—above all—meaninglessly. Their deaths weren't dramatic or heroic; they were routine, registering as little as the cows processed by an abattoir, with the bells warranted by human mortality replaced by impersonal mechanical noise.

Instead of feeling they were sheepdogs protecting a society of sheep, the French soldiers of 1917 used the same image in reverse. Marching to the front lines, they sarcastically 'baaed'—hardened combat soldiers identifying themselves, not as warriors, but as lambs going to slaughter.

The disillusionment of Great War veterans was often attributed to the peculiarities of trench warfare, with men who'd expected thrilling cavalry charges forced instead to crouch knee-deep in mud. But if the grotesque immobility of the war heightened the alienation, it was still only a symptom of a problem that was structural rather than geographical. 'The military is a bureaucratic institution', Goff said, finishing off his coffee. 'That's what everyone has to understand first and foremost. The military is IB fucking M—it's not a bunch of warriors.'

After he left, I stayed in Starbucks alone for a while, in part to use its Wi-Fi to check my email. But I also wanted some time to think. The conversation had convinced me that my approach needed to shift, that a focus on the individual experience of killing was itself a by-product of the warrior mythos. If modern war was anything, it wasn't individual, and even one-on-one killings were necessarily marked by the total context in which they occurred. Today's soldiers might have more mobility than trench fighters, but they were even more enmeshed in a huge organisation, without which their individual tasks were impossible. The army of the Great War was like an Edwardian steel foundry, an old-style factory spouting steam and showering sparks. But as Goff said, today's army was IBM, and that meant that theorising war through personal psychology made as little sense as analysing Windows Vista as if it were handicraft.

With animal slaughter or capital punishment, the organisational structure was more obvious: you couldn't go to the abattoir I'd visited and imagine that slitting thousands of cows' throats each day could be disconnected from the experience of the factory system as a whole. But the mythology of war pushed you to see individual encounters as the archetype of combat, even when that was self-evidently not true. When I thought about it, all the veterans I'd interviewed had said explicitly that their face-to-face experiences had been exceptional. Workman had explained that, before the ambush in which he'd been wounded, he'd killed lots of people, but in a mortar unit and from a distance. Mejía had described most battles as involving soldiers on a Humvee firing at muzzle flashes until they all ran out of ammunition.

'Most of the time', Reppenhagen had said, 'it's so hard to tell who killed who. Most of the firefights involved crew-served weapons, 50 calibre machine guns, Mark-19 fully automatic grenade-launchers, and 240 Bravo rapid-fire machine guns all aiming at an area—just lighting it up. The commander says, cease fire, cease fire; your platoon sergeant says, cease fire, cease fire, but you don't hear anything above all the noise and the shit that's going on, and so all you notice is when somebody stops firing and then everyone else stops firing. Then you go out on a dismount patrol, scour the area, look to see if there's anybody left. Sometimes there is; sometimes there's not—but nobody knows who really got them.'

But one could pull back even further than that. Even firefights from Humvees weren't necessarily representative since, as Goff said, most contemporary killing was done with bombs and missiles and other distance weapons. In twenty-first-century war, you could sit in an airbase in Texas or Arizona or Nevada and tear tribesmen in Afghanistan into bloody shreds with a Predator drone, with the results showing on a video feed delivered from a continent away. Or you could be further removed still. The complexity of the military today, Goff had argued, meant that most recruits never went near the battlefield, but that wasn't to say the support roles weren't vital. The fighting in Iraq depended on a global infrastructure and, in that respect, the attribution of involvement in killing was inherently arbitrary. Who were the killers in the initial 'shock and awe' attacks on Baghdad? The pilots, sure, but what about the designers, the programmers, the military engineers: had they killed more or fewer people than Camilo Mejía?

With that thought, I laughed, a little raggedly and sufficiently loudly that the other customers gave me a worried look. Jeremiah Workman had seemed so much like the quintessential US soldier that I'd been implicitly comparing everyone else with him. But the image forming now was of someone utterly different, someone about whom I hadn't thought for months. Perhaps the archetypical representative of modern war wasn't a muscled-up soldier with a bayonet but someone with glasses and a suit, quietly and efficiently working on more efficient ways to kill, and with so little personal exposure to the bloody mess that contemporary explosives made out of human flesh that killing became entirely a technical challenge. Perhaps, in other words, he wasn't Jeremiah Workman. Perhaps he was Fred Leuchter.

19

WE OURSELVES ARE THE WAR

What makes the green grass grow?
Blood! Blood makes the green grass grow
What is the spirit of the bayonet?
To kill! To kill with cold blue steel!

We were sitting outside the Ruta Maya café, just near St Edward's University in Austin, Texas, where the noticeboard promoted Tai Chi classes and the coffee was all organic and the one-drop bass line of a college reggae band rumbled from the stereo almost in time to the cadences Ronn Cantu was softly chanting, words he'd been taught as a new recruit.

My last day in the USA and I had an evil hangover. It was Texas's fault. The state that spawned George W Bush seemed indelibly associated with the violent masculinity that Goff had described, and all the way to Austin, I was remembering a terrified Henry Smith dragged through the streets on a carnival float, with the mob panting beside him.

Of course, Austin wasn't actually a wild frontier. When the taxi had pulled up outside the hotel lobby the previous evening, the driver had counted his change to the sounds of rhythm and blues playing somewhere in the distance. This city described itself as the live music capital of America, and the kids spilling out into the hot, dry evening weren't a lynch mob but the tail end of Keep Austin Weird, a music festival grown from the local alternative culture.

Everywhere else, weirdness had seemed well and truly on the run, chased out of town by Starbucks and Super 8 motels, so its preservation here in Texas seemed a worthy endeavour. Besides, I was exhausted from the almost daily plane flights and the bad food and a constant preoccupation with death, but was far too keyed up to actually sleep. 'My senses are charred', wrote Owen to Sassoon, less than a month before he was killed. Owen had been through months of combat, so of course the comparison was wildly inappropriate. But still, charred was how I felt, and it was good, then, to be with other people in the enormous park near the Colorado River, hearing Charlie Sexton jam Rolling Stones songs with Alejandro Escovedo on the festival stage, and drinking watery beer in a crowded tent, and muttering drunkenly about wire as the enemy of the hunting man.

Inevitably, in the morning, the intersection between Texas heat and alcoholic dehydration felt markedly less pleasant, and I sipped my Diet Coke and listened to Cantu's chants with a certain nausea.

Like the other Iraq veterans, he came from a family with its own military tradition: a father who'd been in Vietnam. When school ended, he'd initially worked as a computer programmer before tiring of the pressures of the job. Military life seemed to offer something better—or at least a change. 'Being a little, fat computer nerd,' he joked, 'I wanted to do something 100 per cent different. That's why I joined the infantry.'

That was in 1998, and just as Mejía had said, war didn't feel real back then: 'Even though we did the training, it was always, like ... we're doing it because we have to, and so it was always like cops and robbers or cowboys and Indians. Bang, bang: you're dead. OK, lie down. Like an expensive game of paintball.'

The cadences about bayonets and blood served a different function. They didn't teach you how to kill, but they did foster a certain mind-set, which he enthusiastically embraced. 'I gave myself to them,' he said, 'hook, line and sinker. Mentally, where I was when I first came out of the army in 2002 was nowhere close to where I was when I came into the army.'

His youthful liberalism collapsed all along the line. Militarism was structurally conservative, not simply because it honoured tradition and obedience and other traditional values, but also because of the implicit distinction made between soldiers and citizens. Grossman had described the sheep as good, productive people, and assured his audience that the defining quality of a warrior dog was love for such citizens. 'You are the warriors', he'd said, with such emotion he almost seemed to be crying. 'You are the sheepdogs, whose job it is to protect the lambs.'

This was all very well, except that sheepdogs didn't just protect sheep: they controlled them. The model implied that there were soldiers and there were citizens, and one group clearly knew better than the other. Why should warriors worry about the woolly ideas preoccupying the flock? Grossman, for instance, wanted police officers to carry guns at all times, and he had no patience for civilian objections. 'Ain't nothing wrong with a cop who carries a gun off duty!' he'd yelled, berating his absent critics. 'And there's nothing wrong with you, buddy—you're in denial. You're a sheep—say baa-aa!'

The sheepdog–sheep schema was inherently antidemocratic, and its implicit contempt for civilian opinion conditioned a deep military conservatism. 'After my first term', Cantu said, 'I was very much like the Vets for Freedom guys: all gung-ho. I wanted to go to war—I just *wanted* it. So when Iraq broke out, I didn't ask any questions. I was back in school studying journalism, and I waited a full week and a half until I was in the recruiters' office saying, "You've got to get me over there".' And they did.

But because Cantu took seriously the pro-war arguments of people like Colin Powell, his hawkishness was wavering even before his tour began. Cantu initially reacted with disappointment to Bush's 'Mission Accomplished' speech: Iraq had been liberated, he thought, so he'd missed the battles he'd yearned to fight. Then, with Saddam's capture, he was convinced once more that the combat would soon end. The intensification of the violence seemed to him inherently odd: if the invasion had been a liberation, shouldn't the war be winding down?

By the time he arrived, in February 2004, he was already wondering if what he'd been told was true. He was also profoundly troubled by the prevailing attitudes among his fellow soldiers to the Iraqis, the people he was supposedly there to serve. 'Because they don't speak English and they have flies on their food and they wash their clothes in dirty mud holes, there's a perception that they're less than human, more like animals. Because they don't have the nice possessions that we do, they're less than we are. So there's definitely ... if not racism, at least a mind-set that their culture, their religion, is inferior to ours. When people don't speak your language, you feel that they're incapable of communication, just because you don't understand them. In Iraq, that's multiplied a thousandfold—and then you're given a rifle and told that whatever you do, you won't get into any trouble.'

That kind of cultural chauvinism was not uniquely American. Before Gallipoli, the Anzac contingent did its training in Egypt, where the soldiers related to the local Muslims very much in the way Cantu described, and for similar reasons. Australians at that time enjoyed one of the highest standards of living in the world; Cairo was desperately poor, a city of filth and squalor and everything that went along with that. Inevitably, the differences gave rise to racism. 'I was a sure believer in White Australia before I left home, but now I am a perfervid and rabid "White Australian"', wrote one soldier, complaining that the natives were 'filthy beasts'. 'I would not trust a nigger [an Arab]', another said, 'as far as I would a Chinaman, and the latter I would only trust round a corner if he was hobbled, hand-cuffed, and covered with a revolver, loaded and the trigger pulled out'. 'We are learning Arabic,' reported a third, 'and I know one word, "inshi" [sic], clear out, go to blazes etc. That is what we yell at the niggers when they come near the camp.'

You couldn't blame the soldiers, any more than you could hold them responsible for the war. These were ordinary men, with little knowledge of other peoples, abruptly transported thousands of miles from home at a time when White Australia was official policy. But their words also served as a reminder of something often lost in the ahistorical Anzac commemorations: whatever else it was, Gallipoli was also an invasion of a Muslim country by a white Christian coalition, a conflict in which the Turkish soldiers launched their near suicidal bayonet charges with the battle cry 'Allahu Akbar', and the Anzacs responded with Arabic picked up in Cairo, shouting 'Inshi Allah'.

Was that the explanation for a souvenired head? If the trophies from the Pacific were facilitated by perceptions of the Japanese as animals, and if the *haji* label allowed today's soldiers their grisly photos in Iraq, was it not plausible to identify a racial element to the souveniring of a Turkish head? The taboo against depriving a dead man of a Christian burial wouldn't, after all, apply so strongly to someone who'd died in the name of Allah.

This was all pure speculation, of course, but it did seem to explain what had happened after the coroner's inquest. When the authorities decided to repatriate the head to Turkey, the only dissenting voice had been, once more, that of Ramazan Altintas. He was glad, he'd told the papers, to see the dead soldier going home, but he still thought there should be a more thorough inquiry into the head's origins, and he wanted the government to organise a public ceremony to farewell the man. There was a massive and growing interest in the Great War, and given a chance, thousands would attend a public commemoration of a dead Turkish soldier, a service that would also right a historic wrong.

The Turkish ambassador to Australia, Tansu Okandan, disagreed. While he described the soldier as a 'martyr', he insisted that further enquiries into the head were unnecessary. Turkey and Australia enjoyed a very strong relationship. They should not dwell on an unfortunate incident from the past.

As the credentialed representative of his country, the ambassador possessed the most obvious moral claim on the dead soldier and, not surprisingly, his views prevailed. There was no investigation (other than the one carried out by Sergeant Kennedy), and the only ceremony was small, private and low-key. The Australian Minister for Veterans' Affairs, Danna Vale, did not speak: instead, she issued a statement thanking the Turkish government for its graciousness and understanding. A serving Australian naval officer escorted the coffin back to Turkey for its burial on 18 March 2003—which meant the man killed at Gallipoli in 1915 was interred just two days after the Coalition of the Willing invaded Iraq.

Turkey was a traditional US ally. It was also largely Muslim, with a population almost uniformly opposed to the Iraq invasion. On 1 March 2003—less than three weeks before the head's burial—the Turkish parliament, under massive popular pressure, had voted against allowing US soldiers use its soil, the most obvious access point into Iraq. No wonder the Turkish ambassador spoke so carefully. Back in Ankara, the politicians were trying to prevent an open rift with the USA and its allies, while remaining acutely conscious of the growing clout of Turkey's own Islamist parties. In the context of Iraq, and of the ongoing War on Terror, the case of a Muslim man beheaded by a Christian invader involved obvious sensitivities. Much better to get the head home quietly; much better not to look too closely.

That death in Gallipoli was one among tens of thousands, an anonymous corpse that could be swept aside when it became politically embarrassing. But Ronn Cantu didn't have the same luxury. His descriptions of combat were very like Mejía's. 'Our convoy got shot at, and we just rolled through it. They were shooting at us, and I was firing at them out the window. I ended up squaring up to the window so I could shoot with my right hand, and I remember thinking, anywhere but the face. Then I changed that to: anything but the face or the neck. I swear to God: that was the only thing I was thinking. There was no emotion behind it whatsoever.'

The incident that changed everything took place later, on 15 May 2004, in the wake of a subsequent convoy attack. This time, one of the trucks was burning, and the commander insisted that it not be left to be used for insurgent propaganda. So Cantu and his comrades established a strong-point at a particular section of curved road. 'The thing was,' he said, 'you didn't have a whole lot of visibility, and we were scared, because that attack was the first one in which we'd had people hurt. A car came speeding towards us. Afterwards, I asked myself: Couldn't he see the American vehicle burning? Couldn't he hear everybody shouting? Couldn't he see me pointing my weapon? Why did he … but, you see, he just kept coming. So I fired into the vehicle—not trying to hit the driver, but just to stop the car. And it stopped, and I said, thank God; I didn't want to know what would have happened if it had got closer. But then a woman came out and started screaming. And I'm like, uh oh. That was when I saw that the car was full of people.'

'Was anyone hurt?'

'Yeah', he said. 'Yeah, they were. They pulled a man out, and he clearly wasn't alive, since they were dragging him out by his feet, letting him flop down. And I had a mini-freak-out, trying to get the medic. But by the time the medic came, they'd put the guy in the trunk and driven away, so I never had to see face-to-face what I had done.'

In the context of the ruination throughout Iraq, Cantu's was an ordinary, almost trivial story. After five years, there'd been so many checkpoints, so many killings. A car didn't stop; a civilian died: not only would the incident not make the papers, but it probably wasn't even recorded. The US military famously failed to keep a register of civilian casualties, and Iraq Body Count, the group usually quoted on the death toll, relied exclusively on media accounts for its data. When the family took the body away for burial, they erased the death from history—but that didn't make it any less significant for Cantu.

Where his first term with the army had transformed him from a liberal to a pro-war conservative, Iraq sent him back the other way, not just about the war but about everything. 'I think it came from wanting to give all life value. Having become somebody who has taken life away, I was turned back onto religion, not so much in an organised way, but in terms of inner reflection. Why do I value my life more than I value his life? And if I'm going to give his life value, how can I not give everyone else's value, too?' He joked about the change in his social attitudes: 'It was like I went: man, war is *wrong*—and gays *should* be allowed to marry!'

Cantu was still in the army, serving on a military base just out of Austin, even though he was a prominent member of Iraq Veterans against the War. He'd completed a second tour of Iraq, albeit in a non-combat role, and he was due back for a third time. That was why he was seeking conscientious-objector status. But even if he could convince the military to let him leave, he knew his future was uncertain. His computer training was out of date, and there was nothing much else he knew how to do. It was, he said, a common experience for veterans. The young men and women who enlisted to escape dull jobs in dead-end towns found that the army just represented more of the same, since few of the skills acquired in the military were in any way transferable. Most veterans Cantu knew had trickled back to the same menial positions they'd held before enlisting.

Cantu's was, then, the classic disillusionment. But how typical was it? People reacted to war and to killing differently, so generalisations were inherently problematic. Certainly, there were soldiers who came back from combat not only without cynicism but positively energised; there were those who found in killing exactly what they'd been looking for. In J Glenn Gray's account, the Second World War constituted, for some of his comrades, 'the one great lyric passage in their lives'. War promised an alternative to the emptiness of peace, and that was what it sometimes delivered. The most common—or perhaps most palatable—description of its pleasures invoked the camaraderie of the army, but there was also excitement, purpose, responsibility: all of these might be found on a battlefield. Workman's question was a fair one: where else would a twenty-one-year-old man from a small US town find himself in charge of life-and-death decisions every day? The proximity to death provided its own charge. Reppenhagen had explained that he'd never felt more alive than in the moments after a firefight, and survivors of the Great War said the same thing: 'a man who stepped out of the trenches at that moment, and lived through has never in all the ensuing years faced such a climax'.

But if there was a joy in facing violence, so too was there in inflicting it. 'All you do is move that finger', writes William Broyles in an *Esquire* article about his Vietnam service, 'so imperceptibly, just a wish flashing across your mind like a shadow, not even a full brain synapse, and *poof!* in a blast of sound and energy and light a truck or a house or even people disappear, everything flying and settling back into dust'. Broyles's is a description of control, of power. In killing like that, the individual radically asserts himself against others and the world, so that destruction becomes a perverse act of creation. Another Vietnam veteran, this time a sniper, talked of a long-range shot as an aesthetic pleasure, almost like a poem or a great painting: 'A kill at two klicks, that is beautiful. It stays with you … the bullet vaporizes the guy, explodes into him. Satisfying … hitting the target—beautiful.'

The yearning to fight, a lust for war, was not, in that sense, low or base but an expression of humanity's noblest aspirations, albeit radically inverted. People craved companionship; they wanted meaning, needed to express themselves, to leave a mark on their environment. The shame lay not in the desire but in the peace that could offer no outlets for human potential more attractive than a bayonet charge or a sniper duel.

Stan Goff had added a forensic dissection of gender roles in the military to his longstanding critique of the USA's imperial ambitions in the Middle East. He was scathing about warriordom and the rhetoric that accompanied it, as scathing as anyone I'd met. But at the end of our conversation, he'd said, 'I still dream that I'm in the military—and when I dream, I'm right into it, you know. It pulls people back. Sometimes, when I watch the footage from Iraq, I still find myself thinking about what I would do if I was there.'

To that extent, the happy warrior mythos, the vision of becoming in war the person you should have been in peace, could become real—but only sometimes, and only for some soldiers. The great irony of modern war, its awful contradiction, was that it simultaneously confounded the very desires that it stirred. A paradox nestled at the heart, for the structures that allowed war to promise something different from peace also ensured it delivered more of the same.

At the most basic level, every veterans' organisation or peace-time reunion spoke of the camaraderie of the army, and obviously the experience of shared danger built deep friendships. But the actual structures of the military were just as likely to break bonds as to form them. The army was a huge organisation, its hierarchies were externally imposed, and the maintenance of internal discipline entailed as much bastardry as bonding. The camaraderie between the men was forged against the organisation as much as it was created by it, and for every soldier who recalled the good times in uniform, there was another who remembered how he had been forced to wear a LOS insignia because of psychiatric problems, or who had hidden in a toilet cubicle silently crying during boot camp.

As for control, that was precisely what, most of the time, the ordinary soldier lacked. Churchill's comparison of the war to the Chicago stockyards made the point implicitly: just as the slaughter of animals on a mass scale could no longer indulge the individual quirks of people like Demetri, the mass killing of enemy soldiers needed a particular kind of organisation, one that managed its personnel as comprehensively as the meatworkers were controlled.

How did such an organisation kill? Remove the thought; remove the analysis; make the process mechanical: Mejía's description was of the same process that had transformed the master butcher of yesteryear into the one-cut wonder of the modern abattoir, a man who stood in the same position repeating the same task until it became as mechanical as the assembly line itself. The slaughter yard relied on an industrial logic, whereby responsibilities were broken down into their simplest components so that the job got done with maximum efficiency and, if need be, each employee could be quickly and easily replaced by another.

If the trenches of the Great War constituted one enormous factory, then a twenty-first-century army was, as Goff had said, more like IBM, except, of course, that its discipline was harsher and its hierarchies more overt than even the most rapacious of corporations. That was why the enablers that Grossman had described—the rehearsals, the use of teams, the abstraction, the dehumanisation—applied so neatly to death row. It wasn't simply that in both cases the intent was to deliberately take human lives. It was also that the techniques suited a particular institutional structure, that armies and prisons were both huge organisations, and they worked in similar ways.

As soon as you started thinking about mass killing, you stumbled across the *reductio ad absurdum* of warriordom. When genuine knights rode out to battle, each man was responsible for taking down his opponent, and to that extent, he determined his own fate through his strength, his skill, his individual abilities as a fighter. Today the generals could rain down a nuclear devastation on entire cities—perhaps even the planet as a whole—yet in that carnage, a slaughter that would surely represent the zenith of human war-making, the control would belong exclusively to the operator extending a single skinny finger to the launch button. Thousands of engineers and programmers and technicians had laboured to make an Armageddon possible, yet their contribution to a killing on a gargantuan scale would possess no emotional charge whatsoever. They were not Brooke's swimmers leaping into cleanness; they were desk workers coding flight patterns for missile strikes, with the same detachment as the geeks programming new modules for *America's Army*.

Fred Leuchter had been incredulous at the notion that his work might have had an impact on him. I don't kill people, he'd said, and I've never even seen an execution—why would I be affected? The military displayed the same bureaucratic chain as the prison— the same systematic diffusion, the same separation between the designers and the killers—which was why the autistic compartmentalisation demonstrated by Leuchter also informed discussions of

Iraq, and why the figure of a million deaths brought about by the invasion could be accepted by statisticians yet possess almost no emotional force in mainstream politics. Those most responsible for the carnage—the Bushes, the Blairs and the Howards—remained entirely insulated from the emotional force of what they'd wrought.

But the industrial logic necessary for a nuclear strike manifested itself, perhaps more unexpectedly, in individual killings as well. In his 1901 poem 'The Last Hero', GK Chesterton portrays killing as the apogee of the paladin's quest, an intimate act through which two warriors reaffirm each other's humanity: 'You never loved your friends, my friends, as I shall love my foes'. But killing a man with conditioned reflexes didn't involve any thought, any soul-searching, much less any love—and Mejía had shot an insurgent dead without even knowing that he'd done so. 'It was just like training', explained another Iraq veteran. 'I just loaded and fired my weapon from muscle memory. I wasn't even aware what my hands were doing.' Modern training was designed to make that possible. Because combat might be terrifying, because your body might overload with adrenalin in the midst of that noise and that chaos, the act of killing needed to become not profound but mechanical, something so simple and so automatic you could do it without thought and without emotion.

The training was even more necessary given the kinds of wars in which modern armies engaged. An invading army, an army of occupation, with its supply lines stretching across continents, was inherently more bureaucratic than, say, a ragtag militia defending its homeland. More than that, it could not allow its soldiers too much autonomy, since the conversations Mejía had described—the simple chats with locals about their customs—always contained the threat of a broader dialogue, through which the troops might come to identify with the aspirations of the people rather than the goals of the occupation. Hence the need for abstraction, for techniques whereby the job could be done without any human relationship with the enemy.

In the abattoir, in the death chamber, the moments of recognition—the times when abstraction became concrete—damaged the killers the most. When the victim transformed, unexpectedly, from an object to a living creature, the perpetrator needed something other than routine to justify his act. You could kill without thought, just as you could work efficiently in a factory without approving of the particular commodities you produced, yet later you still had to grapple with the question of whether the war was a fucking bullshit lie.

In the maelstrom of war, abstraction broke down far more easily than in the hermetically sealed death chamber, so soldiers were even more vulnerable to moments of identification than executioners. Mejía couldn't even remember the instant he killed an insurgent—but the bloodied corpse dragged away afterwards was imprinted deep in his psyche. It was no wonder that, afterwards, men came undone.

But there was more to it than that. As part of his application for conscientious-objector status, Cantu had collected letters of support, including from his parents. 'I was raised listening to my father's war stories, every single day. In 1998, when I decided to join the military, my father tried to talk me out of it. But I'd never known why. And then, in the letter of support he provided, he wrote that he hadn't wanted me to enlist because he didn't want me to become a murderer like he was; he didn't want me to become a killer like he'd been.' Cantu spoke with a strange wonder, as if this was something about which he'd been thinking a lot. 'My mom never served, but when I went into the army, she was proud; my father served, and when I went into the army, he told me not to go. And I never knew why. But now I understand what my father is wrestling with. Vietnam was forty years ago and he still talks about it every single day—and then says, yeah, I put that behind me. But he didn't. Not when you talk about it every day for forty years—it's not behind you at all.'

Cantu could see that process happening again: 'One of my roommates in Iraq was saying something about how PTSD only affected the weak-minded. It was his first tour and my second. I said to him, "When you get back, every single day, you'll think about Iraq". And now he's back, and that's exactly what he says: "Every single day I see something and it reminds me of Iraq".'

Cantu had been raised a Catholic, but now, he said, he saw himself as closer to Gnostic Christianity or even deism, believing in a higher power but not in any interventionist way, so that he saw no inconsistency between his faith and the teaching of evolution. This, I thought, was the conversation Cantu should have been having. The stereo was still pumping its faux-Jamaican rhythms, and the café clattered with laughter and conversation. Normal students doing normal things: Cantu should have been talking with them, not with me, discussing Gnosticism, arguing about politics, sex and poetry, and everything else that thoughtful young people discussed in university coffee shops.

However, Cantu's religiosity wasn't the result of airy philosophising but a direct consequence of taking a human life—and that made everything different. He smiled, a little sadly. 'You know, I think a large part of my enlistment was that I wanted my stories to tell my own kids one day. And now, if I ever have children, I'm not going to tell them that I served at all.' He went to war for stories— the tales that war traditionally provided—but he came back, not with more to say, but with less. 'I used to do public meetings', he said. 'One time, I was asked to speak in New Mexico after two other veterans, and listening to their stories, the only thing I could say was that there comes a time when talking about your experiences is no longer therapeutic. I apologised: I said, I came up here to tell my story ... but I just can't do it any more.'

For William James, the appeal of war lay in its horror, since violence and romance inevitably walked hand in hand. But in the modern age, horror could just as easily give way to a kind of blankness, a stammering silence. High-tech weapons killed with a terrible indifference for which visions of chivalry were no preparation, so expectations of sacrifice and transcendence might give way to nothing at all.

Some people could, perhaps, accept that nihilism. That was what Goff had meant when he talked of the kids going to Iraq and the minority who would encounter the reality of war and actively embrace it, the ones who would find in that empty space a kind of dark power. In the absence of meaning, a perverse freedom might emerge, in which everything was possible and nothing forbidden, where, in fact, prohibition itself no longer made sense: the logic of massacre and atrocity, of Haditha and My Lai, of endless, escalating violence. 'That was a laugh', said the veteran Friedrich Wilhelm Heinz about being told that the Great War was over. 'We ourselves are the war; its flame burns strongly in us. It envelops our whole being and fascinates us with the enticing urge to destroy.' Heinz's subsequent career with Hitler's Brownshirts possessed, in retrospect, a certain inevitability.

But only a tiny minority could go down that path. Unwilling to embrace the void, but unable to accept the romances they'd been fed, many soldiers were left stranded between what they'd sought and what they'd found. Wasn't that what souvenirs represented? You took a trophy, whether a head or a photo, to show that you'd been there, that, in Reppenhagen's words, you'd 'done the thing'. A token of death for the most profound event of your life, those few minutes in which, amid the clatter of machine guns, everything had seemed obvious and clear and infused with meaning, a too-brief interlude that ended with you confronting the shredded corpse of a man you didn't even recall shooting.

Skull trophies adopted the rituals of recreational hunting, the custom in which the triumphant hunter returned carrying, as Goff would have it, his proof of conquest. In a different era, in an earlier time, such ceremonies wove the fabric of society, and the warrior sang his songs and swung the enemy's severed head for the admiration of his clan. But killing in a modern war—anonymous, automatic, unthinking—was of an entirely different order. The old rites, desperately adopted by men looking for something to which to cling, were as out of place in Iraq or Afghanistan as work songs were in a factory, and there were no new rites with which to replace them.

Back in the USA, Reppenhagen's friends had erased, shamefacedly and silently, the images from their hard drives. But even if they'd kept their trophies, what could they have done with pictures from which loved ones recoiled with pure horror? Even if some people had wanted to look, what then? 'When is a good time to sit around talking about killing people?' Workman had asked. 'What's a good way to bring the subject up? The people who you're talking with, unless they were there, they're not really going to understand.' What meaning did a broken body actually convey? How was one picture of shattered corpses any different from any other? What did your souvenir really express about the pleasures of your war, other than your desire to feel something? That was the dirty secret of modern war: killing might produce not more meaning but less.

The Great War, promised Prime Minister Billy Hughes, would save Australians 'from moral, aye, and physical degeneration and decay, by which we were slipping down with increasing velocity into the very abyss of degeneration. [We] were becoming flabby, and were in danger of losing the ancient qualities which made the race. This war has purged us and is still purging us like the glorious beams of the sun.' And so, once upon a time, a young man, from a country a long way from the main currents of history, signed up to fight, not only to defeat the Teutonic autocracy, but to embark upon a grand adventure, an expedition that would forge the stunted youths and weedy clerks of the factory age into Homeric heroes, into giant men striding forth into destiny.

At Gallipoli, the youth found that death was sudden and random and inexplicable, that men became not bigger but infinitely small, like tiny children, like frightened rabbits, that they fought artillery fire not with lance and shield but by cowering face down in mud, hiding their eyes and mouthing prayers to a God in whom the war itself made belief impossible. 'Glorious charges, magnificent defences, heroic efforts in this or that direction', wrote one Australian from that time, 'all boil down to the one thing, the pitting of human beings against the most scientific machinery, and the result can be seen in the papers'.

What was the vocabulary to express that? How to remember men dying as sheep, killing like slaughtermen? That was the Gallipoli head: mutely eloquent, a trophy of no one, an icon of nothing. What could you say about a souvenir like that? What could it possibly mean? Finally, I thought I understood. It meant everything. It didn't mean a thing.

NOTES

1 No mercy here

Page 1: The head lay ... A Jackson, 'Shock over Gallipoli's grisly memento', *Age*, 3 May 2002; B Crawford, 'Gallipoli "trophy" puzzle', *Australian*, 2 May 2002.

Page 2: controversy erupted about nowthatsfuckedup.com ... See, for instance, San Francisco Chronicle, 'Porn wars', *San Francisco Chronicle*, 2 October 2005. You can still access the site through Wayback Machine at www.archive.org.

Page 3: Prior to the Great War ... P Fussell, *The Great War and modern memory*, Oxford University Press, New York, 1981, p. 189.

Page 5: Wyndham Lewis's reaction ... As quoted in P Fussell, *Doing battle: the making of a skeptic*, Little, Brown & Co., Boston, 1996, p. 63.

Page 5: the poet Vernon Scannell ... As quoted in Fussell, *The Great War and modern memory*, p. 319.

Pages 6–7: The Victorian Returned and Services League president ... D Hoare, 'Turks allowed to join Anzac march', *World Today*, radio program, ABC Radio, 12 April 2006, transcript viewed December 2008, <www.abc.net.au/worldtoday/content/2006/s1614594.htm>.

Page 8: the War Graves Commission ... P Adam-Smith, *The Anzacs*, Penguin Books, Melbourne, 1991, p. 92.

Page 8: All the belligerents ... See, for instance, D Blair, *No quarter: unlawful killing and surrender in the Australian war experience 1915–18*, Ginninderra Press, Canberra, 2005; T Cook, 'The politics of surrender: Canadian soldiers and the killing of prisoners in the Great War', *Journal of Military History*, vol. 70, no. 3, 2006.

Page 8: Private Keith Wadsworth ... As quoted in J Hamilton, *Gallipoli sniper: the life of Billy Sing*, Pan Macmillan Australia, Sydney, 2008, p. 135.

Page 8: Captain Lewis Nott ... LW Nott, *Somewhere in France: the collected letters of Lewis Windermere, Nott, January–December 1916*, ed. D Nott, HarperCollins, Pymble, NSW, 1996.

Page 8: Even Charles Bean ... Blair, *No quarter*, p. 6.

Page 9: Robert Graves suggests ... R Graves, *Goodbye to all that*, revised edn, Penguin, Harmondsworth, Middlesex, 1960 (1929), p. 154.

Page 10: **Detective Sergeant Adrian Kennedy** ... As quoted in Crawford, 'Gallipoli "trophy" puzzle'.

Page 11: **'A Sad Turn'** ... M Ashworth, 'A sad turn', *Riverina Herald*, 6 May 2002.

Page 11: **feminists protesting against rape** ... J Sparrow & J Sparrow, *Radical Melbourne 2: the enemy within*, Vulgar Press, Melbourne, 2004, p. 50.

Page 12: **Inside they found a human skull** ... S Harrison, 'Skull trophies of the Pacific War: transgressive objects of remembrance', *Journal of the Royal Anthropological Institute*, vol. 12, 2006, pp. 817–36.

Page 12: **Private Jake Kovco** ... D Box, *Carry me home: the life and death of Private Jake Kovco*, Allen & Unwin, Sydney, 2008, p. 43.

Page 14: **a PDF of the coroner's report** ... State Coroner's Office of Victoria, *Record of investigation into death*, case no. 1427/02, State Coroner's Office, Melbourne, 15 November 2003.

Page 16: **farmer Archie Barwick** ... As quoted in B Gammage, *The broken years: Australian soldiers in the Great War*, illustrated edn, Penguin, Melbourne, 1982, p. 91.

Page 17: **Australian soldier John Adlard** ... Adlard, John Evan, Diaries, 1915–18, viewed December 2008, <http://users.sa.chariot.net.au/~cadlard/shoestring.htm>.

Page 20: **pertained exclusively to sexual images** ... D Kushner, 'Casualty of porn', *Rolling Stone*, 5 December 2005.

2 Not everyone's cup of tea

Page 22: **Private WR Guest** ... As quoted in Gammage, *The broken years*, p. 66.

Page 25: ***The Face of Battle*** ... J Keegan, *The face of battle*, Cape, London, 1976.

Page 28: **Even the Mongols** ... D Chirot & CR McCauley, *Why not kill them all? The logic and prevention of mass political murder*, Princeton University Press, Princeton, NJ, 2006, p. 53.

Page 28: **British Army had tried inoculating** ... J Bourke, *An intimate history of killing: face-to-face killing in twentieth-century warfare*, Basic Books, New York, 1999, p. 154.

Page 28: **R Wayne Eisenhart** ... Eisenhart, RW, 'You can't hack it little girl: a discussion of the covert psychological agenda of modern combat training', *Journal of Social Issues*, vol. 34, no. 4, 1975, pp. 13–23.

Page 31: Charles Sorley ... Quoted in Fussell, *The Great War and modern memory*, p. 126.

Page 32: 'I froze', the commando recalled ... As quoted in D Grossman, *On killing: the psychological cost of learning to kill in war and society*, Little, Brown & Co., Boston, 1996, p. 115.

Pages 33–4: 'As usual,' wrote Siegfried Sassoon ... S Sassoon, *Memoirs of an infantry officer*, Faber & Faber, London, 2000 (1930), p. 162.

Page 34: the novelist Frederick Manning ... F Manning, *Middle parts of fortune*, ed. S Caterson, Text Publishing, Melbourne, 2000 (1929), p. 13.

Page 35: says Genesis ... Genesis 1:26. See A Cockburn, 'A short, meat-oriented history of the world from Eden to the Mattole', *New Left Review*, vol. 1, no. 215, 1996, pp. 16–42.

3 The kill floor

Page 40: The Lee Enfield rifle ... D Winter, *Death's men: soldiers of the Great War*, Allen Lane, London, 1978, p. 107.

Page 40: Winston Churchill ... As quoted in Bourke, *An intimate history of killing*, p. 154.

Page 41: the Chicago of Upton Sinclair's famous novel... U Sinclair, *The jungle*, Penguin Classics series, Penguin, New York, 1987 (1906), p. 33.

Page 41: animal advocates noted ... M Smith, 'The "ethical" space of the abattoir: on the (in)human(e) slaughter of other animals', *Human Ecology Forum*, vol. 9, no. 2, 2002, p. 51.

Page 41: the Smithfield livestock market ... Smith, 'The "ethical" space of the abattoir', p. 50.

Page 46: wrote Bronson Alcott ... As quoted in M Cartmill, *A view to a death in the morning: hunting and nature through history*, Harvard University Press, Cambridge, Mass., 1993, p. 122.

Page 47: some writers suggested ... N Vialles, *Animal to edible*, Cambridge University Press, Cambridge, 1994.

Page 48: account of an abattoir from the 1940s ... As quoted in D Pick, *War machine: the rationalisation of slaughter in the modern age*, Yale University Press, New Haven, Conn., 1993, p. 185.

Page 48: military theorist Carl von Clausewitz ... CV Clausewitz, *On war*, Kessinger Publishing, Whitefish, Mont., 2004, p. 72.

Page 55: The whole point of factory-style production ... The classic account is H Braverman, *Labor and monopoly capital: the degradation of work in the twentieth century*, Monthly Review Press, New York, 1974.

4 Humane and practical

Page 59: *An Intimate History of Killing* ... Bourke, *An intimate history of killing*.

Page 59: *On Killing* ... Grossman, *On killing*.

Page 60: J Glenn Gray ... JG Gray, *The warriors: reflections on men in battle*, Harper & Row, New York, 1967.

Page 61: Jack Napoleon Tunermenerwail and Robert Smallboy ... J Sparrow & J Sparrow, *Radical Melbourne*, Vulgar Press, Melbourne, 2001, p. 178.

Page 61: when Ned Kelly died ... I Jones, *Ned Kelly: a short life*, new edn, Lothian Books, Melbourne, 2003.

Page 61: Errol Morris film *Mr Death* ... *Mr Death: The rise and fall of Fred A Leuchter, Jr*, documentary, directed by Errol Morris, Channel Four Films, 1999.

Page 65: William Kemmler ... S Trombley, *The execution protocol: inside America's capital punishment industry*, Crown Publishers, New York, 1992, pp. 17–22; see also DW Denno, 'Is electrocution an unconstitutional method of execution? The engineering of death over the century', *William and Mary Law Review*, vol. 35, 1994, pp. 551–692.

Page 66: Jesse Tafero ... Denno, 'Is electrocution an unconstitutional method of execution?', p. 554.

Page 67: Governor David B. Hill ... Denno provides a useful summary in Denno, 'Is electrocution an unconstitutional method of execution?'

Page 67: The electrification of America's convicts ... R Moran, *Executioner's current: Thomas Edison, George Westinghouse, and the invention of the electric chair*, AA Knopf, New York, 2002.

Page 69: gas execution of Donald Harding ... DW Denno, 'The lethal injection quandry: how medicine has dismantled the death penalty', *Fordham Law Review*, vol. 76, 2007, p. 63.

Page 69: the grotesque courtroom dialogues ... Denno discusses these in DW Denno, 'Death bed', *TriQuarterly Journal*, vol. 124, 2006, pp. 141–68.

Page 70: the introduction of lethal injection ... DW Denno, 'When legislatures delegate death: the troubling paradox behind state uses of electrocution and lethal injection and what it says about us', *Ohio State Law Journal*, vol. 63, 2002, pp. 63–128; Denno, 'The lethal injection quandry'.
Page 71: Elsewhere, Fred Leuchter played a role ... Denno discusses Leuchter in Denno, 'Is electrocution an unconstitutional method of execution?', p. 626.

5 The right leg

Page 75: Daryl Holton's execution ... CBJ Allen, 'Tennessee performs first electric chair execution since 1960', *City Paper*, 12 September 2007.
Page 76: *Death Work* ... R Johnson, *Death work: a study of the modern execution process*, Brooks/Cole, Pacific Grove, Calif., 1990.
Page 78: SLA Marshall ... SLA Marshall, *Men against fire: the problem of battle command in future war*, Natraj Publishers, New Delhi, 1997, pp. 50–63.
Page 78: Ardant du Picq ... As quoted in Grossman, *On killing*, p. 151.
Page 79: almost total participation ... D Grossman, 'Human factors in war: the psychology and physiology of close combat', in MEA Ryan (ed.), *The human face of warfare*, Allen & Unwin, Sydney, 2000, p. 19.
Page 79: the importance of the prison structure ... See, in particular, Johnson, *Death work*, p. 27, but also throughout.

6 Close to the fire

Page 87: Brian Turner in his poem 'Sadiq' ... B Turner, 'Sadiq', in *Here, bullet*, Alice James Books, Farmington, Maine, 2005, p. 56. Copyright © 2005 by Brian Turner and reprinted here with the permission of Alice James Books, www.alicejamesbooks.org.
Page 87: Opinion Research Business ... T Susman, 'Poll: civilian death toll in Iraq may top 1 million', *Los Angeles Times*, 14 September 2007.
Page 91: Bob Butterworth ... As quoted in RJ Lifton & G Mitchell, *Who owns death? Capital punishment, the American conscience, and the end of executions*, Perennial, New York, 2002, p. 56.

7 The executioner's paradox

Page 96: Theodore Nadelson's *Trained to Kill* ... T Nadelson, *Trained to kill: soldiers at war*, Johns Hopkins University Press, Baltimore, 2005.

Pages 96–7: article by the neurologist Harold Hillman ... H Hillman, 'The possible pain experienced during execution by different methods', *Perception*, vol. 22, 1993, pp. 745–53.

Page 97: analytical papers by psychologist Michael J Osofsky ... MJ Osofsky & HJ Osofsky, 'The psychological experience of security officers who work with executions', *Psychiatry*, vol. 65, no. 4, 2002, pp. 358–70; MJ Osofsky, A Bandura & PG Zimbardo, 'The role of moral disengagement in the execution process', *Law and Human Behavior*, vol. 29, no. 4, 2005, pp. 371–93.

8 A tremendous secret

Page 107: Gail Eisnitz ... GA Eisnitz, *Slaughterhouse: the shocking story of greed, neglect, and inhumane treatment inside the US meat industry*, Prometheus Books, Amherst, NY, 1997.

Page 107: In Thomas More's *Utopia* ... As quoted in Cartmill, *A view to a death in the morning*, p. 77.

Page 107: John Gay advising ... As quoted in Cockburn, 'A short, meat-oriented history of the world', p. 29.

Page 108: a study of French abattoir workers ... Vialles, *Animal to edible*, p. 79.

Page 108: Piers Beirne ... P Beirne, 'From animal abuse to interhuman violence? A critical review of the progression thesis', *Society & Animals*, vol. 12, no. 1, 2004, pp. 39–65.

Page 109: 'You don't care about people's pain ...' As quoted in Eisnitz, *Slaughterhouse*, p. 92.

Pages 109–10: 'The worst thing ...' As quoted in Eisnitz, *Slaughterhouse*.

Pages 110–11: 'When hogs end up in the catch pen ...' As quoted in Eisnitz, *Slaughterhouse*, p. 69.

Page 112: 'You're standing there night after night ...' As quoted in Eisnitz, *Slaughterhouse*, p. 74.

Page 114: *Skinny Bitch* ... R Freedman & K Barnouin, *Skinny bitch: a no-nonsense, tough-love guide for savvy girls who want to stop eating crap and start looking fabulous!*, Running Press, Philadelphia, 2005.

Pages 114–15: **Human Rights Watch released a report** ... Human Rights Watch, *Blood, sweat and fear: workers' rights in US meat and poultry plants*, Human Rights Watch, New York, 2004.

Page 115: **'There was one night ...'** As quoted in Eisnitz, *Slaughterhouse*, p. 74.

Page 116: **the poet Coral Hull** ... C Hull, *Broken land: 5 days in Bre, 1995*, Five Islands Press, Wollongong, NSW, 1997, p. 63.

Page 116: **A study of Scottish livestock producers...** R Wilkie, 'Sentient commodities and productive paradoxes: the ambiguous nature of human–livestock relations in Northeast Scotland', *Journal of Rural Studies*, vol. 21, 2005, pp. 213–30.

Page 117: **'You may look a hog in the eye ...'** As quoted in Eisnitz, *Slaughterhouse*, p. 87.

9 Just so many of them

Page 120: ***Perpetration-Induced Traumatic Stress*** ... R MacNair, *Perpetration-induced traumatic stress: the psychological consequences of killing*, Psychological Dimensions to War and Peace series, Praeger, London & Westport, Conn., 2002.

Page 123: **in Cabana's memoir** ... DA Cabana, *Death at midnight: the confession of an executioner*, Northeastern University Press, Boston, 1996.

Page 124: **She quotes Fred Allen** ... MacNair, *Perpetration-induced traumatic stress*, p. 36.

10 A button, not a switch

Page 136: **The Coppola execution** ... Denno, 'Is electrocution an unconstitutional method of execution?', p. 665.

Page 139: **Some prisons weighed the corpse down** ... I Solotaroff, *The last face you'll ever see: the private life of the American death penalty*, HarperCollins, New York, 2001, p. 7.

11 Technology

Page 152: **Leuchter's use of autopsy results** ... Trombley, *The execution protocol*, pp. 56–7.

Page 160: the first claim, at least, seemed to be true ... See, for instance, E Morris, interview with Ron Rosenbaum, Museum of Modern Art, New York, fall 1999, viewed December 2008, <www.errolmorris.com/content/interview/moma1999.html>.

Page 164: he'd been represented by Kirk Lyons ... Denno, 'Is electrocution an unconstitutional method of execution?', p. 660.

Page 165: Adolf Eichmann ... H Arendt, *The portable Hannah Arendt*, ed. P Baehr, Penguin, New York, 2000, ch. 5.

Page 166: 'The hardest thing for me ...' As quoted in Osofsky, Bandura & Zimbardo, 'The role of moral disengagement', p. 386.

Page 166: 'I just cannot feel anything ...' As quoted in Johnson, *Death work*, p. 115.

12 Sad celebrations

Pages 170–1: The noise 'did not move ...' As quoted in Winter, *Death's men*, p. 175.

Page 172: Take Robert-François Damiens ... See, for instance, M Foucault, *Discipline and punish: the birth of the prison*, 2nd edn, Vintage Books, New York, 1995, p. 3.

Page 174: the case of Henry Smith ... The description of Smith's execution, as well as the general argument here, comes from D Garland, 'The peculiar forms of American capital punishment', *Social Research*, vol. 74, no. 2, 2007, pp. 435–64.

Page 176: he'd emailed me a poem ... R Johnson, 'Last Supper', in *Burnt offerings: poems on crime and punishment*, Bleak House Books, Madison, Wisc., 2008.

13 Known as killers

Page 180: chronicled in detail in the *Washington Post* ... P Carlson, 'A hero who didn't save himself', *Washington Post*, 4 March 2007.

Pages 181–2: Siegfried Sassoon's two classic novels ... S Sassoon, *Memoirs of a fox-hunting man*, Faber & Faber, London, 1999 (1928); Sassoon, *Memoirs of an infantry officer*.

Page 182: the narrator is solemnly told ... Sassoon, *Memoirs of a fox-hunting man*, p. 106.

14 The anatomy of a kill

Page 194: Australian marksman Billy Sing ... Hamilton, *Gallipoli sniper*, p. 207.

Page 197: eighteen US veterans killed themselves ... A Glantz, 'The truth about veteran suicides', *Foreign Policy in Focus*, 9 May 2008, viewed December 2008, <www.fpif.org/fpiftxt/5219>.

Page 197: more than 650 veterans committed suicide ... J Koopman, 'Vets' growing suicide rate worries officials', *San Francisco Chronicle*, 12 May 2008.

15 Wolves and sheep

Page 199: Grossman accuses the media ... Grossman, *On killing*, pp. 299–316; D Grossman & G DeGaetano, *Stop teaching our kids to kill: a call to action against TV, movie & video game violence*, Crown Publishers, New York, 1999.

Page 201: Lieutenant Colonel Scott Sutton ... JA Vargas, 'Virtual reality prepares soldiers for real war: young warriors say video shooter games helped hone their skills', *Washington Post*, 14 February 2006.

Page 207: an account of that study ... See, for instance, K Springen, 'This is your brain on violence: the first study to look at the direct effect of videogames on teen brains documents functional differences between violent and non-violent play', *Newsweek*, 28 November 2006.

Page 207: boys who didn't play violent games ... A LaMosca, 'Grand theft childhood and the case against media sensationalism', *The Escapist*, 30 April 2008, viewed December 2008, <www.escapistmagazine.com/articles/view/editorials/reviews/4860-Grand-Theft-Childhood-and-the-Case-Against-Media-Sensationalism>; see also CK Olson, L Kutner & EV Beresin, 'Children and video games: how much do we know?' *Psychiatric Times*, vol. 24, no. 12, 1 October 2007, viewed December 2008, <www.psychiatrictimes.com/display/article/10168/54191?pageNumber=1>; L Kutner & CK Olson, *Grand theft childhood: the surprising truth about violent video games and what parents can do*, hardcover edn, Simon & Schuster, New York, 2008. This is not to suggest that video gaming has no impact on behaviour, merely that the relationship is complicated and unclear.

Page 208: the most successful recruiting campaign ... M Power, 'Digitized virtuosity: video war games and post-9/11 cyber-deterrence', *Security Dialogue*, vol. 38, 2007, pp. 271–88.

Page 208: the army funded gaming tournaments ... DB Nieborg, 'Mods, nay! Tournaments, yay! The appropriation of contemporary game culture by the US military', *Fibreculture*, no. 8, October 2006, viewed December 2008, <http://journal.fibreculture.org/issue8/issue8_nieborg.html>; see, more generally, E Halter, *From Sun Tzu to XBox: war and video games*, Thunder's Mouth Press, New York, 2006.

16 Into cleanness leaping

Page 215: the very earth of No Man's Land ... H Barbusse, *Under fire*, Penguin, London, 2003, p. 248.

Page 216: Frederick the Great ... R Holmes, *Acts of war: the behavior of men in battle*, Free Press, New York, 1985, p. 38.

Page 218: With the American practitioners ... The examples come from T Horwitz, *Confederates in the attic: dispatches from the unfinished Civil War*, Pantheon Books, New York, 1998.

Page 220: dismissed his famous research as overtly fraudulent ... For critiques of Marshall, see P Gold, 'Flak for a man and his claim that few soldiers open fire', *Insight*, 27 March 1989, pp. 18–19; F Smoler, 'The secrets of the soldiers who didn't shoot', *American Heritage*, vol. 4, 1989, pp. 37–45; RJ Spiller, 'SLA Marshall and the ratio of fire', *RUSI Journal*, vol. 133, 1988, pp. 63–71; JW Chambers, 'SLA Marshall's *Men against fire*: new evidence regarding fire ratios', *Parameters*, autumn 2003, pp. 113–21. For Grossman's defence of Marshall, see D Grossman, 'Aggression and violence', in JW Chambers (ed.), *Oxford companion to American military history*, Oxford University Press, New York, 1999. There's also an argument that Marshall's observations might have been correct, but not his explanation: see KC Jordan, 'Right for the wrong reasons: SLA Marshall and the ratio of fire in Korea', *Journal of Military History*, vol. 66, no. 1, 2006, pp. 135–62.

Page 220: Captain Kozlov ... VS Grossman, A Beevor & L Vinogradova, *A writer at war: Vasily Grossman with the Red Army, 1941–1945*, Pantheon Books, New York, 2005, p. 109.

Page 221: A revisionist school of historians ... See, for instance, N Ferguson, *The pity of war*, Basic Books, New York, 1999, p. 358.

Page 221: *On Combat* ... D Grossman & LW Christensen, *On combat: the psychology and physiology of deadly conflict in war and in peace*, 2nd edn, PPCT Research Publications, Belleville, Ill., 2007.

Page 221: Rupert Brooke ... As quoted in P Vansittart, *Voices from the Great War*, Pimlico, London, 1998, p. 28.

Page 222: antidote to the diseases of industrial society ... See, generally, EJ Leed, *No man's land: combat & identity in World War I*, Cambridge University Press, Cambridge & New York, 1979, pp. 39–69.

Page 223: The Edwardian militarists developed ... Fussell, *The Great War and modern memory*, p. 21.

Page 223: Grenfell, in particular, was very frank ... As quoted in Bourke, *An intimate history of killing*, p. 141.

Page 224: philosopher William James ... W James, 'The moral equivalent of war', in *William James: the essential writings*, ed. BW Wilshire, State University of New York Press, Albany, NY, 1984, p. 349.

Page 224: soldier-poet Franz Schauwecker ... As quoted in Leed, *No man's land*, p. 55.

Page 225: AD Hope's Vietnam-era treatment ... AD Hope, 'Inscription for any war', in S Cass (ed.), *We took their orders and are dead: an anti-war anthology*, Ure Smith, Sydney, 1971, p. 89.

Page 226: a certain Lieutenant Richards ... As quoted in Gammage, *The broken years*, p. 79.

17 Remove the thought

Page 227: 'I am making this statement ...' Sassoon, *Memoirs of an infantry officer*, p. 244.

Page 227: Camilo Mejía's statements after his 2004 court martial ... See C Mejía, *Road from Ar Ramadi: the private rebellion of Staff Sergeant Camilo Mejía*, New Press, New York, 2007.

Page 231: American pacifist Jane Addams ... J Addams, *A centennial reader*, Macmillan, New York, 1960, p. 270.

Page 231: Christmas truces ... See S Weintraub, *Silent night: the story of the World War I Christmas truce*, Free Press, New York, 2001.

Page 231: informal understandings with the enemy ... T Ashworth, *Trench warfare 1914–1918: the live and let live system*, Macmillan, London, 2000.

Page 231: 'Mr Bosche ain't a bad feller ...' As quoted in Ashworth, *Trench warfare 1914–1918*, p. 30.

Pages 232–3: The Pacific battles of the Second World War ...
CM Cameron, *American samurai: myth, imagination, and the conduct of
battle in the First Marine Division, 1941–1951*, Cambridge University
Press, Cambridge & New York, 1994, pp. 89–129; JW Dower, *War
without mercy: race and power in the Pacific war*, Faber, London, 1986,
pp. 33–93.
Page 233: The sentiment was so prevalent ... Dower, *War without mercy*,
p. 65.

18 A dink for Jo-Jo

Page 238: His last mission ... See S Goff, *Hideous dream: a soldier's
memoir of the US invasion of Haiti*, Soft Skull Press, New York, 2000.
Page 240: *Sex and War* ... S Goff, *Sex and war*, Lulu.com, 2006.
Page 240: less like Sylvester Stallone than Ted Bundy ... Goff, *Sex and
war*, p. 97.
Page 243: the Great War heightened modernity ... This is central to the
argument in Leed, *No man's land*; but see also C Coker, *The future of
war: the re-enchantment of war in the twenty-first century*, Blackwell
Manifestos series, Blackwell Publishing, Malden, Mass., 2004., p. 4.
Page 243: Sassoon, for instance, describes ... On this, see G Dyer, *The
missing of the Somme*, Hamilton, London, 1994, p. 47.
Page 244: A snippet of dialogue ... Barbusse, *Under fire*, p. 302.
Page 244: the French soldiers of 1917 ... Dyer, *The missing of the
Somme*, p. 46.

19 We ourselves are the war

Page 248: 'My senses are charred ...' Wilfred Owen to Siegfried Sassoon,
10 October 1918, in W Owen, *Collected letters*, ed. H Owen & J Bell,
Oxford University Press, London, 1967, p. 581.
Page 250: Before Gallipoli, the Anzac contingent ... S Brugger, *Australians
and Egypt, 1914–1919*, Melbourne University Press, Melbourne, 1980,
pp. 30–47.
Page 251: shouting *'Inshi Allah'* ... Gammage, *The broken years*, pp. 59,
98; Adam-Smith, *The Anzacs*, pp. 90, 99.
Page 251: When the authorities decided ... Australian, 'Mysterious skull
on its way to Gallipoli', *Australian*, 8 March 2003.

Page 254: 'the one great lyric passage ...' Gray, *The warriors*, p. 28.

Pages 254–5: 'a man who stepped out ...' M Eksteins, *Rites of spring: the Great War and the birth of the modern age*, Anchor Books, New York, 1990, p. 141.

Page 255: 'All you do is move that finger ...' As quoted in Bourke, *An intimate history of killing*, p. 14.

Page 255: 'A kill at two klicks, that is beautiful ...' As quoted in Nadelson, *Trained to kill*, p. 72.

Page 258: 'The Last Hero' ... As quoted in D Grossman & LW Christensen, *On combat: the psychology and physiology of deadly conflict in war and in peace*, 2nd edn, PPCT Research Publications, Belleville, Ill., 2007. p. 136.

Page 258: 'It was just like training ...' As quoted in E Wright, *Generation kill: devil dogs, iceman, Captain America, and the new face of American war*, GP Putnam's Sons, New York, 2004, p. 143.

Page 261: Friedrich Wilhelm Heinz ... As quoted in Leed, *No man's land*, p. 213.

Page 262: Prime Minister Billy Hughes ... As quoted in B Walker, *Solidarity forever: a part story of the life and times of Percy Laidler—the first quarter of a century*, National Press, Melbourne, 1972, p. 105.

Page 262: 'Glorious charges, magnificent defences ...' As quoted in Gammage, *The broken years*, p. 81.

Page 262: a trophy of no one ... The lines 'a trophy of no one, an icon of nothing' are from Hull, *Broken land*, p. 46.

BIBLIOGRAPHY

Adam-Smith, P, *The Anzacs*, Penguin Books, Melbourne, 1991.

Addams, J, *A centennial reader*, Macmillan, New York, 1960.

Adlard, John Evan, Diaries, 1915–18, viewed December 2008, <http://users.sa.chariot.net.au/~cadlard/shoestring.htm>.

Allen, CBJ, 'Tennessee performs first electric chair execution since 1960', *City Paper*, 12 September 2007.

Arendt, H, *The portable Hannah Arendt*, ed. P Baehr, Penguin, New York, 2000.

Ashworth, M, 'A sad turn', *Riverina Herald*, 6 May 2002.

Ashworth, T, *Trench warfare 1914–1918: the live and let live system*, Macmillan, London, 2000.

Australian, 'Mysterious skull on its way to Gallipoli', *Australian*, 8 March 2003.

Barbusse, H, *Under fire*, Penguin, London, 2003.

Beirne, P, 'From animal abuse to interhuman violence? A critical review of the progression thesis', *Society & Animals*, vol. 12, no. 1, 2004, pp. 39–65.

Blair, D, *No quarter: unlawful killing and surrender in the Australian war experience 1915–18*, Ginninderra Press, Canberra, 2005.

Bourke, J, *An intimate history of killing: face-to-face killing in twentieth-century warfare*, Basic Books, New York, 1999.

Box, D, *Carry me home: the life and death of Private Jake Kovco*, Allen & Unwin, Sydney, 2008.

Braverman, H, *Labor and monopoly capital: the degradation of work in the twentieth century*, Monthly Review Press, New York, 1974.

Brugger, S, *Australians and Egypt, 1914–1919*, Melbourne University Press, Melbourne, 1980.

Cabana, DA, *Death at midnight: the confession of an executioner*, Northeastern University Press, Boston, 1996.

Cameron, CM, *American samurai: myth, imagination, and the conduct of battle in the First Marine Division, 1941–1951*, Cambridge University Press, Cambridge & New York, 1994.

Carlson, P, 'A hero who didn't save himself', *Washington Post*, 4 March 2007.

Cartmill, M, *A view to a death in the morning: hunting and nature through history*, Harvard University Press, Cambridge, Mass., 1993.

Cass, S (ed.), *We took their orders and are dead: an anti-war anthology*, Ure Smith, Sydney, 1971.

Chambers, JW, 'SLA Marshall's *Men against fire*: new evidence regarding fire ratios', *Parameters*, autumn 2003, pp. 113–21.

Chirot, D & CR McCauley, *Why not kill them all? The logic and prevention of mass political murder*, Princeton University Press, Princeton, NJ, 2006.

Clausewitz, CV, *On war*, Kessinger Publishing, Whitefish, Mont., 2004.

Cockburn, A, 'A short, meat-oriented history of the world from Eden to the Mattole', *New Left Review*, vol. 1, no. 215, 1996, pp. 16–42.

Coker, C, *The future of war: the re-enchantment of war in the twenty-first century*, Blackwell Manifestos series, Blackwell Publishing, Malden, Mass., 2004.

Cook, T, 'The politics of surrender: Canadian soldiers and the killing of prisoners in the Great War', *Journal of Military History*, vol. 70, no. 3, 2006, pp. 637—66.

Crawford, B, 'Gallipoli "trophy" puzzle', *Australian*, 2 May 2002.

Denno, DW, 'Is electrocution an unconstitutional method of execution? The engineering of death over the century', *William and Mary Law Review*, vol. 35, 1994, pp. 551–692.

——'When legislatures delegate death: the troubling paradox behind state uses of electrocution and lethal injection and what it says about us', *Ohio State Law Journal*, vol. 63, 2002, pp. 63–128.

——'Death bed', *TriQuarterly Journal*, vol. 124, 2006, pp. 141–68.

——'The lethal injection quandry: how medicine has dismantled the death penalty', *Fordham Law Review*, vol. 76, 2007, pp. 49–128.

Dower, JW, *War without mercy: race and power in the Pacific war*, Faber, London, 1986.

Dyer, G, *The missing of the Somme*, Hamilton, London, 1994.

Eisenhart, RW, 'You can't hack it little girl: a discussion of the covert psychological agenda of modern combat training', *Journal of Social Issues*, vol. 34, no. 4, 1975, pp. 13–23.

Eisnitz, GA, *Slaughterhouse: the shocking story of greed, neglect, and inhumane treatment inside the US meat industry*, Prometheus Books, Amherst, NY, 1997.

Eksteins, M, *Rites of spring: the Great War and the birth of the modern age*, Anchor Books, New York, 1990.

Ferguson, N, *The pity of war*, Basic Books, New York, 1999.

Foucault, M, *Discipline and punish: the birth of the prison*, 2nd edn, Vintage Books, New York, 1995.

Freedman, R & K Barnouin, *Skinny bitch: a no-nonsense, tough-love guide for savvy girls who want to stop eating crap and start looking fabulous!* Running Press, Philadelphia, 2005.

Fussell, P, *The Great War and modern memory*, Oxford University Press, New York, 1981.

——*Doing battle: the making of a skeptic*, Little, Brown & Co., Boston, 1996.

Gammage, B, *The broken years: Australian soldiers in the Great War*, illustrated edn, Penguin, Melbourne, 1982.

Garland, D, 'The peculiar forms of American capital punishment', *Social Research*, vol. 74, no. 2, 2007, pp. 435–64.

Glantz, A, 'The truth about veteran suicides', *Foreign Policy in Focus*, 9 May 2008, viewed December 2008, <www.fpif.org/fpiftxt/5219>.

Goff, S, *Hideous dream: a soldier's memoir of the US invasion of Haiti*, Soft Skull Press, New York, 2000.

——*Sex and war*, Lulu.com, 2006.

Gold, P, 'Flak for a man and his claim that few soldiers open fire', *Insight*, 27 March 1989, pp. 18–19.

Graves, R, *Goodbye to all that*, revised edn, Penguin, Harmondsworth, Middlesex, 1960 (1929).

Gray, JG, *The warriors: reflections on men in battle*, Harper & Row, New York, 1967.

Grossman, D, *On killing: the psychological cost of learning to kill in war and society*, Little, Brown & Co., Boston, 1996.

——'Aggression and violence', in JW Chambers (ed.), *Oxford companion to American military history*, Oxford University Press, New York, 1999.

——'Human factors in war: the psychology and physiology of close combat', in MEA Ryan (ed.), *The human face of warfare*, Allen & Unwin, Sydney, 2000.

Grossman, D & LW Christensen, *On combat: the psychology and physiology of deadly conflict in war and in peace*, 2nd edn, PPCT Research Publications, Belleville, Ill., 2007.

Grossman, D & G DeGaetano, *Stop teaching our kids to kill: a call to action against TV, movie & video game violence*, Crown Publishers, New York, 1999.

Grossman, VS, A Beevor & L Vinogradova, *A writer at war: Vasily Grossman with the Red Army, 1941–1945*, Pantheon Books, New York, 2005.

Halter, E, *From Sun Tzu to XBox: war and video games*, Thunder's Mouth Press, New York, 2006.

Hamilton, J, *Gallipoli sniper: the life of Billy Sing*, Pan Macmillan Australia, Sydney, 2008.

Harrison, S, 'Skull trophies of the Pacific War: transgressive objects of remembrance', *Journal of the Royal Anthropological Institute*, vol. 12, 2006, pp. 817–36.

Hillman, H, 'The possible pain experienced during execution by different methods', *Perception*, vol. 22, 1993, pp. 745–53.

Hoare, D, 'Turks allowed to join Anzac march', *World Today*, radio program, ABC Radio, 12 April 2006, transcript viewed December 2008, <www.abc.net.au/worldtoday/content/2006/s1614594.htm>.

Holmes, R, *Acts of war: the behavior of men in battle*, Free Press, New York, 1985.

Horwitz, T, *Confederates in the attic: dispatches from the unfinished Civil War*, Pantheon Books, New York, 1998.

Hull, C, *Broken land: 5 days in Bre, 1995*, Five Islands Press, Wollongong, NSW, 1997.

Human Rights Watch, *Blood, sweat and fear: workers' rights in US meat and poultry plants*, Human Rights Watch, New York, 2004.

Jackson, A, 'Shock over Gallipoli's grisly memento', *Age*, 3 May 2002.

James, W, *William James: the essential writings*, ed. BW Wilshire, State University of New York Press, Albany, NY, 1984.

Johnson, R, *Death work: a study of the modern execution process*, Brooks/Cole, Pacific Grove, Calif., 1990.

——*Burnt offerings: poems on crime and punishment*, Bleak House Books, Madison, Wisc., 2008.

Jones, I, *Ned Kelly: a short life*, new edn, Lothian Books, Melbourne, 2003.

Jordan, KC, 'Right for the wrong reasons: SLA Marshall and the ratio of fire in Korea', *Journal of Military History*, vol. 66, no. 1, 2006, pp. 135–62.

Keegan, J, *The face of battle*, Cape, London, 1976.

Koopman, J, 'Vets' growing suicide rate worries officials', *San Francisco Chronicle*, 12 May 2008.

Kushner, D, 'Casualty of porn', *Rolling Stone*, 5 December 2005.

Kutner, L & CK Olson, *Grand theft childhood: the surprising truth about violent video games and what parents can do*, hardcover edn, Simon & Schuster, New York, 2008.

LaMosca, A, 'Grand theft childhood and the case against media sensationalism', *The Escapist*, 30 April 2008, viewed December 2008, <www.escapistmagazine.com/articles/view/editorials/reviews/4860-Grand-Theft-Childhood-and-the-Case-Against-Media-Sensationalism>.

Leed, EJ, *No man's land: combat & identity in World War I*, Cambridge University Press, Cambridge & New York, 1979.

Lifton, RJ & G Mitchell, *Who owns death? Capital punishment, the American conscience, and the end of executions*, Perennial, New York, 2002.

MacNair, R, *Perpetration-induced traumatic stress: the psychological consequences of killing*, Psychological Dimensions to War and Peace series, Praeger, London & Westport, Conn., 2002.

Manning, F, *Middle parts of fortune*, ed. S Caterson, Text Publishing, Melbourne, 2000 (1929).

Marshall, SLA, *Men against fire: the problem of battle command in future war*, Natraj Publishers, New Delhi, 1997.

Mejía, C, *Road from Ar Ramadi: the private rebellion of Staff Sergeant Camilo Mejía*, New Press, New York, 2007.

Moran, R, *Executioner's current: Thomas Edison, George Westinghouse, and the invention of the electric chair*, AA Knopf, New York, 2002.

Morris, E, interview with Ron Rosenbaum, Museum of Modern Art, New York, fall 1999, viewed December 2008, <www.errolmorris.com/content/interview/moma1999.html>.

Mr Death: The rise and fall of Fred A Leuchter, Jr, documentary, directed by Errol Morris, Channel Four Films, 1999.

Nadelson, T, *Trained to kill: soldiers at war*, Johns Hopkins University Press, Baltimore, 2005.

Nieborg, DB, 'Mods, nay! Tournaments, yay! The appropriation of contemporary game culture by the US military', *Fibreculture*, no. 8,

October 2006, viewed December 2008, <http://journal.fibreculture.
org/issue8/issue8_nieborg.html>.

Nott, LW, *Somewhere in France: the collected letters of Lewis Windermere Nott, January–December 1916*, ed. D Nott, HarperCollins, Pymble, NSW, 1996.

Olson, CK, L Kutner & EV Beresin, 'Children and video games: how much do we know?' *Psychiatric Times*, vol. 24, no. 12, 1 October 2007, viewed December 2008, <www.psychiatrictimes.com/display/article/10168/54191?pageNumber=1>.

Osofsky, MJ, A Bandura & PG Zimbardo, 'The role of moral disengagement in the execution process', *Law and Human Behavior*, vol. 29, no. 4, 2005, pp. 371–93.

Osofsky, MJ & HJ Osofsky, 'The psychological experience of security officers who work with executions', *Psychiatry*, vol. 65, no. 4, 2002, pp. 358–70.

Owen, W, *Collected letters*, ed. H Owen & J Bell, Oxford University Press, London, 1967.

Pick, D, *War machine: the rationalisation of slaughter in the modern age*, Yale University Press, New Haven, Conn., 1993.

Power, M, 'Digitized virtuosity: video war games and post-9/11 cyber-deterrence', *Security Dialogue*, vol. 38, 2007, pp. 271–88.

San Francisco Chronicle, 'Porn wars', *San Francisco Chronicle*, 2 October 2005.

Sassoon, S, *Memoirs of a fox-hunting man*, Faber & Faber, London, 1999 (1928).

——*Memoirs of an infantry officer*, Faber & Faber, London, 2000 (1930).

Sinclair, U, *The jungle*, Penguin Classics series, Penguin, New York, 1987 (1906).

Smith, M, 'The "ethical" space of the abattoir: on the (in)human(e) slaughter of other animals', *Human Ecology Forum*, vol. 9, no. 2, 2002, pp. 49–58.

Smoler, F, 'The secrets of the soldiers who didn't shoot', *American Heritage*, vol. 4, 1989, pp. 37–45.

Solotaroff, I, *The last face you'll ever see: the private life of the American death penalty*, HarperCollins, New York, 2001.

Sparrow, J & J Sparrow, *Radical Melbourne*, Vulgar Press, Melbourne, 2001.

——*Radical Melbourne 2: the enemy within*, Vulgar Press, Melbourne, 2004.

Spiller, RJ, 'SLA Marshall and the ratio of fire', *RUSI Journal*, vol. 133, 1988, pp. 63–71.

Springen, K, 'This is your brain on violence: the first study to look at the direct effect of videogames on teen brains documents functional differences between violent and non-violent play', *Newsweek*, 28 November 2006.

State Coroner's Office of Victoria, *Record of investigation into death*, case no. 1427/02, State Coroner's Office, Melbourne, 15 November 2003.

Susman, T, 'Poll: civilian death toll in Iraq may top 1 million', *Los Angeles Times*, 14 September 2007.

Trombley, S, *The execution protocol: inside America's capital punishment industry*, Crown Publishers, New York, 1992.

Turner, B, *Here, bullet*, Alice James Books, Farmington, Maine, 2005.

Vansittart, P, *Voices from the Great War*, Pimlico, London, 1998.

Vargas, JA, 'Virtual reality prepares soldiers for real war: young warriors say video shooter games helped hone their skills', *Washington Post*, 14 February 2006.

Vialles, N, *Animal to edible*, Cambridge University Press, Cambridge, 1994.

Walker, B, *Solidarity forever: a part story of the life and times of Percy Laidler—the first quarter of a century*, National Press, Melbourne, 1972.

Weintraub, S, *Silent night: the story of the World War I Christmas truce*, Free Press, New York, 2001.

Wilkie, R, 'Sentient commodities and productive paradoxes: the ambiguous nature of human–livestock relations in Northeast Scotland', *Journal of Rural Studies*, vol. 21, 2005, pp. 213–30.

Winter, D, *Death's men: soldiers of the Great War*, Allen Lane, London, 1978.

Wright, E, *Generation kill: devil dogs, iceman, Captain America, and the new face of American war*, GP Putnam's Sons, New York, 2004.